**W9-DAN-746**

Living with Leviathan

LIVING WITH LEVIATHAN

Americans Coming to Terms with Big Government

Linda L. M. Bennett
and Stephen Earl Bennett

 University Press of Kansas

Published by the University Press of Kansas (Lawrence, Kansas 66045), which was organized
by the Kansas Board of Regents and is operated and funded by Emporia State University,
Fort Hays State University, Kansas State University, Pittsburg State University, the University
of Kansas, and Wichita State University

Library of Congress Cataloging-in-Publication Data

Bennett, Linda L. M., 1952–
  Living with leviathan: Americans coming to terms with big
government / Linda L. M. Bennett and Stephen Earl Bennett.
     p.   cm. — (Studies in government and public policy)
  Includes bibliographical references and index.
  ISBN 0-7006-0432-4 — ISBN 0-7006-0433-2 (pbk.)
  1. Bureaucracy—United States—Public opinion. 2. Welfare state—
Public opinion. 3. Public opinion—United States. 4. Conflict of
generations—United States. 5. United States—Politics and
government—1933–1945. 6. United States—Politics and
government—1945– I. Bennett, Stephen Earl, 1941–. II. Title.
III. Series.
JK411.B46   1990   90-39015
353′.01—dc20   CIP

British Library Cataloguing in Publication Data is available.

Printed in the United States of America
10 9 8 7 6 5 4 3 2 1

The paper used in this publication meets the minimum requirements of the American National
Standard for Permanence of Paper for Printed Library Materials Z39.48-1984.

To Sherri, Bob, and Jeff
*They and their generation will enjoy the benefits
and bear the costs of big government.*

Contents

Tables and Figures

Preface

One of the most basic themes in American political culture has been popular suspicion of centralized power. Division occurred over many values in the period after the Revolutionary War, but there remained concern that the national government's power had to be used carefully, if at all, lest it become a voracious monster consuming the rights and liberties of individuals and the states. Whether using anecdotal, historical, in-depth interview, or survey data, suspicion of centralized power became an accepted part of most descriptions of American public opinion.

It is time to change that description of American public opinion. Americans have come to accept the wide range of functions and services the national government provides and their suspicion of government's power stops far short of their demands for its withdrawal. In relations between citizen and government, many Americans have come to see themselves more as beneficiaries of its largess than as potential victims of its power. In addition, there is a growing tendency among younger citizens to feel that the largess is that to which they and others are entitled. They have diminished feelings of obligation even to pay attention to what government is doing, let alone to vote. These changes are at the core of American political culture, and their implications are yet to be fully realized.

There will be the temptation among those who favor governmental intervention to solve problems, as well as those who abhor the intrusiveness of government, to cull from the following pages that which most supports their case. There is material in this work that will reassure and infuriate both ends of the ideological spectrum. It was not our purpose to offer a paean to the positive state or a diatribe against national power. In relations between the American people and the central government, the state has been both benefactor and beneficiary. It has dispensed programs, subsidies, and services and broadened its constituent base with each effort. It is not easy to unravel public response to the modern American state, but the effort is worthwhile if we are to assess the quality of relations between the American people and their national government as we head toward the twenty-first century.

In a world where communication depends on being able to boil everything down to a picture, a simple statement, or a sound bite, we know we are taking a risk. Even riskier is our use of a large quantity of public opinion data for which many readers have little patience. We have tried to make the material presented in the following chapters understandable to a wide audience. We hope we have succeeded. For those interested in a good discussion of the complexity of public opinion we suggest a brief, readable volume by Herbert Asher (1988).

In the next six chapters, we attempt to accomplish three important tasks. First, we chart trends in public opinion about big government. Particular attention is paid to the period from the mid-1960s, referred to as the ''Great Society'' years of President Lyndon Johnson, to the administration of President Ronald Reagan and the beginning of President George Bush's tenure in the White House. Second, we discuss what opinions about big government say about changing themes in American political culture. The early months of the Bush administration indicate that the question about big government has been decided for the immediate future. Perhaps the most important consequence of the Reagan years has been to reassure most of the public that big government is here to stay. Finally, there are real age differences in opinions about government and what relations between citizen and government should be. The average college student reading this text probably has very different opinions about federal power and civic obligation than does the professor who assigned the reading.

In Chapter 1, we begin with a historical summary of the growth of the central state and elite contribution to and opinion about that growth, beginning with the Constitutional Convention. V. O. Key (1966) said public opinion often represents a vast ''echo chamber'' of ideas that have their origins among the elite. The ebb and flow of tension between the values of liberty and equality that has characterized political debate in the United States has carried into the modern period and was most evident in the 1964, 1980, and 1984 presidential campaigns. The rhetoric of Ronald Reagan may present the last time the tension between those two values is as clearly articulated for years to come.

We then move to public opinion in the modern United States. After a brief treatment of public opinion during the New Deal era, we focus in Chapter 2 upon the period 1964 to 1989, using a series of public opinion surveys to chart what the public thinks about the power of the central government. Particular attention is paid to the growing trend among Americans since the 1970s to hold no opinion about big government. This tendency says something essential is changing in American political culture: Opinions about big government are increasingly symbolic. The blunt truth is that questions about the central establishment's power are more and more remote to many people's lives. There is less and less connection between these opinions and the programs and services that make up the positive state. The analysis is extended to include a look at various groups in society and how their opinions differ on the central government's power.

An assessment of opinions about government would not be complete without a summary of the impact of ideology. The literature on ideology's impact has become a tangled web. In Chapter 3, we attempt to disentangle the confusing strands of thought about ideology at the grass-roots level by taking another look at the relationships among ideology, partisanship, and opinions about big government. Even with what some claimed was the most ideological president in years occupying the White House in the 1980s, ideology has become less and less important as a guide for people's opinions about big government.

In Chapter 4, we respond to President Reagan's assumption in 1980 that people wanted "government off their backs." By reviewing the basic functions of government that have a direct impact on people (taxing, spending, and regulating), we use a battery of public opinion items to assess what programs people want, what they're willing to pay for, and how much tolerance remains for governmental regulation. Whatever Americans may say about big government in the abstract, they have a healthy and continuing appetite for the programs that make up the positive state.

Age is one of the most important factors determining the willingness to say that one simply does not know or care about the central government's power. In Chapter 5, we take a closer look at seven different age groups beginning with those who came of political age before the New Deal era of the 1930s and extending to those born after the wave of baby boomers. The latter group includes most of the college students sitting in university classrooms today. What are the differences in opinions about government among those who came of age during different political periods? In this chapter, we provide a rare look at what people think not only about their expectations of government but also about their sense of obligation to that government. To the extent that civic obligation is on the wane, particularly among younger Americans, the practice of democratic citizenship is also fading. Although some have described younger citizens as self-absorbed and self-interested, our analysis shows increasing support for egalitarianism but less concern about the power that can enforce it.

In the final chapter, we attempt to weave the findings of Chapters 2 to 5 into a complete cloth. What impact did Ronald Reagan have on Americans' opinions about big government? Ironically, although Reagan came to Washington if not to bury big government certainly not to praise it, he had an impact he had not intended. His partial success in restoring some of the public's confidence in government reinforced a declining fear of big government. Reagan put a "friendly face" on the central establishment and made Americans feel safer with the national government. The implications for this reassurance and the trends we have charted are pondered for a variety of policy areas that are on the political front burner today.

For those who would like to see a more complex treatment of the variables that help us to understand why people have opinions about big government, why many could not care less, and what helps to explain the differences between those who fear big government and those who do not, we included an appendix. This appendix contains multivariate discriminant analyses of the variables that emerge as important predictors of opinions about government. Discriminant analysis is not a complex technique, and we have provided a brief introductory statement to help those without methodological training to understand the tables.

Let us turn now to a brief historical review of governmental growth in the United States, and the people's response to that growth. If we are to chart changes in cultural values on the size of the central government, we must understand the important periods of governmental growth. We begin with the Constitutional Convention and move quickly to the Jacksonian era, through the Populist-Progressive period, and into the twentieth century. Although it is difficult to pick a single important period, we focus on President Franklin Roosevelt's New Deal era in the 1930s as a watershed in relations between the central government and its citizens. The Great Society years of President Lyndon Johnson in the 1960s extended some of the changes begun in the 1930s and set the direction of government into the 1970s. Not until the 1980s and President Reagan was there a serious effort to limit the federal government's reach.

Relations between the national state and its citizens have undergone funda-mental changes as government has grown. As government has become a more important part of our everyday lives, we have changed the way we view the state and our obligations as citizens. Even scholars changed the way they studied the state and public involvement in government. Government's growth has affected everyone.

Acknowledgments

We have benefited from the comments, questions, and encouragement of many individuals whose contributions we gratefully acknowledge. We hope we have remembered them all.

Prof. M. Margaret Conway, now at the University of Florida, invited us to present a paper at the annual meeting of the American Political Science Association, and it evolved into this volume. University of Cincinnati (UC) political scientist David Resnick made helpful suggestions for improving Chapter 1 at an early stage. We also thank Robert Bennett for his comments on Chapter 1.

Dr. Steven R. Howe, of UC's Institute for Policy Research, quickly obtained data from several archives. Roger Stuebing, also of the Institute for Policy Research, helped with data management and statistical analysis. But for Curtis B. Gans, director of the Committee for the Study of the American Electorate, Washington, D.C., we would not have had the data from Gallup's 1987 poll for the Times Mirror Company. Dr. Diane Colasanto and Graham Hueber of the Gallup Organization were very helpful in getting the Gallup data to us. We also wish to thank David Estrin, whose enthusiasm for a book on attitudes about big government in the United States reassured us that the project would see the light of day.

Several people have read the work and their comments have immeasurably improved it: Jarol B. Manheim, now at George Washington University; Sharon A. Sykora, Furman University; and Frank B. Feigert, University of North Texas. We are especially indebted to extensive comments by Michael Margolis, University of Pittsburgh, that improved our presentation of public opinion data.

We are particularly indebted to Fred M. Woodward, director of the University Press of Kansas, and his excellent staff. Debbie Slater at the Type Connection in Yellow Springs, Ohio, converted our figures into camera-ready artwork.

We are also in debt to our respective universities for providing sabbaticals that enabled us to complete this project. Norman C. Thomas, then head of UC's Political Science Department, and Joseph A. Caruso, dean of the McMicken College of Arts and Sciences, engaged in some creative administrative decision making. Dean Caruso also provided funds that speeded the project's completion.

1

A History of Ambivalence

Ronald Wilson Reagan's feelings about "big government" were decidedly unambivalent as he made his first inaugural address on January 20, 1981. Addressing the assembly of guests on the West Front of the Capitol, surrounded by monuments to Washington, Jefferson, and Lincoln, the fortieth president of the United States assessed the state of the national government he would now head and the mandate he perceived was his (Reagan, 1981: 191):

> Our Government has no power except that granted it by the people. It is time to check and reverse the growth of government which shows signs of having grown beyond the consent of the governed.
>
> It is my intention to curb the size and influence of the Federal establishment and to demand recognition of the distinction between the powers granted to the Federal Government and those reserved to the states or to the people.

As he had campaigned to "get government off the people's backs," it was consistent with the new president's optimism to interpret his victory over the Democratic incumbent as a positive statement for action rather than just an overwhelming rejection of President Carter. Ironically, Carter had discussed the American public's restiveness toward big government (and other social institutions) in his televised "Crisis of Confidence" address in July 1979. Relying on his pollster's evidence that Americans were increasingly disillusioned with most big institutions, becoming more conservative, and growing weary of costly big government, Carter reminded his listeners that "the strength we need will not come from the White House, but from every house in America" (Carter, 1982: 121). Hoping to galvanize support for policy to address the "energy crisis," the beleaguered president was soon overwhelmed by the perception that the real crisis was not in every house in America, but in the White House.

1

Was Reagan correct in asserting that government had expanded beyond the consent of the governed? Or have Americans assented to increasing governmental involvement in their lives? What role has the size and power of government played in American politics? How has opinion about the central government changed over time? These are the guiding questions in this book. Extended analyses of various "objective" measures and theories about why government has grown, or whether it has grown more rapidly than the private sector, are left to other studies (but see Berry and Lowery, 1987; Higgs, 1987).

What follows in this chapter is a brief chronological account of growth in American national government and the variety of responses to that growth beginning with the Constitutional Convention and moving to the present. Important periods of change are bounded by the presidencies of Andrew Jackson, Abraham Lincoln, Franklin Roosevelt, Lyndon Johnson, and Ronald Reagan. During each presidency, government grew, whether the sitting president wanted it to or not.

FROM CONFEDERATION TO FEDERATION

The call for less-intrusive government has been well received among the American public at various times in the past. According to political scientists Gabriel A. Almond and Sidney Verba (1963: 441, 494), Americans, as a result of their revolutionary experience with the British monarchy, "tend to be uneasy with a powerful government," and this produces a "tendency to subject all governmental institutions, including the judiciary and bureaucracy, to direct popular control." Samuel P. Huntington (1981) argued that a "pervasive antipower ethic" is an integral part of the American creed and the basis for an American preference for weak central government. Fundamental elements of the American creed such as individualism, a belief in liberty, and a desire for equality lead to an ambivalence toward bigness, particularly in any organization involving the structuring of power. Huntington summarized this ambivalence: "Big buildings, big automobiles, big wealth in the sense of individual wealth, have historically been viewed favorably. Big business, big labor, and, most particularly, big government have been viewed unfavorably" (1981: 39).

Of those fundamental elements of the American creed, the protection of liberty was seen as the surest check on the size and intrusiveness of government. In the years following the Declaration of Independence, there was what Alexander Hamilton described as a "rage for liberty" (Burns, 1982). Under the Articles of Confederation (1781–1789), the national governing system was kept relatively simple with a single-chamber legislature of limited powers. There were no provisions for separate executive or judicial branches of government. States jealously protected their sovereignty against encroachments by other states and particularly by the national legislature. Faced with thirteen independent and often uncooperative states, Congress struggled to establish credible policy with foreign powers and effective control over a growing crisis in public order at home.

By 1787, the rising din from restive Revolutionary War veterans seeking compensation for their services and from farmers whose debts forced them to relinquish their lands to creditors mobilized an increasingly concerned political elite who pondered if liberty could be protected when property was threatened by angry mobs. The enthusiasm that had been missing the previous year in Annapolis, Maryland, to tackle a Constitutional Convention was heightened for the Philadelphia conclave in the spring of 1787. Clearly, in the "rage for liberty," the weak system of national governance was unable to control the rage or to protect liberty.

Ostensibly held to amend the faulty Articles of Confederation, the Convention produced a new Constitution that faced a difficult path to ratification. States that had maintained their supremacy under the Articles would now be asked to relinquish that supremacy to the national government. Furthermore, the national government would grow in size from a single unicameral legislative branch to three separate national branches, including an executive branch headed by a president and a judicial branch composed of a Supreme Court and a system of lower federal courts to be created by a bicameral Congress.

Aware of the uphill battle they faced to garner ratification of the new national system, two of the framers and John Jay took up the new Constitution's cause in a series of essays appearing under the pseudonym "Publius" in New York state newspapers. The *Federalist* essays would not have been necessary had national sentiment been unanimously, or even overwhelmingly, in favor of establishing a new central government. There were responses to the *Federalist* essays, such as those in the Boston *American Herald* from October to December 1787 by an anonymous author who took the pseudonym "John DeWitt" after a seventeenth-century Dutch patriot. Lamenting the haste with which the new Constitution was being considered for ratification, DeWitt counseled, "It is much easier to dispense powers, then [*sic*] recall them" (1986: 193).

The size of a nation-state and its government was a critical component of Anti-Federalist thought. A small republic would best ensure liberty, would best respond to the needs of the people, and would establish sufficiently close relations with the public to educate them to the responsible citizenship necessary to maintain the republic (Storing, 1981: 16). The specter of a larger central structure expanding its powers and reach to distant territories loomed as a serious threat to those who believed that the maintenance of liberty could be guaranteed only when the states had supreme power over the central government, such as in a confederation.

In less than two years, the Federalists triumphed over the Anti-Federalists and the Constitution became the nation's governing document. Part of the reason for the Federalists' victory lay in the nature of their political thought: centralization of organization. Anti-Federalists were in the end too fragmented to mount a decisive campaign against the centripetal force of the Federalists (McDonald, 1979: 362). Neither side was short on charismatic rhetoricians, though the Federalists appeared to have the edge. More than matching the eloquence of a Henry was the brilliance of a Hamilton. Finally, there was the inherent weakness in the Anti-Federalist argument against a large republic when the United States, even then, was not a small republic (Storing, 1981: 71).

To counter Anti-Federalist charges of a central government amassing tremendous power and to guarantee ratification of the Constitution, the Federalists finally accepted a range of limitations on the government's powers. The first ten amendments emerged as a compromise between opposing sides and were offered in the first year of the new government to calm the fearful and uncertain. Still, it was a more powerful and larger entity than that allowed under the Articles of Confederation.

When George Washington became the first president under the newly ratified Constitution, he took over a national government that consisted of a "foreign office with John Jay and a couple of clerks to deal with correspondence from John Adams in London and Thomas Jefferson in Paris; . . . a Treasury Board with an empty treasury; . . . a 'Secretary at War' with an authorized army of 840 men; . . . [and] a dozen clerks whose pay was in arrears" (White, 1956: 1). In the early years of the republic, government grew to meet its new responsibilities, and by the first few years of the Jefferson presidency, the "federal establishment," including the three governmental branches, the military, and a nascent bureaucracy, numbered over twelve thousand (Young, 1966: 29). Even with this growth, it remained small compared with European governments. Few citizens would have come into direct contact with the federal government apparatus since most governmental functions touching upon their daily lives were administered by the state and local governments.

FROM REPUBLIC TO DEMOCRACY

Traveling through the United States in the early 1830s, ostensibly to observe the American penal system, French aristocrats Alexis de Tocqueville and Gustave de Beaumont captured the republic in the middle of its first century. From his voluminous notes contained in fourteen notebooks, Tocqueville framed the classic *Democracy in America,* an effort to develop generalizations about democratic systems based on the lessons learned in Jacksonian America. Although his intent was to instruct a displaced French aristocracy in the wake of a series of revolutions emanating from the lesser estates, Tocqueville made many observations that continue to illuminate aspects of the American system.

Commenting upon the relative equality of most of the citizenry and the absence of an aristocratic class, Tocqueville warned, "When the citizens are all more or less equal, it becomes difficult to defend their freedom from the encroachments of power" (1969: 57). Tocqueville described Americans as "lucky enough to [have] escaped absolute power" and hence standing a good chance to maintain their liberty. Yet he warned of the destructive force to liberty contained in the quest for equality. As more privileges disappear and citizens become more equal, the demand for equality only increases. As demand for equality increases, so does the centralization of authority and power: "Every central power which follows its natural instincts loves equality and favors it. For equality singularly facilitates, extends, and secures its influence" (1969: 673).

If the history of eighteenth-century America is one wherein liberty was the dominant value, then the nineteenth and twentieth centuries have been marked by "rages for equality" and a concomitant growth in the power of the central government. President Andrew Jackson believed that a limited government based upon enumerated constitutional powers was one that best protected liberty as well as equality. Freedom, or liberty, was "equality among the people in the rights conferred by the Government" (Remini, 1984: 92). Citizens were equal with regard to their liberties. When government grew beyond the limits set by the Constitution (as Jackson fervently believed was the case with the National Bank), it then violated equality and liberty. From Jackson's point of view, the essential task of maintaining the union was best served by limiting government's reach, particularly into people's pockets.

The fortieth president could probably have learned a few things from the seventh president. Jackson found the goal of trimming government's size as impossible to attain as would Reagan. Although he succeeded in the controversy over the National Bank, he found that government had remarkable regenerative powers. To large degree, Jackson's policies—particularly his emphasis on the elimination of corruption and on reorganization to improve efficiency—resulted in governmental growth: "In the matter of reducing government, Jackson completely failed. He simply could not have it both ways: he could not reform the government by tightening the administrative process to root out corruption without approving the establishment of bureaus in each department to investigate and oversee operations" (Remini, 1984: 246).

During the 1830s, the federal government experienced a 57 percent increase in civilian employment, from over eleven thousand employees in 1831 to over eighteen thousand in 1841. The sharpest increases came in executive department functions (for example, defense and the post office), but the legislative and judicial branches shared in some of the growth, each expanding their civilian employee bases by 15 percent (U.S. Department of Commerce, 1976: 1103).

Naturally, the federal budget was also expanding, with the largest portion of governmental revenue generated by the controversial tariffs collected by the U.S. Customs and by profits from land sales. Federal budget receipts jumped from $24.8 million in 1829, the first year of Jackson's presidency, to $50.8 million in 1836, Jackson's final year in office. The jump in receipts was due largely to land sales, reflecting a period of national expansion, and receipts would fall the next year to $24.9 million. Federal expenditures also fluctuated widely, doubling from $15.2 million in 1829 to $30.9 million in 1836. For all the fluctuation in the federal budget, Jackson was able to accomplish what Reagan could not: elimination of the federal debt in 1835. The budget was in surplus for every year Jackson was in the White House.

Not everyone applauded Jackson's budgetary accomplishments, however, particularly in South Carolina, where "nullifier" sentiment that the state should refuse to collect the tariffs resulted in an Ordinance of Nullification in 1832. A critical source of revenue for the federal government, tariffs were viewed in the southern states as criminal favoritism of northern over southern interests. The intrusiveness of the federal government into the economic marketplace stirred secessionist talk among the more hot-blooded nullifiers, and leading the intellectual and political charge was South Carolina's John C. Calhoun. Jackson's vice president during his first term, Calhoun resigned to enter the Senate and become the bane of Jackson's existence. Jackson's deathbed wish was that he had executed this leader of the nullifiers for treason during his presidency (Remini, 1984).

Although Jackson's combination of deft political skill and willingness to use force if necessary averted civil war over national tariff policy, his handling of slavery meant Abraham Lincoln would not have as much room to maneuver when South Carolina once again led a secessionist movement. Slave-holding southerners argued for limited government in order to protect their liberty to own human property. Abolitionists, concentrated in the Northeast, argued that equality was a concomitant value guaranteed by the Declaration of Independence. For many of the southern elite, democracy had relatively few attractions and many features that violated their conceptions of liberty and the exercise of power by the chosen few. Jackson viewed the abolitionists as troublemakers and the tools of his Whig opponents, who were bent on weakening or even destroying the Union. Though his rhetoric was steeped in concern for the common man's rights to equality and liberty, slave-holder Jackson had little but contempt for the reformers, who seemed bent on stirring "dangerous" passions among the people.

As the controversy moved west, increasing pressure for a response from the central government was inevitable. Jackson's answer was to straddle the issue, making claims that he would uphold the law of the land but offering little enforcement to support his words. Later, the opportunities to limit the conflict between North and South over economic policy, social values, and political representation would evaporate as regional tensions exploded into a conflict that constituted the most serious threat to the Union since its inception. Nothing expands the size and power of the national government as effectively as war.

FROM CIVIL WAR TO CIVIL SERVICE

Shortly after his inauguration in March 1861, Lincoln was presented with the fall of Fort Sumter and the inevitability of civil war. His response changed forever the dimensions of presidential power and set the stage for the "presidential state" (discussed later in this chapter). Presidential scholar Edward Corwin (1957) described the "wedding" of the "commander-in-chief" clause (Article II, sec. 2) and the "take care that the laws be faithfully executed" clause (Article II, sec. 3) as expanding not only executive power but also legislative power. Defining the new boundaries between the expanded branches was bound to increase and expand the activity of the U.S. Supreme Court. Suspension of habeas corpus, the institution of a draft, and the administration of a war before formal declaration by Congress were all considered departures from "normal" constitutional governance but were accepted as part of the inherent or prerogative executive powers that accrue during an emergency.

With the Union threatened, the ranks of governmental workers grew, never to be diminished to their prewar levels. From 1861 to 1871, there was a 39 percent increase in federal civilian employment, from over 36,000 to over 51,000. Washington-based employees increased from 2,200 to 6,222, a 183 percent jump in a single decade. By the turn of the twentieth century, there would be almost 240,000 civilian employees of the federal government (U.S. Department of Commerce, 1976: 1103), almost half of whom were employed under the provisions of the Civil Service (Pendleton) Act of 1883. Clearly, the organization of government was becoming larger, so Washington, D.C., became more hospitable to its increasing population: Swamplands were drained and streets were paved; only air-conditioning was needed to make the city tolerable year-round.

But the postwar years were significant for more than just the increase in the number of those employed by the federal government or the growth of the budget to pay for the government's war debt and growing expenses. Abraham Lincoln's administration of the war had greatly enhanced the power of the executive branch, and in the years leading up to the turn of the century there was increasing debate about how little or much control the president should have over the burgeoning Washington establishment. The patronage system that Jackson had put into place in the 1830s was assailed for inefficiency and injecting politics into administration. Similar criticisms were made of state and local political "bosses" and their patronage appointments to public offices.

In the Progressive Era, the Pendleton Act began to address concerns about efficiency and honesty in public office by establishing a Civil Service Commission. It would take the assassination of President Garfield to strengthen the civil service system and to begin the movement toward increasing independence from political control of a growing governmental complex, presenting another dilemma to a republican system of representative government. How was a president to be held accountable for the implementation of policy when he had less and less control over administration?

If the number of people working for the government was growing by leaps and bounds, political rhetoric did not echo a "big government" mentality. The years from the end of the Civil War to the turn of the century were the heyday of laissez-fairism. As Leonard White summarized: "During these years there was a general, although not unchallenged, conviction of the virtue of laissez faire. This had been the prevailing temper of the people, despite the Federalist doctrine to the contrary. It survived the Civil War, was congenial to the big business of the postwar years, and was proclaimed by most of the prominent men of the time" (1958: 3).

So powerful was the hold of laissez-faire on the minds of postwar political leaders that President Cleveland could not conceive of a positive role for government even when the evidence of poverty and economic injustices due to the maldistribution of wealth and power became too obvious to dismiss (Hofstadter, 1954: 183–184). All Cleveland would do, in the face of rampant poverty coexisting with superabundant wealth, was to appeal to businessmen to set aside their quest for selfish profits in favor of the public trust. As Hofstadter noted, the key to Cleveland's "mind was his dislike of 'paternalism' in government. The people, he believed, were entitled to economy, purity, and justice in their government, and should expect no more. 'A fair field, and no favor' " (1954: 182).

Proclamations by prominent men aside, folks in the hinterland were not proclaiming the virtues of laissez-faire government. Post–Civil War economic depressions left many southern and western farmers bankrupt; foreclosures on farms were stirring the same kind of restiveness with the political system that they had in the 1780s. Arising from this discontent was the Populist movement, which reached its zenith in the 1890s. Central to Populist philosophy was the necessity of controlling the growing power of big business, particularly railroads and banks. What better check on corporate power than the central government? How could individual liberty be protected in the face of a passive government manipulated by corporate interests? What good was individual effort when it could be wiped away by usurious bank policies and rail freight rates? How can democracy function if the people have no real control over their economic destiny? (Goodwyn, 1978; Pollack, 1962).

Although many have pointed to the Great Depression–New Deal years as the time at which people turned to the central government for relief, and expectations were "nationalized," Franklin Roosevelt reaped a harvest that had been planted in the decades following the Civil War, when seemingly incessant hard times called for action only the national government could deliver. Needed to check big business' power was governmental power that allowed access, however minimal, of the people. The most effective source of governmental power was, of course, national.

The 1896 election ended the Populists' political hopes and marked an important transition point for American politics in general. Speaking of the "Populist Moment," Lawrence Goodwyn (1978: 269) described the "cultural intimidation" of American citizens who increasingly believed that "hierarchical American society could, perhaps, be marginally 'humanized' but could not be fundamentally democratized." Reforms such as the Federal Reserve Act (1913) were designed to satisfy the corporate (banking and large farming) interests whose power had instigated calls for change; they did little to help the small farmer. The belief that the American system could be only "marginally 'humanized' . . . acquired a name, and rather swiftly a respectability always denied Populism. In 1900–1930, it was popularly recognized as 'progressivism.' Later, it became known as 'liberalism' " (Goodwyn, 1978: 270). By 1988, it was the "L word," and some Democrats returned to the term "Progressive" to avoid the negative connotations they thought had been attached to liberalism.

While progressivism borrowed its reform fervor from the Populists, along with some of the latter movement's programs, it was noted for emphasizing the critical role the central government would have to play to provide equality of opportunity, political and economic. As industrialists used the shibboleth of "individual liberty" to counter attempts to rein them in, reformers argued that the brave new industrial world required attention to the need to protect societal, community, or group liberty and equality. In *The Promise of American Life,* Progressive Herbert Croly described the mission of democracy in 1909 as more than merely ensuring individual liberty and equal rights; rather it should be concerned with the "joint benefit of individual distinction *and social improvement*" (1964: 207; emphasis added). Croly further asserted that "a democracy . . . cannot fulfill its mission without the eventual assumption by the state of many functions now performed by individuals, and without becoming expressly responsible for an improved distribution of wealth" (1964: 209).

Progressives were to have more success than the Populists, even though their vibrant spokesman, Theodore Roosevelt, lost his 1912 bid to recapture the White House from Republican incumbent Taft and failed to defeat Democratic challenger Woodrow Wilson. In Roosevelt's "New Nationalism" and Wilson's "New Freedom" was contained a vision of a more active central government. Although Wilson's New Freedom has been judged as more modest than Roosevelt's plan to use big government to check (not to destroy) big business, Wilson would implement many Progressive policies once in office (Link, 1954; Cooper, 1983).

The impact of progressivism, and its later transformation into liberalism, has been profound upon twentieth-century American government at all levels. If the concept of individual liberty was being deemphasized in favor of the common weal, equality was getting increasing attention. The reformers urged not only increasing economic equality but also an extension of the suffrage to women and a widening of voter impact on local, state, and national institutions through referendum, recall, and direct election of U.S. senators. True to Tocqueville's dictum, the central government aided the expansion of equality and its own power.

A tremendous resource to aid in governmental growth was added to the Constitution in 1913 with the Sixteenth Amendment's allowance for the income tax. The tax was generally described as "progressive," though additional deductions and income exclusions made it less progressive as time went by. Not until the 1980s would a successful challenge to the progressive-liberal consensus on the positive state's benefits be mounted. Included in that challenge would be the supply-side charge that the income tax had become progressively unfair and that a 30 percent cut in the rates would do much to trim the size of government.

Government's expanding power and the goals of reformers did not meet with unqualified public approval. Issues such as women's suffrage and temperance generated mixed responses, even from those whom the policies were intended to benefit. It would take over a half-century for women to exercise their franchise in equal proportion to men. Merriam and Gosnell (1924) found that in the first presidential election after the ratification of the Nineteenth Amendment, many women believed politics "was a man's business." Prohibition became federal government policy in 1918, and lawmakers quickly found it necessary to expand the ranks of those charged with its enforcement (for example, the FBI). Eventually, a federal government under a new majority party leadership ended Prohibition under the Twenty-first Amendment, the only constitutional amendment to be ratified by state conventions and to repeal another amendment. The "long thirst" was over, as was the national government's boldest attempt to date to regulate individual behavior.

As a response to the Progressive extension of the "Populist Moment" (Goodwyn, 1978), government grew. But its reach would remain limited by an interest group pressure system that encouraged governmental activity and growth within particular arenas and by public expectations that were only beginning to fathom what the power of the central state could deliver. Already broached, however, was the topic of increasing the government's role in the private economic sphere. It would take an economic crisis of worldwide proportions and the rise of a new majority party in 1932–1936 to implement some of the more far-reaching Progressive reforms, but the public-private dichotomy would never return to a Jeffersonian simplicity, nor would people's expectations of government.

THE PLURALISTS' POSITIVE, PRESIDENTIAL STATE

By the 1930s, events at home and particularly abroad were converging to produce a larger, more powerful, more centralized government in the United States. If Higgs (1987) was correct when he asserted that crises produce a "ratcheted" growth in government that never returns to precrises levels, then the third and fourth decades of the twentieth century were destined to constitute a period of tremendous growth.

Whether one preferred to think of the growing state as "active" or "intrusive" depended upon whether one was "liberal" or "conservative," fairly new ideological labels in Roosevelt's New Deal America (Beer, 1978). In a departure from classic Western tradition, liberalism from the 1930s to the 1960s became associated with support for a growing, "positive" state. The nerve center of the positive state would be the presidency, the only institution with a national constituency capable of checking the special interest constituencies of a "deadlocked" Congress and acting quickly in response to the broader problems the United States had to confront as the premier world power in the wake of World War II.

Clearly, with the chief executive's expanded responsibilities and expectations, "the President need[ed] help" (President's Committee on Administrative Management, 1937). The Brownlow Commission had stipulated that the president needed a "small" staff to help with the increasing administrative burden, but the Executive Office of the President, created in 1939 by executive order, did not stay small for long. What began as a modest White House office with six senior aides, grew to forty-five during the war and continued to balloon in subsequent administrations with a diminution in size only during the post-Watergate Ford years (Pious, 1979: 243). There were almost six hundred staffers in the Reagan White House. In addition, there is a domino effect in staff growth among the three branches. As the White House increased its "expert pool," Congress began, at first in the 1940s and then in earnest in the 1970s, to increase its staff to the current level of over twenty thousand congressional staffers distributed between personal, committee, and administrative (for example, the General Accounting Office and Library of Congress) entities.

More quietly but just as inexorably, the judicial branch was also increasing civilian employment as the number of federal districts grew and the caseloads of the federal courts expanded. Rising tension between the legislative and executive branches was enlarging the role of federal courts in the making of public policy. In a test of wills between a Court reluctant to let go of laissez-faire and a president determined to implement his New Deal policies, the Supreme Court became the last bastion for limited government in the face of increasing demand for governmental response to the Depression. The 1937 "switch in time that saved nine" resulted in a Court that finally abandoned the limited government concept. Moreover, by virtue of his extended tenure, Franklin Roosevelt was granted the opportunity to appoint eight justices to the high court.

Arguably, FDR's most important appointee, Hugo Black in 1937, went on for the next thirty-four years to be the most influential voice from the Court for a "nationalization" of the citizen rights set forth in the Bill of Rights (Abraham, 1985: 214). His interpretation of the Fourteenth Amendment's due process clause (also called "incorporation") has been said to have established a "government by judiciary" (Berger, 1977). Incorporation aside, the Court created by FDR was more sympathetic toward an expansion of the national government's role in economic affairs.

The expansion of the national government's role was reflected in the burgeoning size of its budget and civilian personnel. Between 1933 and 1936, civilian employment rose by 44 percent, to 867,432 (U.S. Department of Commerce, 1976: 1105). There was a 75 percent increase, to almost 123,000, in Washington, D.C.–based employment. Commensurate with expanding employment was an expanding budget. From 1933 to 1936, the national government increased its receipts by 100 percent, taking in almost $4 billion. Simultaneously, the deficit grew to over $4.4 billion (an increase of 70 percent for this three-year period), and the nation's debt increased by 50 percent, to over $33 billion. In addition, government increased its control of the regulation and service functions that were once handled by private institutions (for example, health care for the elderly), other indicants of growing governmental power.

During the Eisenhower years, when Republicans had an opportunity to dismantle parts of the New Deal that they had railed against for years, there was a small decline in the number of civilian government workers, though the budget continued its inexorable climb. Still, the ratcheting up in governmental growth was not reversed, and many of the New Deal programs (for example, Social Security) continued under the Republicans as they had under the Democrats. Furthermore, growth in the national government spurred growth in state governments. Arguments that concern about a growing national government is misplaced in the face of fifty state governments that have grown even more rapidly in personnel and budgets are misleading because they do not take into account how much the growth in state governments is the result of stimuli from the central government.

With the rise of a larger, more centralized national government, where was the discussion about liberty and equality? Tocqueville argued that in the modern democratic state, liberty would be sacrificed in the quest for equality. For the most part, post–New Deal scholarly work, particularly in political science, reflects the accuracy of Tocqueville's prediction. Having survived the wrenching Depression years and the ravages of World War II, scholars sought both a new understanding of what had been wrought by the crises and a sense of continuity with a democratic past.

Arthur Bentley, in a work originally published in 1908, provided the intellectual spark to fire a behavioral revolution. Bentley urged scholars to lift their eyes from the legalistic small-print constitutions and other legal documents and realize that "there are no political phenomena except group phenomena" (1949: 222). Four decades later in *The Governmental Process* (published in 1951), David Truman would absorb Bentley's work into his own and become one of the most prominent "pluralist" theorists.

In pluralist theory, the key political entity is the group, not the individual. Some reduced the state to a "minute factor [that] has served to help give coherent and pretentious expression to some particular group's activity" (Bentley, 1949: 263; see also von Beyme, 1985). From here on, discussion would focus primarily upon relations between groups within and outside of government. As had been presaged by Populist-Progressive thinking at the end of the nineteenth and beginning of the twentieth centuries, the relationship between the individual and the state began to fade as a primary concern: Individuals could have an impact on modern government only by joining groups.

That relations between government and governed were determined by group participation with little focus on the state was reflected in much of the political activity during the 1960s and 1970s. Some worried that the "balkanization" of citizens into groups and their increased access to government as a result of reforms in political parties (especially the Democratic party) and institutions (especially Congress) would lead to a "crisis of governability" for American democracy. Huntington (1981) warned that an "excess" of democracy was undermining governmental authority with dire consequences for the mainte-nance of the American state, but his voice was one of only a few expressing concern about the "democratic distemper." Furthermore, even in his concern Huntington did not prescribe in any of his nostrums for "moderation in democracy" the enhancement of individual liberty.

As concern faded about relations between the individual and the state among political scientists, fewer were comfortable even defining what the state was. While forums for discussing liberty dwindled, anxiety about the possibilities for tyranny from a coercive state was expressed by a few outside the intellectual mainstream (for example, Hayek, 1944). Research noted who joined groups (even institutions) for what reasons, as well as the successes and failures of some groups compared with others, and equality became more important, with the national government as its key promoter. Accepting the ends as desirable and consistent with our national heritage, surely only the most hidebound would question the increasing role of the national government. This shifting emphasis from liberty to equality seemed to make sense given what was happening in the "real world."

One aspect of the real world that would increasingly focus Americans' attention on governmental action, or inaction, dealt with race relations. In the 1940s and 1950s, Americans were slowly awakening to the certainty that after almost one hundred years, slavery's bitter legacy could no longer be denied. If, as pluralist theory argued, government responded to group interests to produce public policy, then could we continue to define America as truly democratic if any group was systematically excluded and discriminated against? Furthermore, if a group had suffered years of deprivation, was a simple declaration of equality sufficient? Was not a more forceful stance necessary? President Lyndon Johnson, working from a report by Daniel Patrick Moynihan, offered a more forceful stance in a commencement address at Howard University in 1965: "It is not enough just to open the gates of opportunity. . . . We seek not just freedom but opportunity. We seek not just legal equity but human ability, not just equality as a right and a theory but equality as a fact and *equality as a result*" (cited in Ravitch, 1983: 161; emphasis added).

President Johnson was the beneficiary of increasingly confident social science research that offered the possibility of understanding the causes of social phenomena. More important, political science research heralded a strong president as the lord protector of democracy. Johnson's 1964 landslide victory over Barry Goldwater was interpreted as a "repudiation" of the conservative attack on the growing welfare state arising from the Kennedy-Johnson War on Poverty–Great Society programs. Conceding that public opinion was sometimes difficult to interpret, Burns (1966: 311) proclaimed that the 1964 victory "strengthened the impression of powerful popular support both for the welfare state and for the modern Presidency." Burns concluded that "it would be a courageous man indeed who would run on a Goldwater platform again."

A CONSERVATIVE RESPONSE

A confluence of disastrous events ranging from Vietnam and Watergate to the first OPEC oil embargo in 1973 left the nation dispirited and anxious as inflation, unemployment, and interest rates soared into double-digits toward the end of the decade. Much attention has been focused on the effects of the Vietnam war and Watergate; less has been said about the effects of the oil embargoes even though their importance is generally acknowledged. The impact of these embargoes on the American economy was profound and lasting. The inflationary 1970s are still being felt in real estate values that rose sharply and stayed sufficiently high to price a young working class out of the housing market or into bankruptcy. The increase in farmland value crashed in the early 1980s and, in the process, brought an end to many small family farms.

Commentators and academicians worried about a growing "crisis of confidence." Assessing the public's mood toward government concerned even the White House during the 1970s. President Carter's crisis of confidence speech on July 15, 1979, was a less-than-successful attempt to respond to that mood. Carter's admonition to Americans to "expect less" from government did not play as well as Reagan's offer to "get the government off the backs of the American people." Preaching a gospel of limited expectations may have been what was needed to "build down" public expectations of government and particularly of the president (see Lowi, 1985), but few enjoyed the sermon. Americans, it was said, were becoming more conservative, dubious of liberal reforms, moving to the right, and growing weary of costly big government.

If 1964 was the wrong year for a conservative candidate to win the presidency,

1980 was the right year. Taking up the cause for conservatism was Ronald Reagan whose 1964 televised address in California brought in a record $1 million for conservative Republicans that year (Cannon, 1982). His 1980 campaign promise to get government off the backs of the people was a well-timed appeal if pollsters were right about the "public malaise." Here amid a foreign policy crisis and a disastrous domestic economy was a candidate who conveyed that he was as upset with Washington as were many among the public. The question that would take some time to answer was, Were they upset about the same things?

Lipset and Schneider warned that public disenchantment with Washington would abate with "more intelligent and skillful leadership and more effective government" (1987: 351). They asserted that people were more disillusioned with the competence of those running the large institutions and particularly with the government's inability to address chronic economic problems such as high inflation and unemployment rates. President Carter's 1979 appeal was correct in its recognition of a "crisis of confidence," but his response (that leadership would have to come from somewhere other than the White House) failed to grasp the source of the crisis. *In the president-centered positive state, people looked to the White House for solutions, not more problems.* Carter's failure to perceive this doomed his presidency to a single term and led some scholars who had been chastising an "imperial presidency" to begin lamenting the "imperiled presidency."

Whether Ronald Reagan's 1980 victory over the incumbent president was a mandate for less government will be discussed later; however, his coattails were longer than any other presidential victor's since Lyndon Johnson in 1964. Gaining twelve seats in the Senate lifted the Republicans to majority status in that chamber for the first time since 1954, and winning thirty-three seats in the House generated a crisis of confidence for the remaining Democratic members, particularly those, usually from the Northeast, whose records were more liberal than those of their conservative party colleagues from the Sunbelt. The "conservative coalition" of Republicans and conservative Democrats got a tremendous boost in November 1980. Certainly, the new Reagan administration behaved as if it did have a mandate and, with the help of "Boll Weevil" Democrats, took full advantage of the "honeymoon period" to push through Congress a double package of budget cuts and large income-tax reductions.

Observers began characterizing the Reagan years as a return to isolated individualism at home, or, as some preferred to call it, "selfishness." The American public, in general, was said to be in a more conservative mood. Even the young, particularly college-educated whites among whom Reagan garnered surprising levels of support, were characterized as self-absorbed and increasingly materialistic. Individualism, a value that had been deemphasized in modern political theory, appeared to be flourishing among segments of the populace. Were Americans just being manipulated by corporate advertising techniques designed to present a nostalgic mythic picture of small-town America? Irving Howe argued that the countercultural excesses of the late 1960s resulted in a "yearn[ing] for a return to 'traditional values' even if that return was being sponsored politically by a *nouveau riche* class which in its pinched little heart aspired most of all to conspicuous consumption" (1986: 416).

The claim that the Republican party appealed to "selfishness" while the Democrats appealed to "compassion" was used by Walter Mondale in his 1984 bid to oust incumbent Reagan from the White House. During the general election campaign, Mondale chided his opponent for his "social Darwinism" and added, "I'd rather lose a campaign about decency than win one about self-interest" (*Newsweek,* Nov. 5, 1984: 29). After the election there was hurt and sometimes angry confusion among Democrats and their intellectual supporters. How could the American people desert them?

The presidential elections of 1980 and, to a lesser extent, 1984 provide some of the clearest examples since 1964 of pro- and anti-government rhetoric by candidates of the two major parties. By 1984, however, the edges of the debate had blurred and the candidate who announced, "We're taking care of more people than . . . ever . . . before by any administration. . . . We are today subsidizing more than 10 million people, and we're going to continue along that line"(Broder, 1984), was none other than Ronald Reagan.

In his first four years in the White House, President Reagan had begun to learn about the unambivalent nature of people's attitudes toward government. He had also learned the lesson Andrew Jackson had confronted: In any attempt to trim the size of government, it only seems to grow larger. By 1986, the Census Bureau reported that governmental employment was growing, with federal employment increasing more rapidly than any other level, to over three million civilian employees (*New York Times,* Oct. 14, 1986: Y13). Reagan could not repeat Jackson's record with the budget, however, and his administration proposed the first trillion-dollar budget while requesting Congress to approve higher debt ceilings. Republicans, now in congressional leadership positions, had the embarrassing task of sponsoring legislation for higher debt ceilings. For years, from the haven provided by their minority status, they had assailed the Democrats for growing deficits and debts. Now there was a certain glee among Democrats to see their Republican colleagues' discomfort.

In his observation of Jacksonian democracy, Alexis de Tocqueville expressed the hope that the centralizing and leveling effects of an increasing quest for equality would be tempered by the people's desire to maintain their liberty. What Tocqueville did not anticipate was that a centralized democratic state would provide services (either in benefits or protection) beyond increasing equality that would come to be taken by the public as entitlements—rights to be protected as vigilantly as those guaranteed by the Constitution. In many ways, the positive, welfare state amended the social contract; it changed the fundamental "relationship between government and society in the United States" (Huntington,

1981). The amended contract stipulated the provision of a variety of benefits that recipient ("clientele") groups had come to expect as theirs by group entitlement. Nothing much was expected in return for these benefits and, indeed, governmental transfer programs have been characterized as "permissive" in that they required only that one "fit [a] deserving category" (Mead, 1986).

It was the amendation of the old social contract that caught the Reagan administration off guard as it sought to trim the size of government during the honeymoon months of the first term. Relying upon rhetoric that emphasized the danger to individual liberty presented by a bloated, wasteful national government, President Reagan found that proposing cuts in a series of domestic programs stirred equally rousing rhetoric from a variety of groups in defense of entitlement programs. His administration's attempt to reform Social Security was probably the strongest lesson in entitlement politics. The battering the White House took from Congress, the Gray Panthers, Cong. Claude Pepper, and the media was sufficient for Reagan to declare the largest transfer payment program to the nation's wealthiest age group (over sixty-five) as off-limits.[1] Afterward, the director of the Office of Management and Budget (OMB), David Stockman, noted wryly that Chief of Staff Jim Baker "carried around a bazooka, firing first and asking questions later of anyone who mentioned the words 'Social Security'" (1987: 14).

That lesson was not lost on Reagan's Republican successor, George Bush. Bush's ascension to the Oval Office was not accompanied by the antigovernmental rhetoric that had marked Reagan's campaigns. His January 1989 inaugural address (1989: 207–211) mentioned "hard choices," but trimming the government's size was not one of them. Mention of cutting the deficit elicited only the suggestion that leaders need to be "looking at what we have, perhaps allocating it differently, making our decisions based on honest need and prudent safety." Nor was Bush's first year in office characterized by the same attacks on governmental spending that marked Reagan's first term. Instead, Bush frustrated Washington observers, while still maintaining a relatively high level of popularity, with little in the way of domestic policy initiatives. In his first year as president, George Bush relied on the aura of statesmanship that presidential visits to foreign capitals can bestow.

If the Bush presidency got off to a slow start, there appeared to be no mandate from the people to do anything else but wait for politically opportune moments when a Republican president could strike bargains with the Democrat-dominated Congress. The Supreme Court has become the most likely source from which the debate about the appropriate role of government will spread to the legislative and executive agendas. Its 1989 ruling in the abortion case of *Webster v. Reproductive Services* has the potential to mobilize (and polarize) public opinion and place the issue of how much government people want back on the political front burner.

Just as the political world seemed to be coming to terms with the persistence of the positive state, political science turned up the volume on a debate between pluralists and "statists." The latter argue that pluralistic political science has ignored for too long the autonomous, coercive, even manipulative power of the state. In a recent exchange between pluralist and statist theorists (Almond, 1988; Nordlinger, Lowi, and Fabbrini, 1988), both sides acknowledged the state's ability to act, even in the absence of organized demand. Where they diverge appears to be on the implications for that autonomy, with the statists more critical of state power.

CONCLUSION

By the beginning of his second term, Ronald Reagan had come to terms with big government. Although V. O. Key believed that popular opinion usually echoed elite opinion, in the course of the Reagan years the public voiced its views, which were mimicked by the presidency. The first two hundred years of this republic's history has seen the government grow for a variety of reasons. What began with the Constitutional Convention as an attempt by the elite to limit the role of government was soon lost to popular demands for government to increase equality as well as benefits and services. Even James Madison lived to see the growing call for governmental involvement in the development of roads and canals, something he felt was not a federal power without constitutional amendment (McCoy, 1989).

The public's growing acceptance of government is most readily charted by the availability of public opinion data beginning in the 1930s. It is not a coincidence that the most important moment of governmental growth should occur at the same time as the establishment of public opinion surveys. Beginning with FDR, presidents became increasingly interested in taking the public's pulse on issues and their personal popularity. A president's popularity rating has become the foundation of his legitimacy to shape policy. Popularity or approval ratings in national surveys have become a standard by which the responsiveness of government is measured. Governmental responsiveness to public opinion in turn has become the standard for measuring the extent of democracy. Therefore, if government is responsive to public opinion and its leadership is popular, it meets the modern test for a democracy. Government grows only because it meets public needs and demands and thus remains democratic. To question this linkage is to question the democratic fiber of the state.

But is the government's responsiveness to group demands and maintenance of its leadership's popularity enough to establish the claim of a democracy? Increased concern in political science about the role of the state has been extended to the relationship between public opinion and the state. Benjamin Ginsberg summarized his concern that modern Western governments manipulate the "captive public's" opinions and that scholars have missed the implications of this manipulation:

> Contemporary students of public opinion assume that the citizenry was the only beneficiary of the linkage that was forged between government and opinion in the West. But in some respects the ultimate beneficiary was the state. Expansion of the role of mass opinion in political life opened the way for expansion of the size and power of the state. The power of the traditional state had been limited by the narrowness of its constituent base (1986: 28).

As government exhibits responsiveness to popular opinion, it justifies the expansion of its power. This is remarkably similar to Alexis de Tocqueville's argument that as citizens demand more equality, the central government happily responds with an expansion of its power to guarantee this equality. To question the expansion is to question the goal. The role of the citizen is more to express preferences to which government can respond than to monitor the appropriateness of governmental activity. Ginsberg called the channeling of political energies into safer activities for the state the "domestication," or taming, of public opinion. (He argues that voting is an example, but nonvoting is even less disruptive to the state.) The implications for the maintenance of meaningful democratic citizenship are profound if Ginsberg is even partially correct.

We will return to this argument later, but first we need to take a closer look at how public opinion has changed since the 1930s. What impact have fifty years and two significant periods of governmental growth (the 1930s and the 1960s–1970s) had on how people respond to the size and power of the national government?

2

Changing Views about Big Government, 1935–1989

In this chapter, we will take a closer look at what people have thought about the central government since the New Deal years. Careful interpretation of polls from the 1930s reveals that although there was not overwhelming endorsement of New Deal programs, people generally approved of governmental involvement in economic affairs and of President Franklin Roosevelt. From 1964 to the present, we are able to chart trends in people's opinions about the size and power of the central government with a single survey item that has been asked, with little change in wording, for nearly a quarter-century. Items about big government asked by other survey organizations essentially confirm the messages derived from our main vehicle.

The most significant trend from 1964 to the late 1980s is the increase in the percentage of people who offer no opinion on this item. Clearly, the size and power of the national government is becoming less significant to the modern American citizen. We then look at the varying importance of social class, race, and partisanship on how people feel about the central government. For all three variables, differences in opinion narrowed between subgroups from the 1960s to the 1980s. Those expressing no opinion on government's power were most likely to come from the lower social classes. A more thorough analysis of why more people are opting out of expressing an opinion about the size and power of government is offered in the appendix.

After all the data have been examined, what are the implications for relations between people and government? Do people think differently about government today than they did a half-century ago? What follows suggests strongly that opinions have changed and that the ambivalent tradition in American political culture might be coming to an end. Does the lessening of a healthy stock of suspicion mean that Ginsberg's warning about the "domestication" of public opinion by government is now a reality? Although that may be too pessimistic a conclusion, certainly the weakening in the perception that government merits a watchful eye has implications for democratic citizenship.

FROM THE 1930s TO THE 1960s

As noted in Chapter 1, the Depression and the Roosevelt administration's efforts to cope with massive unemployment during the 1930s led to a substantial increase in Washington's involvement in society. According to Ekirch, "More than in any other comparable period of the American past, the years from 1929 to 1941 transformed the traditional values and attitudes of the American people, conditioning them to look, as never before, to the national state as the basic arbiter and fundamental factor in their lives" (1969: viii). Based on FDR's landslide reelection in 1936 and his unprecedented election to a third term in 1940, the temptation is to assume widespread public endorsement of the New Deal and its accumulation of power in the national capital. Actually, as one can see in Table 2.1, polls conducted by the newly created Gallup organization and *Fortune* magazine show that Americans were divided over Roosevelt's policies during the 1930s and early 1940s.[1]

Gallup polls in late 1935 and early 1936 indicate that although the balance of public opinion disapproved of the president's policies during his first two years, the New Deal was favored by a five-to-four margin (questions 1 and 2). A November 1939 *Fortune* poll found Americans slightly more favorably disposed. Just over half of the public thought that the New Deal should either be continued without change or be kept with some improvements (question 8). Still, there was substantial opposition. One-fifth of the 1939 public gave the New Deal some credit but believed it had done enough wrong that a new administration was needed. Finally, one-sixth of the public believed the New Deal had had such a negative influence on the nation that it "will take years of good government by others to clean up the mistakes." According to Gallup and Rae, despite polls revealing Roosevelt's "tremendous personal popularity, the people have not blindly endorsed every New Deal measure. They were for the C.C.C. [Civilian Conservation Corps], for social security, for wages-and-hours legislation; but they voted [*sic*] against the N.R.A. [National Recovery Administration] and the A.A.A. [Agricultural Adjustment Administration] shortly before these laws were declared unconstitutional, and they steadfastly refused to go along on Supreme Court change" (1940: 133).

If the public was ambivalent about various New Deal programs, how did it feel about the growth of power in the central government? Gallup polls from the late 1930s and early 1940s suggest that Americans favored it. In March 1936 and June 1937, the public favored concentration of power in Washington by a margin of four-to-three (questions 3 and 4). However, Devine (1972) pointed out that

Table 2.1 Public Opinion about Big Government during the New Deal Era

1. Question: "Do you approve of the acts and policies of Roosevelt's first two years?" (Gallup, 11/35)

   Yes 44%   No 56%

2. Question: "Are you in favor of the New Deal?" (Gallup, 1/36)

   Yes 50%   No 46%   No opinion 4%

3. Question: "Which theory of government do you favor, concentration of power in the federal government or concentration of power in the state government?" (Gallup, 3/36)

   Federal government 42%   State government 34%   No opinion 23%

4. Question: "Which theory of government do you favor, concentration of power in the federal government or concentration of power in the state government?" (Gallup, 6/37)

   Federal government 43%   State government 33%   No opinion 23%

5. Question: "Should state governments transfer more of their powers to the federal government?" (Gallup, 6/37)

   Yes 26%   No 54%   No opinion 20%

6. Question: "In the division of government power between the federal and state governments, do you think the federal should have more power and the state less, or the state more and the federal less?" (*Fortune*, 7/38)

   Federal more 27%   State more 32%   Same as now 20%
   No opinion 21%

7. Question: "Do you think the federal government will have more power or less power ten years from now, than it has today?" (Gallup, 5/39)

   More 48%   Less 19%   Same 16%   Don't know 17%

8. Question: "Which of the following statements most nearly represents your idea of the New Deal: (1) The New Deal has been the kind of government best suited to our times, and it should be continued without modification (whether under Mr. Roosevelt or someone else). (2) Although the New Deal has not worked perfectly in many ways, it has done a lot of good and should be continued with some modificiation and improvements. (3) The New Deal may have done some good, but it has done so many bad things that now we need a different administration. (4) The New Deal had a bad influence upon the nation, and it will take years of good government by others to clean up the mistakes." (*Fortune*, 11/39)

   (1) 10%   (2) 45%   (3) 21%   (4) 16%   Don't know 8%

9. Question: "Do you think there is too much power in the hands of the government in Washington?" (Gallup, 4/41)

   Yes 32%   No 56%   No opinion 12%

10. Question: "After the war do you think the aims and programs of the New Deal will be entirely done away with, partly done away with, continued along the same lines, or made stronger than ever?" (*Fortune*, 6/43)

Entirely done away with	8%
Partly done away with	42%
Continued along same lines	18%
Made stronger than ever	14%
Don't know	18%

Table 2.1, *continued*

11. Question: "Do you think the government program during the past few years for [the measures listed below] goes too far, not far enough, or is just about right?" (*Fortune,* 1/45)

	Goes too far	Not far enough	Just right	Don't know
Providing pensions under				
Social Security	6%	41%	38%	15%
Providing low-cost housing	14%	33%	36%	17%
Preventing too low wages	14%	28%	36%	12%
Trying to help the farmer				
make a decent living	14%	32%	40%	14%
Regulating things so that the				
sale of stocks and bonds is				
done honestly	4%	13%	35%	47%

Sources: Hadley Cantril, with Mildred Strunk, eds., *Public Opinion, 1935–1946* (Westport, Conn.: Greenwood Press, 1978), pp. 815, 978–986; Donald J. Devine, *The Political Culture of the United States* (Boston: Little, Brown & Co., 1972), p. 169.

when the respondents to the June 1937 poll were asked if state governments "should transfer more of their powers to the federal government," half the public disapproved and only one-fifth approved (question 5).

Devine (1972: 169–170) believed that the discrepancy between the two questions on the same 1937 poll could be resolved by interpreting responses to the first as satisfaction with the status quo while opposing any further growth in the federal establishment. He claimed that his interpretation was supported by results from a July 1938 *Fortune* poll that asked whether the federal government should have more power and the state governments less, or the state governments more and the federal government less (question 6). Just over a quarter of the public favored strengthening the central government, a third would have given the states more power, and a fifth wanted things left as they were.

These polls are useful, but they do not answer how the public felt about the federal government's power per se. By May 1939, almost half of the public expected Washington to become more powerful in the future, whereas only one-fifth predicted a less powerful central establishment (question 7). According to an April 1941 Gallup poll, more people would have supported increased power for the central establishment than would have opposed it (question 9). Only a third of the public claimed that Washington had too much power, while slightly over half said it did not. It is difficult to say how much views of governmental power were influenced by the growing possibility of American involvement in World War II. Still, it may have played some part, as three-fifths of the respondents to the same poll thought there was too much power in the hands of a few rich men and large corporations, and three-quarters believed labor union leaders had too much power (Gallup, 1972: 277). In any event, polls in the late

1930s and early 1940s showed a public divided over whether Washington was too powerful, with a slight majority inclined to say it was not.

There is some evidence that FDR's switch from "Dr. New Deal" to "Dr. Win the War," and his association with the Allied struggle against the Axis powers, led to a retrospective judgment in favor of the New Deal. A June 1943 *Fortune* poll asked, "After the war do you think the aims and programs of the New Deal will be entirely done away with, partly done away with, continued along the same lines, or made stronger than ever" (question 10). Less than one-tenth of the public believed the New Deal would be entirely jettisoned, two-fifths thought it might be partially abandoned, about one-fifth thought it would be continued along the same lines, and one-seventh believed it would be made stronger than ever. Based on a follow-up question, "Do you think [your initial response] will be a good thing or a bad thing," the overwhelming bulk of the wartime public made it clear that some continuation of the New Deal would be satisfactory (Cantril, with Strunk, 1978: 985). By January 1945, a *Fortune* poll showed that only small minorities of the public thought such basic New Deal programs as Social Security, low-cost housing, minimum wage legislation, and farm assistance programs had gone too far; whereas one-third to two-fifths judged them as just right, and similar proportions believed they did not go far enough (question 11).

Although the Republicans gained substantially from their 1946 off-year slogan, "Had Enough?," they badly misjudged the postwar public's willingness to put the nascent welfare state at risk in the next presidential election. According to Ross, "Truman's supporters reaffirmed their loyalty to the New Deal and endorsed the more ambitious program of governmental intervention in the private sector which Truman offered [in the Fair Deal]" (1969: 245). But after snatching defeat from the jaws of victory in 1948, Republicans muted their opposition to a powerful federal establishment in the 1952 and especially the 1956 campaigns.

To some historians, the Eisenhower administration represented a Republican acknowledgment of the New Deal's legitimacy while at the same time holding the line against its extension (Alexander, 1975). Hamby pointed to two important reasons the Eisenhower Republicans accepted the Democrats' welfare state programs: "The New and Fair Deals were too woven into the fabric of society to be torn out; moreover, it was obviously unwise to contemplate such a step. The dispensing of benefits throughout society, whether or not it was just and enlightened, had surely been politically popular; any effort to take them away would be doubly unpopular" (1985: 122). But while the GOP was making its peace with the New Deal, the Democratic party was in the hands of centrists: two-time presidential nominee Adlai Stevenson, House Speaker Sam Rayburn, Senate Majority Leader Lyndon Johnson, and, later, President John F. Kennedy. Hence, the issue of Washington's power was not a major factor during the 1950s and early 1960s.

A PRELIMINARY RECONNAISSANCE: 1964–1988

In *The Conscience of a Conservative*, Barry Goldwater decried the growth of power in Washington: "The federal government has moved into every field in which it believes its services are needed. . . . The result is a Leviathan, a vast national authority out of touch with the people, and out of their control" (1960: 19–20). This theme would be articulated again and again throughout his unsuccessful quest for the presidency. From 1964 on, the federal government's role in American politics and society has been at the center of political struggle. It has been a factor in virtually every presidential election since Goldwater made his assault on big government in the 1964 campaign.

Slightly over twenty years later, in his second inaugural address, President Reagan, in many ways Goldwater's ideological successor, said, "[Americans] asked things of government that government was not equipped to give. We yielded authority to the national government that properly belonged to states or to local governments or to the people themselves" (1985: 186). The president went on to promise a continuation in his second term of efforts to curtail Washington's power. In almost every presidential election between 1964 and 1984, at least one serious candidate for the presidency, whether perceived to be of the right (Wallace, 1968; Reagan, 1980 and 1984), left (McGovern, 1972), or center (Carter, 1976), has sounded similar warnings against excessive concentration of power in the central government. The 1988 campaign was a departure from this pattern as neither major party candidate campaigned on the curtailment of centralized government.

If the issue of big government has agitated political elites since 1964, has it also been important to ordinary people in the United States? Survey data from 1964 on offer the opportunity to plumb what Americans have been thinking about the role of the federal government. Most of the data used here come from the University of Michigan's Survey Research Center–Center for Political Studies' (SRC-CPS) National Election Studies (NES) of 1964, 1966, 1968, 1970, 1972, 1974, 1976, 1978, 1980, 1984, and 1988.[2] Also included are polls by the American Institute of Public Opinion (Gallup), two done for the Advisory Commission on Intergovernmental Relations (ACIR) by the Opinion Research Corporation (ORC) of Princeton, New Jersey, as well as other national polling organizations.

Since the primary data for assessing American views about governmental power are the SRC-CPS's National Election Studies, let us consider the University of Michigan's vehicle first. Beginning in 1964, the SRC posed this question:

Some people are afraid the government in Washington is getting too powerful for the good of the country and the individual person. Others feel that the government has not gotten too strong for the good of the country.

Have you been interested enough in this to favor one side over the other? [If yes] What is your feeling, do you think: (1) the government is getting too powerful; or (5) the government has not gotten too strong?

The question has been asked on the SRC-CPS's National Election Studies since 1964, except in 1974, 1982, and 1986. Although the item's placement on the questionnaires has shifted from time to time, its wording has remained unaltered. The only change occurred when the filter was simplified in 1976: "Do you have an opinion on this?" Finally, in 1978, the CPS began posing an additional question to those who replied either that the federal government had not gotten too strong or that "it depends": "Do you think the government should become more powerful, or should it stay the way it is?" Although even slight variation in question wording or questionnaire context can vex comparisons over time (see Schuman and Presser, 1981), this is not a serious problem here. We are fortunate to have an identically worded item, except for a small change in its filter, over nearly a quarter-century during which a great deal changed in American culture and politics. Rarely does the student of public opinion have even one item that has been asked repeatedly in the same way to survey respondents over an extended period.

Figure 2.1 presents the American public's opinions on the power of the central government from 1964 to 1988. Although much could be said about these data, a few observations will suffice. The first thing that strikes the eye is the large percentage of adults who claim to be uninterested in or have no opinion about Washington's power or don't know what their opinion is. These answers are called "nonsubstantive responses" (Francis and Busch, 1975). Between 1964 and 1988, the percentage of Americans not expressing an opinion ranges from 26 to 47. The average over the twenty-four years is 35 percent. Moreover, the trend in the late 1970s and 1980s has been upward. Since 1978, an average of 42 percent of the public has not taken a position on the federal government's power.

Could the changed filter, introduced in 1976, be behind the increase in nonsubstantive responses? Experiments show that changing the filter from the 1964–1972 form ("Have you been interested enough in this to favor one side over the other?") to the 1976–1988 form ("Do you have an opinion on this?") does not account for the increase in don't know/no opinion responses that began in 1978. If anything, the former version should have screened out more respondents than the latter (Bishop, Oldendick, and Tuchfarber, 1983: 543).

Public opinion analysts have often commented on Americans' willingness to express opinions on policy issues, even when offered the opportunity to admit that they either have no interest or have not thought much about a given issue (P. E. Converse, 1970; J. M. Converse, 1976–77; Schuman and Presser, 1981). Despite assurances by interviewers that it was perfectly acceptable not to have an opinion on every question about public policy, many individuals insisted on

Figure 2.1 Public Opinion about the Federal Government's Power, for various years, 1964–1988

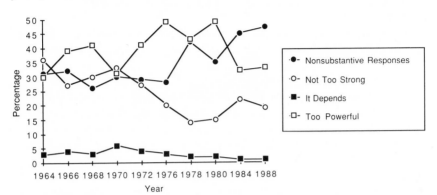

Source: University of Michigan's Survey Research Center–Center for Political Studies' National Election Studies

responding to each query as a test of civic knowledge or virtue and therefore felt compelled to express an "opinion" (P. E. Converse, 1970: 177). A sizable percentage felt compelled to express an opinion on fictitious issues (Bishop, Oldendick, Tuchfarber, and Bennett, 1980; Bishop, Tuchfarber, and Oldendick, 1986). Opinions invented in an interview are called "non-opinions."

Undoubtedly, some of the opinions depicted in Figure 2.1 fall into this category. Still, the percentage of Americans who have been willing to admit that they are without an opinion on the central government's power is remarkable. For one thing, questions about Washington's role tap elements of American political culture. As noted in Chapter 1, Almond and Verba (1963: 493–494) believed that Americans' disquietude with a strong central government can be traced to the revolutionary era. Samuel Huntington contended that "the distinctive aspect of the American Creed is its antigovernment character. Opposition to power, and suspicion of government as the most dangerous embodiment of power, are the central themes of American political thought" (1981: 33).

Second, since the 1930s, differing views about the role of the federal government have been at the core of ideological cleavage between liberals and conservatives. As Nie and Andersen noted, "It is true that for many years 'that government is best which governs least' has been a central tenet of the American conservative position, and that at least from the time of the New Deal, American liberalism has held equally strongly that the desirable role of government is to enter as many areas of social life as necessary to rectify social and economic injustices" (1974: 554). Although Nie and his colleagues argued that this liberal-conservative split on the big government issue broke down in 1972 (Nie, with Andersen, 1974: 557; Nie, Verba, and Petrocik, 1979: 125–128), Ronald Reagan's emergence as the premier conservative spokesman in the late 1970s restored the older left-right rift over Washington's power.

Moreover, the big government issue has partisan overtones. Noting the "Democratic [party's] emphasis on Washington, D.C., and [the] Republican emphasis on state capitals," Kessel observed that "these references capture one of the most important partisan distinctions of our era" (1972: 463). Finally, between 1964 and 1988, several major political figures—Goldwater, Wallace, McGovern, Carter, and Reagan—campaigned more or less *against* the federal establishment. In short, questions about Washington's role in American society and politics touch upon elements of our political culture, ideology, and partisan politics. Nevertheless, over the past quarter century an average of slightly over one-third of the American public has remained mute when confronted by the SRC-CPS's question.

Previous analyses of public opinion about the federal government's power have either ignored or missed the significance of so many people not having had an opinion (Nie, with Andersen, 1974; Nie, Verba, and Petrocik, 1979; Maddox and Lilie, 1984). Failure to determine who those without opinion are, or why one-quarter to two-fifths of the public take no position on the question, may lead to misinterpretation of public opinion on this issue. The appendix presents detailed analyses of the factors that best explain why people do not express an opinion on the federal government's power (see also Bennett and Bennett, 1986). Those most likely to express an opinion about Washington's power have remained constant from 1964 to 1988: the politically interested, college graduates, men, strong ideologues, the well-to-do, and the elderly. One interesting change has been the decline of region as a determinant of don't know/ no opinion responses, probably due to the muting of Washington's direct involvement in racial issues as the major factor in domestic politics.

Perhaps the most important trend is the decreased interest of the young in the question of Washington's power. During the 1960s, less than a third of those under thirty years of age had no opinion about the central government's power, which was no different from individuals over sixty-five. By 1988, 61 percent of persons under thirty did not express an opinion on the question, compared with 47 percent of those over sixty-five. Glenn speculated that many of the age differences in surveys reflected generational differences in experience: "Younger people are likely to evidence the newer attitudes and behavior whereas older people are likely to exemplify the traditional culture" (1969: 33). The major battles surrounding expansion of the central government's role in our society were fought twenty-five to fifty years ago. Those issues are likely to be relevant to people who either experienced them as adults or at least were politically aware when they were occurring. People who have recently come of age, after the battle has stilled and its refuse has been removed from the field, may find the issue unimportant and thus either be content to avoid the question or be disinclined to upset the status quo. We will explore young Americans' views about Washington's power at greater length in Chapter 5.

There are two key points to keep in mind about the failure to express an opinion about Washington's power. First, these individuals are not randomly distributed through the population. If Bishop and his associates (1983) are correct, the fact that those with opinions about the central government's power are not a representative subset of the total public could significantly affect the distribution of views expressed on the issue, a point overlooked by previous researchers. For this reason, we occasionally describe percentages of various subgroups that express no opinion as well as percentages of those *with opinions* about Washington's power. Second, since don't know/no opinion responses are unlikely to occur on issues that are personally relevant (J. M. Converse, 1976–77: 529), it is possible that larger percentages of "no opinion" responses are an indication that the big government issue is perceived as increasingly remote and personally irrelevant. We discuss this point in Chapter 6.

Returning to Figure 2.1, the distribution of opinions on the federal government's power is also interesting. In the beginning, the public was about evenly divided between those who believed Washington had gotten too powerful and those who thought it had not. Had the election of 1964 been fought solely on the question of the federal government's power, Goldwater would still have lost, albeit by a much smaller margin (Converse, Clausen, and Miller, 1965). Although less than a third of the public was convinced that the national government had already become too strong by 1964, things quickly changed. By the end of 1966, a year after the passage of Lyndon Johnson's Great Society legislation, more people had become disturbed by Washington's power. Just under two-fifths now thought government had grown too big, just over one-quarter believed it was not too strong, and a small portion said, "It depends."

The period between 1966 and 1970 was filled with social and political turmoil. American involvement in Vietnam, which had been a relatively small matter to the public in November 1964 (Mueller, 1973: 54–55), was a major issue by 1966, and by 1968 it was considered the most important problem confronting the country (Bennett and Tuchfarber, 1975: 435). Along with the importance attached to U.S. participation in the war itself, the divisiveness engendered by domestic protest against the war contributed substantially to public discontent (Scammon and Wattenberg, 1971). Racial conflicts also contributed to political unrest, as riots scorched dozens of cities, and white backlash inflamed political nerves already rubbed raw. Perhaps it is not surprising that public opinion on Washington's power became more polarized and volatile. Although a plurality of the electorate in 1968 thought the central government was too big, just two years later public opinion was evenly divided. Given the violence of these years, it is understandable that 1970 was the only time that more than 5 percent of the electorate believed that the question of Washington's power depended on the respondent's frame of reference.

Some public opinion analysts have commented on a conservative trend during the 1970s (Davis, 1980; Robinson, 1984), although civil rights for blacks (Smith and Sheatsley, 1984; Schuman, Steeh, and Bobo, 1985) and civil liberties for left-wing groups (Davis, 1975; Nunn, Crockett, and Williams, 1978) became more popular.[3] Certainly, the years from 1972 to 1980 saw a decline in the proportion still believing the federal government was not too powerful, from just over one-fourth in 1972 to only about one-seventh by the decade's end. At the same time, between two-fifths and nearly one-half of the public believed Washington had become too powerful.

These were the years in which opinions about governmental leaders and institutions soured considerably (A. Miller, 1974a; Citrin, 1981; Abramson, 1983; Citrin and Green, 1986; Lipset and Schneider, 1987). Whether the substantial decline in the public's trust and confidence in political leadership amounted to a "crisis of confidence" (A. Miller, 1974a, 1974b; Cadell, 1979) or merely fashionable clichés (Citrin, 1974; W. Miller, 1979) is a very important question. The best evidence suggests that cynical views of government are closely tied to perceptions of political leaders' poor performance in office (Abramson and Finifter, 1981; Citrin and Green, 1986; Lipset and Schneider, 1987). As we discuss in Chapter 6, it is not coincidental that the same period also witnessed mounting concern about concentration of power in Washington.

Someone looking at Figure 2.1 might be tempted to conclude that Ronald Reagan's calls for curtailment of the federal establishment had a receptive audience in the late 1970s and early 1980s. In any event, once elected, President Reagan acted as though he had widespread support to cut governmental programs. However, critics charged him with slashing federal spending for programs that had substantial backing among the citizenry (Ferguson and Rogers, 1986). Whatever the truth of such claims, by 1984, belief that the central government was too powerful had fallen to a third of the public, while a fifth believed it was not too strong. The Reagan years witnessed a substantial shift away from Reagan's long-cherished proposition that the federal establishment was too big. By 1984, two decades after Barry Goldwater had run against what he had called "a vast national authority out of touch with the people, and out of their control" (Goldwater, 1960: 20), and four years after Reagan made curtailment of government a centerpiece of his campaign, Americans were no more likely than they were in 1964 to subscribe to the belief that Washington had grown too powerful. As the data in Figure 2.1 show, the situation at the end of the Reagan era was the same as it had been at the end of his first term.

In fairness, it should be pointed out that the SRC-CPS's question suggests that there has been very little support for expanding the national government's power. In 1978, 1980, 1984, and 1988, the CPS asked those with opinions who did not think Washington was too powerful whether they thought the federal government should become more powerful or merely remain as it was. On each occasion, only about 5 percent of the public supported granting additional authority to the federal establishment. The overwhelming bulk of those who did not think Washington was already too big were content to leave well enough alone.

Thus three basic themes can be detected in Figure 2.1. First, a sizable minority has consistently opted out of expressing an opinion on what is supposed to be a fundamental question of American political culture, ideology, and partisan politics. Moreover, during the period that Reagan emerged as a national leader, the proportion without an opinion increased by approximately 10 percent. It appears that although Reagan and others before him had sought to place the question of Washington's power at the forefront of the political agenda, such efforts left one-third to two-fifths of the public out of the discussion. (It is possible that the absence of candidates running on an anti–big government platform during the 1988 campaign reflected pollsters' appreciation of lessened public interest in the issue.) Moreover, Tom Smith (1985b) shows that with the exception of the Watergate era, Americans rarely mention big government as an important national problem, even when the context is broadened to include corruption, inefficiency, and red tape.

Second, Figure 2.1 shows there was an increase during the 1970s in the percentage of those who believed government was too powerful. The late 1970s and early 1980s were characterized by a strong sentiment against big government. For example, Harris polls showed that the percentage agreeing with the dictum that "the best government is the government that governs least" rose from 32 in 1973 to 59 in early 1981 (*Public Opinion,* 1982: 36). Indeed, the early 1980s may have marked the height of a quarter-century-long shift away from support of a powerful central government. Recall that Gallup polls in 1936 and 1937 showed that Americans favored concentration of power in the federal government over state governments by a ratio of four to three (Table 2.1). In September 1981, only 28 percent of a Gallup poll favored concentration of power in Washington, whereas 56 percent favored concentrating power at the state level (Gallup, 1982: 235–236). A decision-making information survey conducted in April 1987 for the GOP showed only a slight shift toward more support for more concentration of power in Washington; 63 percent of the public still wanted more power at the state level, while 34 percent favored more power in the central government (White, 1988: 131). By the late 1980s, however, anti–central government sentiment had substantially waned. A Gallup poll in April and May 1987 showed the public almost evenly divided over whether "the federal government should be able to overrule individual states on important matters." Forty-four percent agreed that Washington should be able to overturn state actions, whereas 47 percent disagreed (*Times Mirror,* 1987: 126).

The third finding in Figure 2.1 is that after the early 1980s, the percentage worrying about too much power in Washington fell, so that by 1984 and 1988 the percentage of the public predisposed to agree with President Reagan's call for more cuts in Washington's power was no larger than in 1964, at the height of

LBJ's popularity. The latter point raises an intriguing question: Did a sizable percentage of the public believe that unlike his immediate predecessors, Reagan was dealing successfully with some of the vexing problems facing the country? If so, would this belief make it safer for big government in the United States? We return to this question in Chapter 6.

Although the data in Figure 2.1 tell some interesting tales, alone they leave much untold. An unfocused item can be read to suit the ideological and/or partisan interests of the observer. It would help if, over the years, the SRC-CPS (or some other survey agency) had plumbed public sentiment about the national government's power with more focused questions. If they were available, would our tale pale by comparison?

ANOTHER LOOK AT THE CENTRAL GOVERNMENT'S POWER

In two 1964 polls—one in late September and early October, the other in late October—the Gallup organization asked 3,175 Americans the following question (Free and Cantril, 1968: 19):

Which one of the following statements listed on this card comes closest to your own views about Governmental power today?

1. The Federal Government today has too much power.

2. The Federal Government is now using just about the right amount of power for meeting today's needs.

3. The Federal Government should use its powers even more vigorously to promote the well-being of all segments of the people.

The same question was asked for the ACIR by the ORC on its May 1978 caravan. The ORC asked it for the ACIR again in 1982. In 1984, 1985, and 1986, the ACIR commissioned the Gallup organization to include the item on its personal omnibus. Although there is a gap of fourteen years between Gallup's initial use of the item and its use by the ORC, we are fortunate to have an item that seems similar to the SRC-CPS question over essentially the same period covered in Figure 2.1. The Gallup and ORC data are depicted in Figure 2.2.

The Gallup question differs from the SRC-CPS item in two important respects.[4] First, it has no filter to eliminate those without opinion. For that reason, no more than 14 percent reply "don't know" to the Gallup question; this category averages 8 percent over the six observations. This is far below the average of "no opinion" on the SRC-CPS question. Research indicates that the level of don't know/no opinion responses depends upon the remoteness and

Figure 2.2 Public Opinion about the Federal Government's Power, for various years, 1964–1986

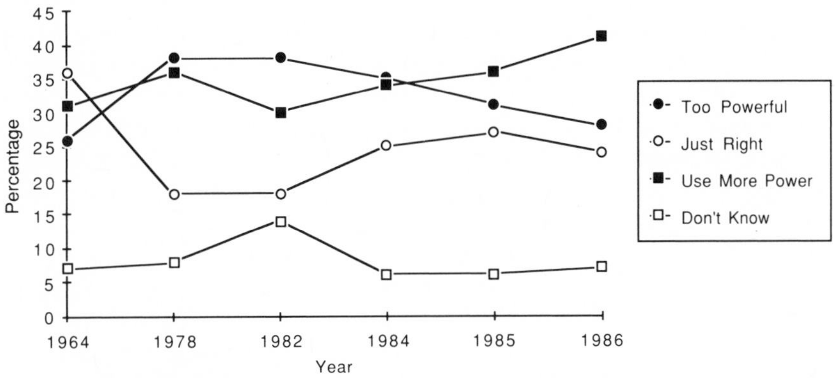

Source: For 1964, Free and Cantril (1968): 185–186; for 1978, ACIR (1983): 52; for 1982–1986, ACIR (1986)

abstractness of the topic and the stringency of the filter used (J. M. Converse, 1976–77; Schuman and Presser, 1978, 1981; Bishop, Oldendick, and Tuchfarber, 1980, 1983). "On topics which are very familiar, or on which public sentiment has become highly intensified (*e.g.*, abortion, death penalty), the use and wording of a filter will have little impact on the expression of opinion" (Bishop, Oldendick, and Tuchfarber, 1980: 345), but "the more remote or abstract the issue, the greater will be the effect of a more strongly worded filter question" (Bishop, Oldendick, and Tuchfarber, 1983: 535), such as those used by the SRC-CPS. That the SRC-CPS's filtered question screens out more than three times the percentage saying "don't know" to the Gallup item strongly suggests that the question of the central government's power is seen by many Americans as highly abstract and/or personally remote.

On the other hand, there is a considerable difference between the two questions in the option calling for the federal government to enhance its power. As noted above, beginning in 1978, the CPS added the following query, which was posed to only those who had said either that the government had not gotten too strong or that it depends: "Do you think the government should become more powerful, or should it stay the way it is?" Compare this with the Gallup option that says: "The Federal Government should use its powers even more vigorously *to promote the well-being of all segments of the people*" (our emphasis). Whereas the CPS question leaves the reason for favoring a bigger national government up to each respondent, the Gallup item specifies the purpose for Washington's undertaking more vigorous action.

Wars or international crises aside, whether a situation can be conceived in which an expanding national government could redound to the benefit of all population segments or whether governmental growth to benefit some must occur at the expense of others is a philosophical question, but moot for our purposes. However, the wording of the Gallup item makes it much easier than the SRC-CPS question for respondents to opt for greater government action. So it is in the data. In 1978 and 1984, an average of 35 percent of the Gallup poll's respondents favored increased governmental power "to promote the well-being of all segments of the people." On the other hand, only 4 to 6 percent of the CPS's respondents to the 1978, 1980, 1984, and 1988 National Election Studies thought "the government should become more powerful," while 10 to 20 percent believed the national government "should stay the way it is." In this sense, Bishop and his associates (1983) are supported. We are still left wondering which of the two items' estimates of support for enhanced central government power is closer to the mark.

Until now we have stressed the differences between the SRC-CPS and the Gallup questions. Different though they are, they reveal important similarities in opinion trends. The most important is that both questions show a growth between 1964 and 1978 in the percentage of the public believing the central government had grown too powerful. According to the SRC-CPS item, the percentage saying too powerful went from 30 to 43. The Gallup version indicates that the percentage went from 26 to 38. What is particularly important is that the magnitude of the shift was the same for both items. When two items that are worded differently reveal identical shifts over the same period, we can have greater confidence in the results.

The SRC-CPS and Gallup items also reveal another common trend, although comparisons must be more tentative since the questions were not always asked in the same years. As noted above, between 1980 and 1984 the CPS item shows a large drop in the belief that government was too powerful and a small increase in the belief that Washington had not become too strong. The Gallup version indicates nearly stable distributions between 1978 and 1982. After 1982, a decline in the percentage believing the federal government was too powerful set in. The Gallup data also show an increase after 1982 in the percentage thinking the central government should exercise its powers even more vigorously. By 1986, two-fifths of the public thought Washington should expand its powers, a higher proportion than at the peak of LBJ's popularity.

In one sense, the Gallup question provides a bit more leverage than the SRC-CPS item. Since the SRC-CPS offers only two options (either Washington is or is not too powerful), while Gallup offers a third alternative (calling for yet bigger government), we should not be surprised when Gallup uncovers much greater support for expansive central government. Experiments have shown that when "middle response alternatives"—in this case, offering all respondents the option that government was just the right size rather than making this option available only as a follow-up for those who already believed Washington was not too powerful—a much larger percentage will select it than when the middle alternative is not asked (Bishop, 1987). Even though that finding may be relegated to the "so what else is new" category, it is more important to discover that when the middle alternative is not available, the resulting opinion distribution will often be significantly different. As a result, public opinion will seem very different when the middle alternative is available than when it is not.

Such is the case here. Looking at the data in Figure 2.1, one might be tempted to think that support for big government eroded substantially between 1964 and 1980. Looking at Figure 2.2, however, we see that what may have happened instead was a shrinkage in the percentage who believed Washington's power was just right while the percentage who called for more vigorous usage of federal powers remained fairly constant. The fly in the ointment is that the Gallup item had no filter for don't know/no opinion responses, thereby making comparisons with the SRC-CPS question difficult. Still, the key point is that both questions suggest that the height of support for President Reagan's views about excessive governmental power occurred sometime between 1978 and 1982, and that the percentage of Americans who favored more expansive government may have grown since the early 1980s.

THE BIG GOVERNMENT THREAT

Does this mean that cries that big government constitutes a threat to American liberties are diminishing? Not necessarily. In 1959 the Gallup organization began asking: "In your opinion, which of the following will be the biggest threat to the country in the future—big business, big labor, or big government?" The question has been repeated at intervals ever since. In some ways, the data from this question dovetail with those of the first two questions. In other ways, they tell different yarns (see Figure 2.3).

In 1959, only one-seventh of the public selected big government as the most likely future culprit; an identical proportion picked big business, two-fifths chose big labor, and almost one-third had no opinion. That 30 percent of the public had no opinion on the Gallup item in the twilight of the Eisenhower era tends to corroborate the SRC-CPS data. However, in the 1960s, 1970s, and 1980s, the Gallup polls showed a much smaller percentage of the public without opinion, because absence of a filter on the Gallup item did not give the respondent the same easy out the SRC-CPS's question did (Schuman and Presser, 1981; Bishop, Oldendick, and Tuchfarber, 1983). In addition, use of the adjective "big" by Gallup (Lipset and Schneider, 1987) induced a much higher response rate. It is also possible that Goldwater's campaign in 1964, U.S. involvement in Vietnam, and Reagan's campaigns in 1976, 1980, and 1984 sensitized some people to potential problems with big government.

The Gallup data after 1959 show another interesting trend. From early 1967 to

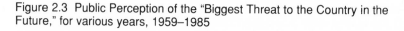

Figure 2.3 Public Perception of the "Biggest Threat to the Country in the Future," for various years, 1959–1985

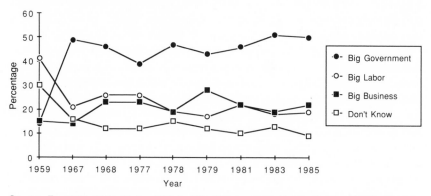

Source: For 1959–1983, Gallup (1984): 127–128; for 1985, *Public Opinion* (1987): 26

late 1981, the percentage identifying big government as the most likely national threat never falls below 39 and averages around 45. From the late 1960s to the early 1980s, just about the same proportion, roughly one-fifth, picked either big labor or big business. Moreover, midway through Reagan's first term (May 1983) and in the first year of his second, big government was seen as slightly more threatening than it had been under either LBJ or Carter.

Although the data in Figure 2.3 can be interpreted as providing additional, slightly divergent information on opinions about the central government's power, others may see them as no more illuminating than the data in Figures 2.1 and 2.2. The question presumes a threat to the nation in some unspecified future. Also, not only is it impossible to discern what people may have in mind by a threat, but also inclusion of the adjective ''big'' is known to sound warning bells in the American political psyche (Almond and Verba, 1963; Huntington, 1981; Lipset and Schneider, 1987). Still, it is worth remembering that under appropriate goads, the big government issue may be relevant to a broader segment of the public than the SRC-CPS data suggest. Finally, the Gallup data from 1981, 1983, and 1985 suggest that in the Reagan era, fears of big government had not receded. If anything, they seem to have increased slightly.

NO ORWELLIAN VISION

If, midway through the Reagan era, half of the American public thought big government was the most likely future threat to the country's well-being, did it mean that George Orwell's vision of omnipresent totalitarianism struck a responsive chord with many Americans? Not really, if a Gallup poll taken in December 1983 is any indication. In that poll, respondents were reminded that Orwell had written *1984* in 1948 and that he had made several predictions about a future in which people had lost all freedom. Respondents were then asked if they thought each prediction was already happening in the United States, was very likely to happen, was somewhat likely, or was not at all likely.

When it came to expectations that the country would be ruled by a dictator or that criticism of the government would be severely punished, 66 to 70 percent of Americans believed they were not at all likely, while only one-tenth said they either were already happening or were very likely to happen. Similarly, three-fifths did not think it ever likely that the government would urge its citizens to hate people in other countries, whereas only one-sixth thought it either was already doing so or was very likely to do so. In addition, half of the public thought it was not at all likely that the government would "urge people to surrender freedom in order to gain greater security," while one-tenth believed it was already happening and another one-tenth thought it was very likely to happen (*Gallup Report*, 1984: 46). On the other hand, two-fifths believed government was already falsifying data to "hide bad news about the economy," one-sixth thought it was very likely to happen, and one-seventh dismissed the idea altogether. Half of the public believed people were already being asked to make "great economic sacrifices" while "government officials themselves live in luxury." Almost half (47 percent) believed there already was "no real privacy because the government can learn anything it wants about you."

Although the December 1983 Gallup poll contains mixed evidence concerning Americans' views about their freedom, the bottom line is that very few Americans were worried. When asked how much freedom people have in the United States, four-fifths thought Americans enjoyed a great deal of freedom, one-tenth said they enjoyed only some, and trace elements said they enjoyed either very little or none at all (*Gallup Report*, 1984: 58). According to Lane (1962: 145), the working-class men of Eastport did not fear government because, unlike Thomas Paine (n.d.), who emphasized government's punitive and restrictive capacities, they thought of government as "a benign, helpful organization, one working *for* the people, not merely restraining them."

Lane's research was done during the halcyon years of the Eisenhower era, when overwhelming majorities were proud of their political institutions, trusted their political leaders, and believed governmental actions were mostly beneficial to themselves and the country (Almond and Verba, 1963). Although the public's trust in government increased during Reagan's first term (A. Miller, 1983; Citrin and Green, 1986; Lipset and Schneider, 1987), Americans still take a much more jaundiced view of government and politicians today than in the late 1950s (Sussman, 1988: 54–55). Nevertheless, very few are concerned about losing their freedom, which may be one reason why worry about big government does not mean that Americans are thinking in Orwellian terms.

Data from a May 1988 poll by CBS News–*New York Times* indicate that Americans are again in a fairly expansive mood concerning big government. The poll asked the following question: "In general, government grows bigger as it provides more services. If you had to choose, would you rather have a smaller government providing fewer services or a bigger government providing more services?" In the twilight of the Reagan era, the public was evenly divided; slightly over two-fifths favored a smaller government, and an identical proportion wanted bigger government. That constitutes a significant shift in opinion from what a CBS News–*New York Times* poll found in March 1980, when just over half of the pre-Reagan public wanted smaller government while slightly less than a third wanted it to grow bigger (*National Journal*, 1988: 1824). Almost seven years of Reagan had produced more support for a bigger government providing more services. Indeed, a CBS News–*New York Times* poll taken in the final days of Reagan's presidency (January 12–15, 1989) found that nearly half of the public favored bigger government (Roberts, 1989), a figure not seen since the heyday of the Great Society.

THE BIG GOVERNMENT THREAT: ANOTHER LOOK

Increased public concern about big government as a future threat during the administration of a president committed to its reduction is intriguing. Perhaps it was due to the steady calls by Reagan and the Reaganauts for yet greater reductions in government. It could also have stemmed from waning public belief that the Reagan administration would actually succeed in shrinking government. For example, just after the 1980 election, before Reagan had even taken the oath of office, half of the public believed he would be able to reduce the size of government, a third thought he would not, and one-sixth offered no opinion (Gallup, 1982: 262). In May 1981, after the president's early successes, two-thirds of the public had concluded that he would reduce the size of government, and one-fifth was pessimistic (Gallup, 1982: 127). Early public optimism quickly waned, however. Seven months into the first Reagan term (August 1981), 56 percent believed his administration would be able to cut government's size while 30 percent now thought the president would not succeed (Gallup, 1982: 198). In the spring of 1985, when asked for a retrospective judgment on the first Reagan administration's successes and failures in dealing with foreign and domestic problems, only 5 percent of the public thought "the chances of reducing the size of the federal government" had gotten much better, 24 percent believed they were somewhat better, 26 percent thought they had stayed the same, 19 percent opined they were somewhat worse, and 12 percent said they were much worse (*Gallup Report*, 1985b: 24).

Undoubtedly, the public has had a number of things in mind when identifying big government as the most likely future threat. Polls taken by Yankelovich,

Skelly, and White in 1978, 1981, and 1982 make it clear that people were more likely to blame government than business and labor unions combined "for the economic problems this country is facing," and that the tendency to lay the primary responsibility at government's doorstep increased once Reagan became president (*Public Opinion*, 1983: 26). A September 1980 poll by the *Los Angeles Times* found that when asked whether business, government, or labor was the most responsible for inflation, unemployment, and declining productivity, Americans were more likely to blame government for each. In addition, the same poll found that more people (43 percent) picked government to cut back its power "for the good of the country" than picked business and labor combined (37 percent) (*Public Opinion*, 1987: 27). It would have been helpful if either the SRC-CPS or Gallup had added another question to those in Figures 2.1, 2.2, and 2.3: "What do you mean by that?" No such follow-up exists. It would also have been useful if either a battery of items focusing on various facets of the central government's activities or, failing that, a more focused item had been asked from 1964 on. Again, no luck.

Fee (1981) suggested that when responding to questions about big government, people respond in terms of four essentially independent clusters of ideas: "welfare-statism," that is, welfare programs, big spending, and socialism; "corporatism," that is, government for the wealthy; "federal control" at the expense of state and local governments; and "bureaucracy," to the detriment of democracy. Unfortunately, the size and composition of the sample Fee relied on caution against complete confidence in the results. Hence, those wishing to study public opinion on the central government's power from 1964 on are left mainly with the item displayed in Figure 2.1. Despite the problems associated with working with just one item, much can be gleaned from the SRC-CPS data—for example, how have important population subgroups changed their views about big government during the past two decades or so.

WHO THINKS GOVERNMENT IS TOO BIG
AND WHO DOES NOT, 1964–1988

As we noted, the big government issue has been an important part of elections since 1964. Presumably, this means differences of opinion exist among major population subgroups. In *The Political Beliefs of Americans*, which was based on the Gallup surveys of September and October 1964, Free and Cantril (1968: 20–21) provided a brief description of group differences on the Gallup question about Washington's power. They noted that the divergent opinions were based substantially on socioeconomic class, with the college-educated, the well-to-do, and businessmen and professionals believing Washington was too powerful, and the less educated, the lower income, and blue-collar, especially union, workers more in favor of an expansive central government (Free and Cantril, 1968:

218–219). These clear-cut class differences reflected the patterns of the New Deal era, when battles over the extension of governmental power into the nation's economic affairs sharply polarized the working class and the so-called higher orders of society (Ladd, with Hadley, 1978: 64–74). Class polarization in American politics has softened considerably since the 1940s (Lipset, 1981: 511–515), but the fault lines created by the New Deal–Fair Deal era were still readily detectable in the mid-1960s.

Class was not the only basis for divergent views about big government in 1964. Interestingly, there was a linear relationship between age and opinions about Washington's power. Americans under thirty, who had come of age after the most strident battles over the federal government's involvement in the economy during the New Deal era were long past, were less likely than the middle-aged or the elderly to think government was too powerful and were the most likely to favor a more energetic national entity. People over fifty were the most concerned about big government and the least likely to favor a more potent national establishment. This will not be the last we see of age-related differences of opinion about big government (see Chapter 5).

Free and Cantril also pointed to newer battle lines over big government. Although the New Deal had seldom directly challenged Jim Crow practices in the South (Ladd, with Hadley, 1978: 59), and Washington had made only sporadic efforts to cope with de jure segregation in the first fifteen years after World War II, civil rights issues came to the fore in the 1960s. The central government's more forceful efforts to improve the lot of southern blacks cleaved the population along regional and racial lines. Free and Cantril (1968: 21, 219) noted that just over half of the Gallup poll respondents living in southern states who had backed Goldwater in 1964 thought Washington was too powerful, compared with only about one-fifth of those living in the East and Midwest. But the most dramatic cleavage in the 1964 Gallup samples was racial. Whites were more than ten times as likely as blacks to believe Washington had too much power (29 percent versus 2 percent) and less than half as likely to say that the central government should use its powers even more forcefully (22 percent versus 52 percent). Carmines and Stimson (1989) detected, at just about this time, a racial reorientation of American politics that is clearly reflected in the 1964 Gallup data.

So much has changed in American politics since 1964 that we need to explore how the snapshot of group differences about big government provided by Free and Cantril has withstood the passage of time. As we shall see, some of the images they depicted have faded; but others remain remarkably distinct. We first take up class-based views of big government (see Table 2.2). Socioeconomic status (SES) is measured separately by education, occupation, and income. The codes for the first two are self-explanatory. However, since the codes for income have changed so much over the years, we present family income by quintiles. There are two figures for each category in each year.

Table 2.2 Public Opinion about the Federal Government's Power, by Socioeconomic Status, for various years, 1964–1988[a]

	1964	1966	1968	1970	1972	1976	1978	1980	1984	1988
Education										
Grade School	38/18	26/32	32/30	36/27	26/37	21/34	16/28	23/30	11/24	16/22
Some High School	38/26	25/39	33/33	37/24	25/37	16/46	11/36	15/39	12/33	14/28
High School Graduate	40/31	33/37	30/44	39/32	31/41	21/51	12/42	15/47	21/31	18/30
Some College	41/41	33/48	34/48	42/40	41/44	23/59	18/49	16/58	31/34	24/37
College Graduate	36/49	38/50	36/55	52/38	34/56	31/59	22/59	20/61	34/38	25/44
Occupation										
Professional	38/47	33/49	32/58	50/34	38/52	34/52	21/55	16/58	41/29	23/40
Business	33/46	33/55	27/58	38/40	36/46	23/63	17/53	17/62	31/40	27/42
Clerical and Sales	41/38	28/48	33/39	38/34	31/48	22/51	13/42	15/44	21/33	22/30
Skilled and Semi-skilled	51/26	33/32	33/41	34/32	32/41	21/54	16/39	15/51	22/34	18/31
Farmers	44/28	15/42	37/51	22/50	41/32	21/48	3/64	8/71	9/55	6/47
Unskilled	53/9	36/24	43/22	51/22	22/36	19/45	18/40	23/44	13/30	13/39
Service	38/13	36/27	34/23	50/17	28/34	17/44	16/34	13/39	21/20	17/26
Housewives	34/25	19/38	30/36	35/30	26/39	18/42	10/41	17/44	18/27	15/26
Income										
Lowest Quintile	38/21	24/32	32/29	37/26	30/35	21/33	13/33	18/38	13/32	18/25
Second Quintile	42/25	34/33	31/35	40/30	28/42	22/47	16/31	21/44	23/30	17/33
Middle Quintile	43/26	30/39	35/40	37/37	32/41	23/51	15/46	16/53	26/34	20/37
Fourth Quintile	33/36	30/33	33/45	43/32	31/45	25/54	18/49	18/52	25/38	21/38
Highest Quintile	38/42	37/46	34/51	44/38	39/49	23/64	16/53	17/58	34/32	28/37

Source: Adapted from the University of Michigan's Survey Research Center–Center for Political Studies' National Election Studies.

[a] Entries above the diagonal are the percentage in each year who said the federal government had not gotten too powerful; those beneath the diagonal are the percentage who said it had gotten too strong. To find the percentage of no opinions, add the figures above and below the diagonal, and subtract that value from 100.

There are three important messages in the table. First, socioeconomic status affected respondents' views about big government throughout the twenty-four years covered in the table, although in ways more complex than Free and Cantril's analysis suggested. The chief complicating factor is the tendency for persons from the lower social orders to express nonsubstantive responses at a much higher rate than middle-class and higher SES individuals. In the late 1970s and thereafter, it was not unusual for 40 to 55 percent of lower SES individuals to express no opinion. By contrast, only between a quarter and a third of upper SES persons do not have opinions about big government. As a result, assessments of the impact of SES on opinions about Washington's power should take the class skew of don't know/no opinion responses into account.

Second, regardless of which dimension of SES is considered, class makes a difference in the way people feel about a powerful central establishment, although there have been changes over the years. Moreover, the impact of class is much clearer when it comes to belief that government has become too big. In the 1960s, there was a definite tendency for the college-educated and the well-to-do to think that Washington had become too strong. However, class differences have narrowed considerably over the years, a point to which we shall return shortly.

Note that class is seldom a good predictor of belief that Washington has not become too strong. One is just as likely to find this opinion among the upper classes, who are normally thought to oppose a powerful central government, as among those from the lower and middle social strata. Indeed, in three years— 1970, 1984, and 1988—upper SES individuals were more likely than those in the lower classes to think that Washington was not too strong. (Keep in mind that since large portions of the lower social orders express nonsubstantive responses on this question, any discussion of the division of opinions about big government leaves out a large proportion of these people.)

As Ladd was aware (1976–77, 1978a, 1978b, 1979b), in recent decades the relationship between social class and views about big government has become much more complex. Although "in the New Deal context, the working class provided the main support for the growth of government," since the end of World War II "a large segment of the *working class* has become (lower) *middle class*. . . . To the degree that it is 'embourgeoised,' [the working class] can be expected to worry about its pocketbook, about inflation, and about the impact of new public spending programs on its economic positions" (Ladd, 1978a: 50, 51). Ladd also pointed to the rise of a "New Class": "the college educated, professional stratum—people in research and development, in education, in public bureaucracies, and the like—[who] are directly dependent upon government for their income and for the support of their professions and institutions" (1978a: 51). As a result, the New Class is often much more supportive of governmental spending for domestic programs than is the traditional working class (Ladd, 1978a: 52). The New Class is also more likely than the working class to support an expansive government on behalf of newer issues such as the environment (Ladd, 1979a: 111). It is not surprising, therefore, that the relationship between SES and views about big government has become much less clear-cut than in the 1960s. The surveys done for the ACIR by the ORC in 1978 and 1982 and by Gallup in 1984, 1985, and 1986, which use the Gallup version of the big government question, also show that SES has a more muted effect than in 1964 (ACIR, 1986: 24-25). Moreover, the ACIR data show class becoming less important between 1978 and 1986; this lends additional credence to Ladd's argument.

Realization of the complexity in the relationship between social class and responses to the SRC-CPS's question about Washington's power brings out the third message in Table 2.2. Maddox and Lilie (1984: 42) believed that this question taps "the public's response to taxes, regulation, government spending, and other economic issues." We think the SRC-CPS's governmental power item can resonate with noneconomic issues as well, such as race relations, law and order/social control, and, occasionally, even foreign affairs. As Lipset noted, "It is necessary to distinguish between so-called economic liberalism (issues concerned with the distribution of wealth and power) and noneconomic liberalism (issues concerned with civil liberties, race relations and foreign affairs)" (1981: 318). Although the lower classes have usually favored governmental intervention in the economic realm to redistribute wealth, and the upper classes have just as often been opposed, when it comes to noneconomic issues one often sees these class relationships reversed (see Lipset, 1981: 92-97).

In the mid- and late 1960s, race was the primary noneconomic source of domestic discord over Washington's role. Students of American racial attitudes in the 1960s and 1970s have noted the paramount importance of the federal government's involvement in changing blacks' status in our society, and some have argued that, as a result, opinions about Washington's power affected opinions about specific policies on blacks' behalf (Jackman, 1978, 1981a, 1981b; Margolis and Haque, 1981; Kuklinski and Parent, 1981; however, see also Merriman and Parent, 1983). The data on racial differences in views about Washington's power are depicted in Figures 2.4 (blacks), 2.5 (nonsouthern whites), and 2.6 (southern whites). Given the historic role of regional differences in racial attitudes and behaviors, the opinions of whites have been divided to reflect those living in the states of the Old Confederacy and those in nonsouthern states.

The message of the figures is straightforward. In the 1960s and early 1970s, there was a major gulf between black and white views about Washington's power. Two points should be made about black feelings in these years. First, even during the peak years of the civil rights movement and the racial crisis in American society (1964-1968), about two-fifths of blacks expressed nonsub-

Figure 2.4 Blacks' Opinions about Big Government, for various years, 1964–1988

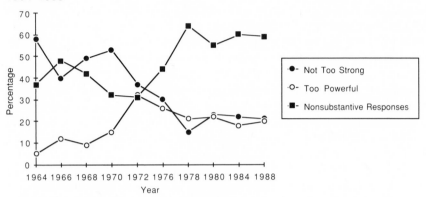

Source: University of Michigan's Survey Research Center–Center for Political Studies' National Election Studies

Figure 2.5 Nonsouthern Whites' Opinions about Big Government, for various years, 1964–1988

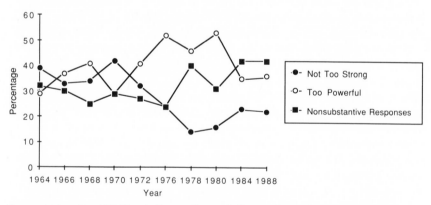

Source: University of Michigan's Survey Research Center–Center for Political Studies' National Election Studies

Figure 2.6 Southern Whites' Opinions about Big Government, for various years, 1964–1988

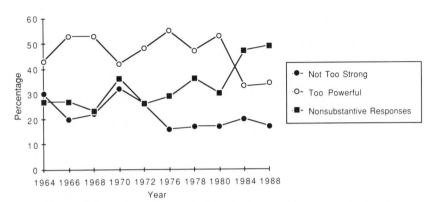

Source: University of Michigan's Survey Research Center–Center for Political Studies' National Election Studies

stantive responses on the question, probably as a result of their low levels of formal schooling. More important, between 1964 and 1970, very few blacks believed the central government had become too powerful.

Among whites, the impact of region on views about big government was very clear from 1964 to 1970. Nonsouthern whites were not only less likely to say Washington was too powerful, they were also slightly less likely to express nonsubstantive responses on the issue. America's racial crisis of the 1960s is clearly mirrored in these data. Reflecting Washington's role on their behalf in these years, blacks overwhelmingly rejected the view that it was too strong. Just as obvious was the tendency of southern whites to be considerably more likely than nonsouthern whites to believe Washington had gotten too powerful.

The years after 1970 show some very interesting trends. Blacks manifested two changes. First, after 1972 there was an increase in nonsubstantive responses, from 44 percent in 1976 to 55–64 percent in the late 1970s and 1980s. The growth in "no opinion" responses among blacks was much larger than among whites and probably reflected the reduced salience of race and the national government's diminished role as a primary agent of racial change during the Reagan era. Second, there was a decrease in the belief that government had not gotten too big. Much of this stemmed from the growth in don't know/no opinion responses, but some of it reflected a slight increase in agreement among blacks that the federal establishment had grown too powerful. Although one is tempted to ascribe this to a belief that a federal government controlled by a conservative Republican administration could become a potential threat to the black community (as in 1972, 1984, and 1988), blacks were still slightly more likely to view Washington as too big when Carter was president (in 1978 and 1980) than they had been with LBJ in the White House (in 1964 and 1968). (Attempts to determine if changes in blacks' social status since 1964 had any impact on their opinions about big government are frustrated by the small number of blacks interviewed in the National Election Studies.)

The reduced salience of racial politics during the 1970s and 1980s was reflected in the white community in a slightly different way. Although there had been substantial differences between the way white southerners and white nonsoutherners had viewed the central government's power in the 1960s and early 1970s, by the late 1970s there was no difference in their views. The confluence in white opinions about big government occurred during both Democratic and Republican administrations. Indeed, white southerners were even more likely to worry about big government when one of their own was president (1978 and 1980) than they were once Carter had been replaced by Reagan. This tendency was not due simply to southern whites' approval of conservative Republican racial policies, because nonsouthern whites' opinions changed at just about the same rate between 1980 and 1988.

All in all, the data in Figures 2.4, 2.5, and 2.6 show two distinct periods in racial views of big government. Between 1964 and 1970, the impact of racial conflict and Washington's role in changing the position of blacks in our society was clearly demonstrated. But the period from 1972 through 1984 showed the lessened salience of race and the perceived reduced role of Washington as the agent of racial change. Even so, there is one constancy over the twenty-four years: Blacks were less likely than either southern whites or nonsouthern whites to think the central government is too powerful. Gallup surveys for the Advisory Commission on Intergovernmental Relations reinforce this point (ACIR, 1986: 24). In 1982, 1984, and 1986, nonwhites were considerably less likely than whites to believe the federal government had too much power and were more inclined to think it should use its powers more vigorously to promote the well-being of all people (ACIR, 1986: 24). Only for 1985 did the ACIR polls show no substantial racial difference in responses to the Gallup question about big government. In short, Carmines and Stimson's racial reorientation of American politics can still be seen in NES and Gallup data.

SES and race have been important determinants of opinions about big government, but they are not the only factors behind differing views about Washington's power. As noted above, Kessel (1972: 463) pointed out that although the Democrats have favored expanding Washington's role in our society, Republicans have stressed the importance of maintaining state and local control of public policy. Differences in Democratic and Republican opinions about governmental power can be traced back to the New Deal era. A March 1936 poll showed that 72 percent of the Democrats responding favored concentration of power in the federal government, compared with only 35 percent of the Republicans (Cantril, with Strunk, 1978: 815). The 1964 Gallup polls used by Free and Cantril (1968: 219) showed that partisanship had a strong impact on responses to the Gallup version of the big government question. Only 14 percent of the Democrats felt that Washington had too much power, whereas 38 percent thought it had about the right amount and another 38 percent thought it should use its powers even more energetically. Thirty-two percent of the independents believed the central government was too big, 38 percent said it had the right amount of power, and 26 percent thought it should become more powerful. Finally, among Republicans, 46 percent believed the federal government was too big, 32 percent said it had the right amount of power, and 18 percent thought it should become more powerful.

If partisanship was a strong determinant of opinions about governmental power in the 1930s and mid-1960s, has it continued to be? SRC-CPS surveys contain the information necessary for an answer. See Figures 2.7 (Democrats), 2.8 (independents), and 2.9 (Republicans). There are essentially four patterns in the figures. Not surprisingly, given Goldwater's crusade against big government in 1964, partisanship played a major role in what people thought about big government. At no other time during the twenty-four years covered in the figures were opinions about Washington's power as clearly differentiated by partisanship as in 1964. Partisanship continued to have an effect throughout the 1960s, albeit at a slightly reduced level in 1966 and 1968, chiefly because Democrats became slightly more leery of big government.

A new pattern manifested itself in the early and mid-1970s, once the Republicans gained control of the White House: The impact of party affiliation was much reduced. It is particularly important to pay close attention to changes in party identifiers' opinions about big government between 1968 and 1970. Although, in the aggregate, no change occurred among Democrats, Republicans had become much less likely to think Washington was too powerful. This suggests that although fearful of big government when a Democrat lives at 1600 Pennsylvania Avenue, Republicans become a good deal more sanguine when one of their own, and a conservative at that, moves in.[5]

The 1972 and 1976 data continue this pattern, but with some new elements added. In 1972, there was no difference between Democratic and Republican opinions about Washington's power, chiefly because Democrats had become a good deal more likely to think it was too strong, although Republicans evinced the same tendency at a slightly lesser rate. It is not difficult to understand why Democrats might have become wary of big government between 1970 and 1972: A conservative Republican administration aggressively exercised its powers at home and abroad, from the impoundment of congressionally appropriated funds to appointment of conservative Supreme Court justices. All the while, there was a continuation, albeit at a reduced rate, of American participation in the Vietnam war. It is more difficult to understand why Republicans became slightly more worried about big government during the same period. Were they simply returning to their normal wariness of a powerful central establishment after the

Figure 2.7 Democrats' Opinions about Big Government, for various years, 1964–1988

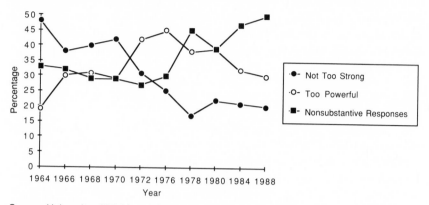

Source: University of Michigan's Survey Research Center–Center for Political Studies' National Election Studies

Figure 2.8 Independents' Opinions about Big Government, for various years, 1964–1988

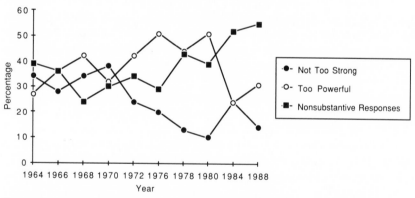

Source: University of Michigan's Survey Research Center–Center for Political Studies' National Election Studies

Figure 2.9 Republicans' Opinions about Big Government, for various years, 1964–1988

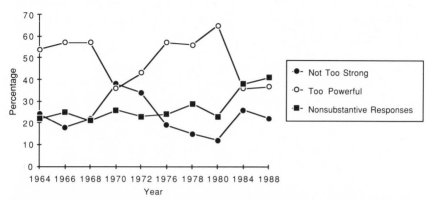

Source: University of Michigan's Survey Research Center–Center for Political Studies' National Election Studies

initial euphoria of having one of their own in the White House for the first time in almost a decade had worn off?

Tempting though it is to ascribe the 1972 data to Watergate, the best evidence seems to indicate that although a substantial segment of the public was aware of the break-in by September, there is "no evidence that, for the most part, citizens were outraged and prepared to charge the Nixon administration the price for its various trespasses" (Lang and Lang, 1983: 32). According to the Langs, "Only a minority [of the public] were personally concerned about . . . [Watergate's] implication for civil liberties or saw in what they had learned evidence of corruption in the administration" (1983: 34).

By 1976, however, the full story of Watergate and its aftermath had come out, with some evident consequences for Democratic and Republican views about big government. Even though Gerald Ford was president, Republicans had become as concerned about too much power in the central government as they had been in the 1960s. Furthermore, slightly over two-fifths of the Democrats, a larger percentage than at any time between 1964 and 1984, claimed Washington was too big. Over half the independents also said government was too strong.

With the Democrats back in control of the White House in 1978 and 1980, we see the third pattern in Figures 2.7–2.9. In some ways, it is reminiscent of the 1960s, with the Republicans considerably more likely than the Democrats to claim Washington was too powerful. But the late 1970s were not the 1960s, for the Democrats were now a bit chastened in their opinions about big government. Whether this was due to the effects of Watergate or to Carter's rhetoric about limits to governmental accomplishments cannot be immediately determined.

In 1984 and 1988, the final pattern emerged. As in 1972, partisanship had no impact on views about big government. But unlike 1972, and quite important, large percentages of Democrats, Republicans, and independents expressed no opinion on the big government item. It was as if all political camps had exhausted their ideas about big government thereby eliminating partisanship as a factor shaping opinions on the question.

The data in Figures 2.7–2.9 provide telling clues about how people view a powerful central establishment. For Republicans, the normal tendency since the 1930s to fear concentration of power in Washington is exacerbated when a Democrat is president, although it can be somewhat overcome when a conservative Republican is chief executive. The pattern among Democrats is a bit more complex. In the 1930s and 1960s, they were more likely to think that Washington had not become too powerful rather than that it had, and this tendency did not end during the first two years of Nixon's presidency. (Looking at just white Democrats does not change the data in Figure 2.7 in any substantial way.) But from 1972 on, Democrats were more likely to think that government was too big than that it was not, even when Carter was president. There was a similar shift among independents. Hence, most of the changes between 1964 and 1980 occurred among Democrats and independents. As important as party affiliation is, it does not provide the complete story. Another critical factor, ideology, will be discussed next.

3

The Tangled Web of Ideology

The data in Chapter 2 show that at different times opinions about Washington's power have been influenced by, among other things, race and party identification. Here we take up a factor that is related to both and has long been alleged to be a major determinant of opinions about big government: ideology. An ideology is a set of beliefs and opinions about how government and society should be organized and how the "good society" can be achieved (Lane, 1962; Erikson, Luttbeg, and Tedin, 1988: Chap. 3). Ideology is said to help people organize specific opinions into a coherent political belief system (P. E. Converse, 1964, 1970, 1975; Sniderman and Tetlock, 1986). Ideologies, therefore, can serve as shorthand devices for helping people organize and retain information to make sense of the political universe. They can also serve as guides to political action, such as voting.

But how much do ordinary citizens use ideology to organize political dispositions, particularly opinions about the central government? There has been sharp disagreement among scholars over whether the public is ideologically naive (called the SRC model after the University of Michigan Survey Research Center) or capable of using ideological labels to shape political judgments (called the revisionist model). There is a lengthy examination of the substantive and methodological differences between these two models focusing primarily upon the work of Angus Campbell et al. (SRC model) and Norman Nie et al. (revisionist model).

Our analysis finds some support for both models. Returning to V. O. Key's contention that the public tends to echo elite opinion, we find that when parties and candidates avoid talking about ideology, as they did in the 1950s, only a tiny fragment of the electorate views public affairs within an ideological framework. When, as in the 1960s, candidates and parties campaign on ideological bases, a much larger proportion of the public echoes those ideological themes. At the center of this process is the president, whose party becomes the focus of reassurance to fellow partisans and often of concern for the other party's followers. It is partisan control of the White House, not Nie et al.'s revisionist argument for increased ideological sophistication among the public, that has affected the twists and turns of liberal and conservative views about Washington's power since the 1970s. As conservative Republicans have moved into the White House and exhibited a willingness to use governmental power on behalf of a conservative agenda, the response of Republican partisans has been to worry less about big government. After all, one of their own is in charge.

THE NEW DEAL DEFINITION

In the United States, at least since the 1930s, ideology has meant liberalism and conservatism. The liberal-conservative polarity encapsulated the major social and political conflicts that arose during the transition from industrialization to mature industrialism (Ladd, 1970: 203; Beer, 1978: 13–15). In its classic New Deal sense, liberals espoused change toward a society led by the people, or by those claiming to speak for them, in favor of more equitable distribution of society's values, while conservatives resisted change and championed the leadership of the well-to-do (Ladd, 1970: 203–204, 1972: 155–157). The fundamental difference between New Deal liberals and New Deal conservatives was their views of big government; the former favored and the latter opposed expansion of the central government (Free and Cantril, 1968: 5). During the 1930s and 1940s, liberalism was a nationalizing force. Using the power of the presidential office and the national government's capacity to tax and spend, liberals centralized power not only by dealing "with problems that had previously been left to state or local governments, or had not been dealt with at all," but also by integrating "into the national community groups which had previously been marginal or excluded" (Beer, 1965: 158), chiefly the urban working class.

Many students of politics think liberalism and conservatism are "the fundamental conceptual yardsticks for measuring political life" (Neuman, 1986: 18). Neuman contended that "most" political parties, leaders, arguments, policy positions, and even court decisions "can be located along these traditional dimensions." Analogous to monetary units in economics, "the liberal-conservative continuum spans the specific issues of politics and serves as its primary, if less precise, unit of analysis. Thus, as understanding of economics is impossible without a concept of price, political life is incomprehensible without some sense of its central continuum" (Neuman, 1986: 18).

Beer (1978) believed that the New Deal ended as the nation's public philosophy in the early 1960s. Similarly, Ladd argued that since the mid-1960s, changes in America's social structure and political alignments have fundamentally altered the meanings of liberalism and conservatism and the social bases of their respective supporters (1976–77, 1978a, 1978b, 1979b, 1982; Ladd, with Hadley, 1978). Ladd identified three major social changes that are at the root of ideological transformations: (1) the decline of entrepreneurial businessmen and their replacement by managers more likely to identify with their professions than with older business values; (2) the growth of a college-educated class tied to government as either educators or government workers ("New Class"); and (3) the transition of the working class from have-nots dependent on government for improved living standards to moderately well-off haves worried about preserving the status quo. As a result, although the 1930s saw the cutting edges of ideological cleavage between a working class which backed liberal demands for an expanded federal apparatus that would transfer wealth from a middle class which resisted change at all cost, the 1970s and 1980s witnessed battles between a college-educated upper middle class seeking change while being opposed by an "embourgeoisified" working class.

Ladd also pointed to changes in the issues that divide liberals from conservatives, and the clientele groups allied with each. Essentially, the old battles between those who would use an activist state and those who favored a passive central government are over (see also Lowi, 1979; Hamby, 1985). Except for the vestige of 1930s economic royalists, all sides today seek to use the federal government to their own ends. What is different, according to Ladd, is that contemporary liberalism no longer seeks to use the federal establishment to achieve majoritarian goals. Rather, liberals now pursue policies designed to help minorities, especially the black underclass, often expecting the costs to be borne disproportionately by the white working class (Ladd, 1976–77: 590–592; 1979a: 92–94; 1982: 47–48; Beer, 1978: 26–32; Hamby, 1985; 325–326, 345–346). In addition, the emergence of new issues tied to changing views about sex, marriage and the family, and lifestyles have often pitted the college-educated upper middle class against a high school–educated working class that still believes in older notions of right and wrong. Further complicating ideological alignments was the reemergence in the 1960s of a romantic impulse extolling the virtues of emotion over reason and placing its faith in the popular will rather than in bureaucratic expertise (Beer, 1978: 22–28).

There are two primary consequences of the ideological transformation since the mid-1960s (Beer, 1978; Ladd, 1978b). First, there are now several varieties of liberals and conservatives. For example, a small group of "orthodox" conservatives still refuses to accept the positive state, whereas a larger group of "moderate" conservatives now accepts it. Liberals are divided into the "old" liberals (sometimes called "neo-conservatives"), who endorse the New Deal but say they have learned the limits of politics, and the "new" liberals, who advocate greater governmental intervention on behalf of different clientele groups in order to achieve not equality of opportunity but equality of result.

Second, and for our purposes more important, the composition of the groups arguing over the expansion of the federal government and the ends to be served by governmental growth have changed. In the 1930s, the working class was the pro-government group and it sought the creation of a positive state to achieve equality of opportunity. Today's pro-government class is the New Class intelligentsia, not only because they are dependent on government for their livelihood, but also because they wish to use the state on behalf of groups they see as still outside the American mainstream: blacks, women, gays, and other unpopular minorities (Ladd, 1978a: 51; 1982: 37–45). In addition, one finds moderate and neo-conservatives attacking big government in the name of decentralization and greater efficiency, while new liberals assail it out of "a romantic distrust of power and faith in 'the people' " (Beer, 1978: 41).

THE DEBATE OVER GRASS-ROOTS IDEOLOGY IN THE UNITED STATES

Students of public opinion once naively assumed that most Americans were aware of liberal-conservative ideologies and understood the elaborate conceptual schemata employed by politicians to tie specific policy opinions into relatively consistent bundles. Thus it was not unusual to find pollsters asking questions such as that posed by Gallup in June 1938: "During the next two years, would you like to see the Roosevelt administration be more liberal or more conservative?" When 28 percent of those polled replied "More liberal," and 72 percent said, "More conservative" (Cantril, with Strunk, 1978: 979), the answers were taken at face value. This tendency was reinforced when it was routinely found that only small percentages of the public expressed don't know/no opinion on this and similar questions (see Cantril, with Strunk, 1978: 979, 987).

It was also common to interpret the outcomes of presidential elections as reflecting meaningful shifts in public support for liberalism or conservatism. For example, when, after twenty years out of power, the Republicans recaptured the White House by a landslide in 1952, the election was interpreted as signifying "a nation turned conservative" (Lubell, 1956: 3). Such interpretations do not belong to a benighted past. At least two recent works claimed to be able to identify clear-cut ideological patterns in public opinion. Both denied that public opinion has become more conservative. After a review of poll data between 1980 and 1984, Ferguson and Rogers concluded that "if American public opinion drifted anywhere over Reagan's first term, it was toward the left, not the right" (1986: 28). Based on much flimsier evidence, such as rock-and-roll lyrics, McElvaine (1987) heralded "the end of the conservative era."

Serious students of public opinion have long since jettisoned such broad interpretations. Drawing largely on the Survey Research Center's 1956 National Election Study, Campbell, Converse, Miller, and Stokes searched in vain for evidence of highly differentiated, wide-ranging, and coherent liberal-conservative ideologies. They concluded that "the typical American lacks a clearly patterned ideology of such breadth. He may feel strongly about a variety of individual issues, but there are severe limitations on our ability to predict his position in one issue area from his position in another" (1960: 197). Like other scholars at the time (for example, McClosky, Hoffman, and O'Hara, 1960; Key, 1961: 171–172; McClosky, 1964), Campbell et al. (1960: 253) claimed that the overarching liberal-conservative ideologies that influenced the thinking of the political elites were too abstract and complex to be meaningful to the masses. Conceding the claim of critics that American politics in the mid-1950s was largely issueless (see Mills, 1956), Campbell et al. nonetheless contended that lack of ideological sophistication among the public stemmed mainly from ordinary people's limited intellectual abilities (1960: 180–181).

The SRC's seminal study of grass-roots political thinking and the basis of the SRC model, is Philip E. Converse's "The Nature of Belief Systems in Mass Publics" (1964). Using data from National Election Studies in 1956, 1958, and 1960, he sought to prove that the liberal-conservative continuum, which had been the primary basis for elite struggles since the 1930s, was largely missing among the American public of the 1950s. His proof came in four parts. First, only 3 percent of the public in the mid-1950s appeared to evaluate political parties and presidential candidates in ideological terms, and 9 percent employed ideological terms in a very limited and imprecise way. Most people judged the parties either by the clientele groups that benefited from their policies or by associating prosperity with the Democrats and hard times with the Republicans, or war with the Democrats and peace with the GOP (P. E. Converse, 1964: 215–216).

Second, when asked to explain what they had in mind when they judged one of the political parties as more liberal or more conservative than the other, only 17 percent of the public in 1956 had "an understanding of the [liberal-conservative] distinction that captures much of its breadth" (Converse, 1964: 223). Third, the inter-item correlations between the policy opinions of the respondents to the 1958 National Election Study and those of congressional candidates showed a fairly high level of consistent policy opinions (called "issue constraint") among the latter, but much lower consistency at the grass-roots level. Inconsistent policy opinions indicate that "the organization of more specific attitudes into wide-ranging belief systems is absent" among ordinary people (P. E. Converse, 1964: 228–229).

Fourth, when issue opinions measured in 1958 were retested in 1960, there were basically two patterns (P. E. Converse, 1964: 238–245; see also P. E.

Converse, 1970): A tiny portion of the public had almost perfectly stable opinions over time; and an overwhelming majority manifested essentially random opinion change from time-one to time-two. Converse concluded that "these longitudinal data offer eloquent proof that signs of low constraint among belief elements in the mass public are not products of well knit but highly idiosyncratic belief systems. . . . Great instability in itself is *prima facie* evidence that the belief has extremely low centrality for the believer" (1964: 241). His central proposition was that "where any single [ideological] dimension is concerned, very substantial portions of the public simply do not belong on the dimension at all" (1964: 245).

How might American politics have been different had substantial portions of the public organized their policy opinions along ideological lines? With an ideological orientation, "new political events have more meaning, retention of political information from the past is far more adequate, and political behavior increasingly approximates that of sophisticated 'rational' models, which assume relatively full information" (P. E. Converse, 1964: 227). Because the public in the 1950s was ideologically unsophisticated and without a backlog of politically relevant information, political controversies were beyond the ken of the average citizen. With elites and masses speaking different political languages, meaningful communication between them was seriously hindered. As a result, popular control over governmental policy was reduced.

Although the SRC's characterization of an ideologically innocent public became the standard view among academics throughout the 1960s (Bennett, 1977), given the nature of American politics during the 1960s and 1970s and the dialectical tendency of scholarship, new views emerged to contest the SRC's interpretation. Some alleged that "confusion" had been superseded by "clarity" (Pomper, 1972). So voluminous has the literature on mass belief systems and ideology become (see, for example, Kessel, 1972; P. E. Converse, 1975; Kinder, 1983; Kinder and Sears, 1985; Sniderman and Tetlock, 1986; Luskin, 1987; E. Smith, 1989), no comprehensive survey can be attempted here. Rather, our goal is to provide only the outlines of the revisionist argument favoring clear ideological divisions among the public.

Many revisionist scholars accept the basic theoretical framework and methodologies of the SRC but argue that its findings apply only to the placid 1950s. However, when new issues such as race (Carmines and Stimson, 1989) and more ideologically pure candidates such as Barry Goldwater or George McGovern emerged in the mid-1960s, the American public's political dispositions changed dramatically. Studies by Field and Anderson (1969), Pierce (1970), and Nie, Verba, and Petrocik (1976) showed Goldwater's ideological candidacy significantly increased the percentage of the public using ideological terms to describe political parties and presidential candidates. Most important in the revisionist view was a sudden, major increase in consistency among the public's policy opinions (S. E. Bennett, 1973; Nie, with Andersen, 1974;

Miller, Miller, Raine, and Brown, 1976; Nie, Verba, and Petrocik, 1976). The leap in issue constraint in 1964 produced a very different portrait of grass-roots political thinking, one that persisted into 1968, although overall consistency fell after 1972 (Nie, Verba, and Petrocik, 1979).

It was not long before the revisionist position was under assault. Much, but not all, of the criticism focused on alleged methodological weaknesses in revisionist scholarship. For example, critics pointed out that although the authors of *The American Voter* had analyzed the original interview code sheets, handwritten by survey interviewers, the revisionists (for example, Field and Anderson and Nie, Verba, and Petrocik) employed simplified codes from the computer-readable versions of National Election Studies that are provided to scholars by the Inter-University Consortium for Political and Social Research. This, the critics argued, could have artificially inflated the estimates of the use of ideological dimensions of judgment (Luskin, 1987). Later, when researchers analyzed the actual interview code sheets from the same National Election Studies on which the revisionists had relied, they reported much more modest increases in active usage of ideological terminology (Klingemann, 1979; Hagner and Pierce, 1982). These studies support the conclusion that "the active usage measure is situationally elastic" (P. E. Converse, 1975: 91). Still, replications of the SRC's 1956 analysis indicated that the elasticity in the public's reliance on ideology to judge parties and candidates was rather limited (Miller and Miller, 1976; Flanigan and Zingale, 1987: 111–112).

Other researchers, often relying on question-wording experiments, contended that increased issue constraint in 1964 and thereafter was artifactual and not substantive (Bishop, Tuchfarber, and Oldendick, 1978a, 1978b; Brunk, 1978; Sullivan, Piereson, and Marcus, 1978). Changes in the SRC's question wording and format between 1960 and 1964 were alleged to account for the leap in issue constraint. Some critics have concluded that the public was just as ideologically unsophisticated in the 1960s and 1970s as it had been during the Eisenhower era. New issues, new leaders, and new politics had evidently not led to a fundamental improvement in grass-roots ideological sophistication. Clarity had not replaced confusion, for confusion had been followed by confusion (Margolis, 1977). Apparently, the American voter was unchanged from his or her counterpart of the 1950s (E. Smith, 1989).

The question-wording thesis was met by spirited counterthrusts (Petrocik, 1978; Nie and Rabjohn, 1979a), which produced another round of replies (Bishop, Tuchfarber, Oldendick, and Bennett, 1979; Sullivan, Piereson, Marcus, and Feldman, 1979), which led to two last parries (Nie and Rabjohn, 1979b; Petrocik, 1980). With that, most of the contenders left the field, more in exhaustion than in triumph. The result was to leave the study of mass belief systems in even worse disarray than W. Lance Bennett (1977) had thought (compare Kinder, 1983: 395–396, with W. L. Bennett, 1980: 53–56). Thus, although some public opinion analysts claim that the picture of the public as ideologically unsophisticated has been definitively drawn (Kinder, 1983; Luskin, 1987), new studies supporting the revisionist view of an ideologically aware electorate continue to appear (Judd and Milburn, 1980; Jackson, 1983; Inglehart, 1985; Peffley and Hurwitz, 1985). Also, critics continue to fault the methodological shortcomings of revisionists (see P. E. Converse, 1980, and Martin, 1981, on Judd and Milburn, 1980) while the latter continue to defend their work (Judd and Milburn, 1981).

As different as they are in their claims about the public's ideological innocence or sophistication, the SRC and most revisionists agree that liberalism and conservatism are the antipodes of a single continuum. However, we have seen in Chapter 2 that Seymour Martin Lipset (1981: 92, 318) identified at least two dimensions of ideology where domestic issues are concerned: the economic and the civil liberties–racial dimensions. In a similar vein, Maddox and Lilie argued that the liberal-conservative bipolarity was inadequate for understanding grass-roots ideology because American belief systems are organized along two distinct dimensions: feelings about governmental intervention in the economy, and opinions about personal freedoms (1984: 4).

Based on these two underlying dimensions, Maddox and Lilie identified four ideological orientations in contemporary America: (1) liberals, who favor governmental intervention in the economy and the expansion of individual freedoms; (2) libertarians, who oppose governmental involvement in economic affairs and in regulating personal affairs; (3) conservatives, who oppose governmental involvement in the economy but favor regulation of personal affairs; and (4) populists, who favor governmental action in the economy but oppose expansion of individual freedoms. According to Maddox and Lilie (1984: 67–69), between 1972 and 1980, one-sixth to one-quarter of the American public could be classified as liberals, another one-sixth were conservatives, one-tenth to one-sixth were libertarians, one-fourth to just under one-third were populists, and the remainder were either inattentive or had divided ideological orientations.

Despite their rather cavalier handling of methodological and historical questions (Lekachman, 1985–86), Maddox and Lilie offered a useful corrective to the bipolar characterization of American ideology. American politics is too complex to be encapsulated by a single overarching, bipolar conceptual dimension.[1] Those who would seek to impose a unidimensional liberal-conservative framework upon the mass public often make a priori assumptions based on how they perceive the general principle(s) used to organize opinions into coherent belief systems (Lane, 1973; Marcus, Tabb, and Sullivan, 1974). Moreover, it is possible that the presence of multiple organizing principles indicates conceptual complexity in political thinking (Marcus, Tabb, and Sullivan, 1974; Jackson and Marcus, 1975) rather than low cognitive ability, as has been alleged (Stimson, 1975).

IDEOLOGY IN THE UNITED STATES:
WHERE DO WE STAND?

What sense can be made of all this? More, we think, than initially meets the eye. What all the evidence presented during the past twenty-five years and all the controversies since the early 1970s establish is that most Americans are indifferent to the liberal-conservative ideologies that undergird elite political discourse. Much, although not all, of the increase in issue constraint in mass belief systems during the 1960s is artifactual, and a good deal of the genuine enhancement in opinion consistency evident today is due to the emergence of racial, law-and-order, and lifestyle issues in the 1960s and 1970s. A careful reading of Philip E. Converse (1964: 234–238) would have anticipated this development. In addition, ideology plays only a limited role in what goes on inside the voting booth on election day (Luttbeg and Gant, 1985; however, see also Miller, Miller, Raine, and Brown, 1976, Levitin and Miller, 1979, and Miller and Shanks, 1982).

Still, some scholars continue to argue that American public opinion is comprehensible in ideological terms (Davis, 1980; Holm and Robinson, 1978; Robinson and Holm, 1980; T. W. Smith, 1981, 1985b; Robinson and Fleishman, 1984; Exter and Barber, 1986). For example, between 1974 and 1988, the National Opinion Research Center (NORC) asked respondents to its General Social Surveys (GSS) to locate themselves on a seven-point ideological scale, running from extremely liberal to extremely conservative. About 95 percent of the public were able to place themselves at some point on the GSS's liberal-conservative scale. It might be tempting to argue that because only about 5 percent of GSS respondents said they did not know where they belonged on a liberal-conservative scale, the contemporary public is thoroughly comfortable with ideology. We think not, for three reasons.

First, roughly 40 percent of GSS respondents opted for the moderate, middle-of-the-road category, which may indicate a nonideological tendency. Second, and more important, NORC did not include a screen for don't know/no opinion responses on its liberal-conservative self-placement measure. When a screen is included on an otherwise identical liberal-conservative scale, a much different picture of grass-roots ideology appears. Since 1972, the CPS has asked respondents to its National Election Studies to place themselves somewhere along the same seven-point liberal-conservative continuum used by NORC, except the CPS included a stringent screen for nonsubstantive responses ("or haven't you thought much about this"). Between 1972 and 1988, the CPS data show that when offered the opportunity, 25 to 36 percent of the public admit they have not thought much about liberalism or conservatism. In addition, another 25 percent place themselves in the moderate, middle-of-the-road category.

Could it be contended that even with a screen for don't know/no opinion responses and eliminating those in the middle-of-the-road, from 42 to 47 percent of the American public have placed themselves in either a liberal or a conservative category since the early 1970s? Yes, but those figures very likely overestimate the extent of ideological commitment among ordinary people. Fewer than 5 percent selected the extremely liberal or extremely conservative categories, and an average of only 23 percent of the public have placed themselves in the four outermost categories on the scale. Perhaps what the CPS data best illustrate is Scammon and Wattenberg's (1971) dictum that the only attractive ideological extreme to ordinary Americans is the extreme center.

Third, although Luttbeg and Gant reported an increase between 1956 and 1980 in the ability of Americans to define liberalism and conservatism in ways "which are consistent with the terms of public debate" (1985: 82), they warned that the 1980 data did not suggest that the public was now capable of sophisticated ideological reasoning. Moreover, in a similar analysis of the 1976 National Election Study, Conover and Feldman found that "the meaning of ideological labels is largely symbolic in content and nondimensional in structure" (1981: 636). The definitions put forth most often indicate that the public perceives the core meaning of liberalism-conservatism as "change vs. the preservation of traditional values" (Conover and Feldman, 1981: 643).

Conover and Feldman established that ideological self-placement is influenced much more by feelings about liberals and conservatives than by issue opinions. They concluded that "ideological labels, and consequently self-identifications, have largely symbolic, nonissue-oriented meaning to the mass public" (1981: 641), which is in keeping with the views of Levitin and Miller (1979; however, see also Sanders, 1986). That substantial proportions of the contemporary public are capable of at least a symbolic understanding of ideology, even if it is largely devoid of issue content, has important consequences. Ideology becomes, in this way, a handy device for simplifying sociopolitical conflict. "The public's usage of ideological labels is more a simplification than a distortion of reality, and . . . ideological identifications constitute more a symbolic than issue-oriented link to the political world" (Conover and Feldman, 1981: 644).

In short, it would be a mistake to conclude that ideology is completely foreign to American thinking. Even when a screen for don't know/no opinion responses is used, and people who say they are moderates are excluded, a sizable percentage of the public admits to some ideological tendency. Even if this tendency is largely symbolic and based on affect rather than cognition, it has important consequences. Just as party identification helps ordinary people to better understand politics (Campbell, Converse, Miller, and Stokes, 1960), "ideological labels may create links that help many citizens make sense out of the remote world of politics, even though they attach little systematic content to those labels" (Levitin and Miller, 1979: 752; see also Conover and Feldman, 1981: 642–644).

IDEOLOGY AND OPINIONS ABOUT BIG GOVERNMENT

If a substantial portion of the mass public relies upon ideological labels as a means of making sense, even if in a symbolic, simplified way, of the political world, does this have any bearing on the way they approach questions about the power of the central government? Generally speaking, the answer is yes, but the details differ depending upon whom one consults. In their study of American public opinion in the mid-1960s, Free and Cantril distinguished between operational and ideological spectra. The first deals with opinions about specific governmental programs. According to Free and Cantril, from the New Deal to the Great Society, the consensus was that at the operational level of specific programs, "the Federal Government should act to meet public needs" (1968: 13). Free and Cantril defined the ideological spectrum as the abstractions Americans hold about "the nature and functioning of our socioeconomic system" (1968: 25). When it came to these abstractions, Americans were much more conservative. Hence, in the 1960s, Americans were alleged to be ideologically conservative because they took a dim view of big government, but they were also operationally liberal, favoring specific governmental programs (Free and Cantril, 1968: 36–38).

In 1964, there was a modest association between self-identification as liberal, middle-of-the-road, or conservative and opinions that the central government was too powerful, had about the right amount of power, or should become even stronger (Free and Cantril, 1968: 48–49). Of self-proclaimed liberals, 11 percent thought Washington was too strong, 44 percent thought it had about the right amount of power, and 45 percent believed it should use its powers even more energetically. Among moderates, the respective percentages were 24, 44, and 32. Of people who called themselves conservative, 48 percent said government was too big, 29 percent thought it had about the right amount of power, and 23 percent believed it should become even more powerful. That almost a quarter of self-professed conservatives called for even bigger government led Free and Cantril to argue that when people called themselves liberal, they had the operational spectrum in mind. It was less clear whether conservatives referred to the operational or the ideological spectrum (1968: 49). For that reason, Free and Cantril did not explore any further the relationship between ideological self-placement and views about big government (1968: 50).

Another view is provided by Nie and his associates (Nie, with Andersen, 1974; Nie, Verba, and Petrocik, 1976, 1979; Nie and Rabjohn, 1979a), who believed that the relationship between ideology and opinions about Washington's power changed from the 1960s to the 1970s in response to shifts in the meaning people attached to the SRC's big government question. According to Nie and Andersen (1974: 556), "the size of the government issue split the population along classical liberal/conservative lines" in 1964. Conservatives viewed big government as anathema, just as they had since the New Deal, while liberals saw a powerful central establishment as a useful vehicle for rectifying social and economic injustices. Although the big government issue still divided liberals and conservatives in 1968, ideological differences had narrowed, by virtue of a more than 20 percent jump in liberals viewing Washington as too powerful and a 10 percent drop in conservatives saying the national government was too big (Nie, with Andersen, 1974: 555–556). By 1972, however, "a monotonic [linear] relationship no longer existed between liberalism and conservatism and attitudes towards the size of government" (Nie, with Andersen, 1974: 556). The figures differ depending upon which version of Nie's research one consults (compare Nie, with Andersen, 1974: 555; with Nie, Verba, and Petrocik, 1976: 125–128; and Nie, Verba, and Petrocik, 1979: 125–128, 371). The point is that "by 1972 liberals were more opposed to big government than were conservatives" (Nie, Verba, and Petrocik, 1976: 127).

The explanation for the change in the relationship between ideology and big government opinions differs slightly from one version of Nie's research to the next. Nie and Andersen contended that "sometime in the late 1960s, a sense began to emerge among the leadership of the liberal community that big government was merely acting to reinforce existing injustices," that "the core of these ideas has indeed taken hold in the mass public" (1974: 554), and that this accounts for the increase in the perceptions of grass-roots liberals that Washington was too powerful. To account for growing liberal skepticism about big government between 1968 and 1972, Nie and Andersen argued that "given Vietnam, the failure of the New Deal and Great Society welfare programs, and the resurgence of the notion of 'returning the government to the people,' such a finding is only surprising in terms of the *extent* to which this ideological redefinition has penetrated to the mass public" (1974: 557).

Nie, Verba, and Petrocik (1976: 125–128) proposed a slightly different explanation for the transformation of the relationship between ideology and views about big government. The new version of the SRC question about Washington's power initially tapped general dispositions about governmental intervention in the economy (see also Maddox and Lilie, 1984). However, "from 1968 to 1972, the [SRC] question appears to take on a mixed meaning. Big and powerful government no longer appears to refer only to the economic interventionist governments of the New Deal; it comes to connote as well a government involved in the Vietnam war and in the harassment of protesters. Such a change in meaning would create opponents of 'big and powerful' government on both the left and the right" (Nie, Verba, and Petrocik, 1976: 126). Nie and Rabjohn claimed that the big government item tapped, in addition to the Vietnam war and the suppression of antiwar dissenters, the Nixon administration's "stiffening position on a variety of civil liberty issues ranging from how to handle urban riots to the rights of criminals and penalties for those smoking marijuana" (1979a: 142–143).

Interestingly, both Nie and his associates and Maddox and Lilie saw two dimensions to political ideology and opinions about specific issues and big government: an economic interventionist dimension and a civil libertarianism–personal freedom dimension. However, Maddox and Lilie believed that the SRC's big government question "certainly taps the public's reaction to taxes, regulation, government spending, and other economic issues" (1984: 42) between 1964 and 1980, whereas Nie and his associates claimed that the item shifted from economic interventionism to civil libertarianism and back between 1964 and 1976.

To show that the SRC's big government question had changed from one concerning purely governmental economic interventionism to one concerning economic activism as well as civil libertarianism, Nie and his associates conducted a question-wording experiment in late 1973, which they say supported their view (1976: 127–128). They also believed their interpretation was supported by public attitudes in 1976. With the end of the Vietnam war and the cessation of the Nixon administration's harassment of antiwar protesters, the civil libertarian aspect of government had receded and the economic interventionist component had reasserted itself. Conservatives were again more likely than liberals to believe Washington was too strong (70 percent versus 50 percent; see Nie, Verba, and Petrocik, 1979: 370–371). One should note, however, that the pre-1972 pattern did not completely reassert itself in 1976, for moderates were just as likely as liberals to claim that government was too big (Nie, Verba, and Petrocik, 1979: 371).

Nie et al.'s argument that the relationship between ideology and opinions about Washington's power changed with the emergence of new issues is interesting, but it has some problems. First, it is predicated on the belief that Americans had become ideologically sophisticated, a premise that has been hotly contested. Second, the contention that American involvement in Vietnam, governmental harassment of protesters, and the Nixon administration's hard line on civil libertarianism and counterculture lifestyles affected opinions about big government has not been tested, even though there are appropriate data available. There are also problems with the measure Nie and his associates relied on to tap ideology, although it can be used.

Although the SRC did not ask about ideological self-placement before 1972, beginning in 1964 it did ask respondents to locate political personalities and groups on an opinion thermometer (OT), depending upon how warm or cold the individual felt. The thermometer ranges from 0° to 100°. Included among the political groups were liberals and conservatives. To create their measure of ideology, Nie and his associates subtracted opinion thermometer ratings of conservatives from those of liberals and recoded the resulting scores to obtain liberal, moderate, and conservative categories (Nie, with Andersen, 1974: 555n; Nie, Verba, and Petrocik, 1976: 126).[2] Figure 3.1 presents the relationship between ideology, as measured by the opinion thermometer, and opinions about

Figure 3.1   Opinion That the Federal Government Is Too Powerful, by Ideology, for various years, 1964–1988

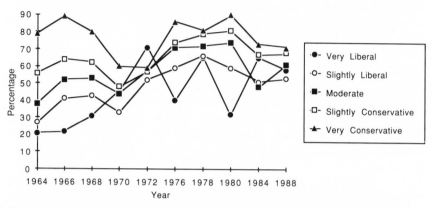

Source: University of Michigan's Survey Research Center–Center for Political Studies' National Election Studies

big government between 1964 and 1988. The figure depicts the percentage of those with opinions who said that Washington had gotten too powerful.[3]

The most important message in Figure 3.1 is that the relationship between ideology and opinions about big government went through several changes over the twenty-four years.[4] Just as Nie and his associates contended, in the mid- and late 1960s there was a robust, linear relationship. Extreme conservatives were 50 to 60 percent more likely to think Washington had become too powerful than were extreme liberals. Those who were slightly liberal or slightly conservative were a bit less inclined to adopt the opinion on Washington's power to which their more extreme ideological brethren subscribed, and moderates fell right in the middle. As indicated by tau-c coefficients,[5] the relationship between ideology and big government opinions was quite respectable in 1964 and 1966 (.34 and .31), although it had slightly weakened as early as 1968 (.24). It sagged to .16 in 1970. Just as Nie claimed, moreover, by 1972 the relationship had disappeared ($t_c = .02$). In fact, extreme liberals were now slightly more likely than extreme conservatives to believe the central government was too big, although, given the small numbers involved, the difference is within sampling error. The temptation is to conclude that the data in Figure 3.1 confirm Nie et al.'s analysis, which should not be surprising since we are using the same data sets and nearly the same operational definitions.

Closer inspection of the data between 1964 and 1988 suggests, however, that the interpretation of Nie et al. was too facile. First, except for extreme liberals, who remained adamantly unconvinced, opinion that Washington had become too powerful increased among the slightly liberal, the moderates, and all conservatives between 1964 and 1966. The increase was 14 percent among moderates and the slightly liberal, and 8 to 10 percent among the two conservative categories. The 10 percent increase in anti–big government opinions among extreme conservatives, coupled with the unchanged views among the very liberal, explains why the value of the tau-c coefficients remained unchanged from 1964 to 1966.

From 1966 to 1968, the only meaningful shifts were a 9 percent rise in anti-big government feelings among extreme liberals and a 7 percent drop among extreme conservatives, which contributed to an overall weakened relationship between ideology and views of Washington's power. In the four years between the height of Lyndon Baines Johnson's popularity and his fall from public grace (Mueller, 1973: 200–201), the neat, ideologically based pattern of opinions about big government had already begun to erode, although its essential characteristics remained intact even in the twilight of Johnson's presidency.

Recall that Nie et al. contended that the SRC's question came to mean economic interventionism plus involvement in Vietnam and harassment of protesters sometime between 1968 and 1972, and this allegedly created anti–big government feelings on both the right and the left. The data in Figure 3.1 may not overturn this contention, but they suggest that the timetable may be off. Not only had some liberals begun to manifest increasing queasiness about big government as early as 1966, but also one can see residues of the old New Deal ideological alignment as late as 1970. Indeed, the shifts in public opinion that Nie et al. claimed would culminate in 1972 were well under way by 1970. Not only had the very conservative become 22 percent less likely to believe the central government was too powerful, but also slightly over two-fifths of extreme liberals now thought Washington was too big. As a result, what had been a 50 to 60 percent gap in big government opinions between the ideological extremes in the 1960s had narrowed to only a 15 percent difference.

Closer inspection reveals a more complicated pattern to the 1970 data. Extreme liberals were more inclined than the slightly liberal to believe Washington was too big. Also, there had actually been a decline in anti–big government opinions within every group except the extreme liberals. In Chapter 2, we pointed out that 1970 had witnessed a temporary reversal of a growth in anti–big government opinions from 1964 through 1968. In addition, 1970 was the only time that the SRC's big government question elicited more than a small percentage of people replying, "It depends." We shall return to this unusual pattern, but first let us complete the chronological overview that Figure 3.1 provides.

Recall that Nie and his associates' initial analyses carried the tale through 1972, when they believed the SRC's big government item had taken on multiple meanings: For conservatives, it continued to conjure up images of the activist state created by the New Deal; for liberals, it now connoted a government pursuing war in Southeast Asia and violating the civil liberties of its domestic critics (Nie, with Andersen, 1974: 554–557; Nie, Verba, and Petrocik, 1976: 125–128). In the revised edition of *The Changing American Voter,* Nie, Verba, and Petrocik carry the story through 1976. As they see it, by 1976, with the United States out of Vietnam and political unrest stilled, the public's attention turned elsewhere. "As partisan quarrels focused upon unemployment, inflation, and medical services, the more typical relationship between one's self-identification as a liberal or conservative and the size of government question reasserted itself" (Nie, Verba, and Petrocik, 1979: 371).

Our data in Figure 3.1 for 1976 agree with those of Nie et al. in general but differ in important specifics. Certainly the old gulf between the big government views of extreme liberals and extreme conservatives had reasserted itself, by virtue of a 31 percent drop in the view among extreme liberals and 27 percent increase in the belief among extreme conservatives that Washington was too big. However, note that there had been a slight increase in anti–big government beliefs among liberals, which was accompanied by even larger increases in anti–big government sentiments among moderates and conservatives. Although the 1976 data do depart from the 1972 pattern, their similarity to the pattern of the mid-1960s is almost entirely limited to the ideological extremes. As a result, the tau-c for the relationship in 1976 is only .17.

If Nie and his coauthors had had access to the 1980 data, however, they might have clung even more tenaciously to their interpretation of the big government question. The year 1980, after all, was the heyday of Jimmy Carter's "national malaise" (Carter, 1982: 121). It was also a time of serious economic problems: high inflation, high interest rates, high unemployment. Altogether, they meant severe stagflation. Not surprisingly, the public's concerns reflected the country's straitened economic conditions. Economic issues were listed as major national problems by slightly over half of the public in 1980, compared with only a quarter in 1972 (Abramson, Aldrich, and Rohde, 1983: 121–122).

Perhaps it is also not surprising that the relationship between ideology and opinions about big government in 1980 looked initially like the mid-1960s pattern. Whereas only a third of the small group of extreme liberals believed Washington was too powerful, fully 90 percent of extreme conservatives were convinced that the national government had grown too big. At a glance, the 1980 data appear to buttress the argument of Nie et al., although the tau-c for the relationship is .24, somewhat weaker than in 1964–1966, but well above 1978's .13. However, three-fifths of the liberals, along with three-fourths of the moderates, believed government had grown too powerful by 1980. Long after Vietnam and its accompanying civil turmoil had receded from public consciousness, the relation of ideology to big government opinions bore little resemblance to the mid-1960s pattern (compare Abramson, Aldrich, and Rohde, 1983: 121–122, with Bennett and Tuchfarber, 1975: 435). Something had changed, but perhaps not in the fashion described by Nie and his associates.

The proof of the pudding can be found in the 1984 and 1988 data. Although half of the 1984 public still listed economic issues as the country's most important problem (Abramson, Aldrich, and Rohde, 1987: 165–168), the relationship between ideology and big government opinions was closer to the pattern in 1972 than to the ones in either the mid-1960s or 1976–1980. The tau-c was .17 in 1984 and .14 in 1988. It is true that conservatives were more likely than liberals to say the federal establishment was too powerful, but the differences were far smaller than in any year save 1972. Moreover, just as in 1972, the small group of extreme liberals was a little more likely than the slightly liberal to say Washington had grown too big.

Could the 1984 data be a fluke, due perhaps either to the CPS's asking the big government question of only a part of the NES or to the large number of don't know/no opinion responses that year? Just a few months after the CPS completed its last interview, NORC asked a subset of its 1985 GSS respondents whether they thought labor unions, business and industry, and the federal government had too much power or too little power. When opinions about the central government are broken down by NORC's ideological self-placement variable,[6] the NORC data are virtually the same as the 1984 NES data. Among liberals, only 5 percent said the federal government had too little power, whereas 41 percent believed it had "about the right amount" and 54 percent thought it had too much power. Among moderates, 4 percent thought Washington had too little power, 40 percent said it had the right amount, and 56 percent felt it was too strong. As might be expected, only 4 percent of the conservatives believed the federal government had too little power, whereas just over a third said it was exercising about the right amount and 62 percent believed it was too powerful. Although the 1985 GSS shows conservatives more worried than liberals about power being concentrated in Washington, the differences are statistically and substantively unimportant. Even though the NORC question is worded differently from the SRC's item, the similarity between the 1984 NES and the 1985 GSS lends confidence that the relationship between ideology and big government opinions midway through the Reagan era was much closer to what it had been at the peak of Richard Nixon's presidency than what it had been at the height of Lyndon Johnson's popularity. Final confirmation of this point comes from the 1988 NES. With the exception that moderates were slightly more likely than moderate liberals to believe Washington was too strong, the 1988 data mirror those from 1984 almost perfectly. Indeed, given the number of cases involved, the two data sets can be treated as substantively equivalent.

Thus, something is wrong with the argument of Nie et al. Recall that their interpretation of the shifting relationship between ideology and big government opinions was couched within the framework of their theory of increased ideological sophistication among the mass public. Hence, they took pains to show that the decoupling of the linear relationship between ideology and big

government opinions between 1968 and 1972 did not reflect a decline in ideological sophistication but, rather, hinged on the ambiguity of the SRC's item.

As we have noted, the argument about the growth of ideological sophistication
among the mass public has come under severe attack. We concur with Neuman's
(1986: 45–50) judgment that the evidence of increased political sophistication at
the grass-roots level is enmeshed in a methodological imbroglio from which it is
unlikely to be extricated. With the exception of increased consistency in public
policy opinions brought about by the racial reorientation of American politics
(Carmines and Stimson, 1989), or the increased nonideological usage of
ideological phraseology by a public acting as an echo chamber for elite rhetoric,
today's electorate is just as sophisticated, or unsophisticated, as its predecessor
of the 1950s (Kinder, 1983; Kinder and Sears, 1985).

ASSESSING THE INFLUENCE OF PARTY IDENTIFICATION

An alternative to the explanation of Nie et al. is needed, and the best place to
begin is with party identification. Interestingly, the study that first established
ordinary people's ideological unsophistication (Campbell, Converse, Miller,
and Stokes, 1960) also confirmed an earlier SRC study showing that people's
psychological attachment to one of the major parties played a major role in how
they voted and in how they responded to political figures and issues (Campbell,
Gurin, and Miller, 1954). Although scholars contend that party identification has
weakened among the electorate since the mid-1960s (see, for example, Wattenberg, 1986), most of the adult population continues to manifest some affinity for
one of the two major political parties. NORC's General Social Surveys between
1983 and 1988 show that an average of 88 percent of the public has at least some
level of partisanship; this percentage is only slightly lower than the percentage
found during the 1950s by the SRC National Election Studies (see Miller,
Miller, and Schneider, 1980: 81). The 1988 NES shows that 87 percent of the
public expressed some degree of identification with either the Democrats or the
GOP.

For our purposes, what is important about partisanship is that there is
substantial overlap between one's party identification and one's ideological
tendency (Flanigan and Zingale, 1987: 115–116). Even though many of those
who identify with the Democratic party say they are conservative, Democrats
are on the whole more likely to be liberals than conservatives. Independents are
about evenly split between moderates and conservatives. And, at least since the
mid-1960s, Republicans are much more likely to be conservatives than liberals.

The affinity between partisanship and ideology raises an intriguing possibility.
Recall that when a Democrat is president, as in the mid-1960s, 1978, and 1980,
grass-roots Republicans are much more likely than Democrats to say Washington has too much power. On the other hand, when a Republican resides at 1600

Pennsylvania Avenue, as in 1970, 1972, 1984, and 1988, Republicans become less concerned about big government while Democrats become more so. Is it possible that hidden beneath the surface of Figure 3.1, as well as undetected by Nie et al., partisanship is shaping ideology and views of big government? The answer is contained in Table 3.1, whose data show the percentage of liberals, moderates, and conservatives with opinions who say Washington has grown too strong (partisanship is controlled).[7] Note the paucity of liberals among Republican identifiers (see the numbers in the parentheses). Democrats, on the other hand, tend to be more liberal than conservative, but they are much more evenly balanced than the Republicans.

Table 3.1 Public Opinion That the Federal Government Is Too Big, by Party Identification and Ideology, for various years, 1964–1988 (in percentages)

	Democrats[a]			Independents[b]			Republicans[c]		
	Lib.	Mod.	Cons.	Lib.	Mod.	Cons.	Lib.	Mod.	Cons.
1964	20	23	41	35	36	67	58	58	77
	(218)[d]	(235)	(163)	(20)	(31)	(21)	(38)	(106)	(212)
1966	32	47	50	42	53	74	60	66	83
	(146)	(185)	(133)	(26)	(38)	(35)	(37)	(80)	(180)
1968	35	47	52	65	52	55	57	67	79
	(193)	(221)	(167)	(23)	(46)	(49)	(46)	(120)	(224)
1970	35	48	47	40	37	55	33	40	55
	(199)	(144)	(189)	(25)	(43)	(56)	(30)	(82)	(227)
1972	53	53	57	50	69	65	61	55	56
	(125)	(94)	(119)	(22)	(26)	(26)	(38)	(47)	(164)
1976	53	70	70	75	73	80	65	73	79
	(274)	(242)	(223)	(44)	(94)	(73)	(40)	(143)	(381)
1978	63	70	72	71	70	92	71	77	87
	(209)	(202)	(137)	(31)	(53)	(47)	(45)	(111)	(280)
1980	50	72	71	88	82	84	68	73	89
	(137)	(99)	(142)	(17)	(34)	(43)	(25)	(51)	(268)
1984	54	65	70	50	33	75	48	43	67
	(105)	(51)	(54)	(10)	(24)	(16)	(31)	(67)	(143)
1988	57	66	65	64	61	81	35	55	69
	(157)	(96)	(136)	(11)	(31)	(32)	(42)	(85)	(291)

Source: Adapted from the University of Michigan's Survey Research Center–Center for Political Studies' National Election Studies.

Note: Except in 1978, ideology is measured by the opinion thermometer rating of liberals–opinion thermometer rating of conservatives. In 1978, ideology is a recoded version of the CPS's seven-point self-anchoring scale.

   [a] Democrats include strong and weak identifiers plus independent leaners.

   [b] Independents include only those who do not lean toward either party.

   [c] Republicans include weak and strong identifiers plus independents who lean toward the Republicans.

   [d] The figures enclosed by parentheses are the number of cases for each category.

Much more important, Table 3.1 shows that partisanship and ideology have independent effects on opinions about Washington's power. (For the moment, we shall ignore the independents, since small numbers often complicate analyses.) Especially in the 1960s, one sees the dual effects of ideology and partisanship. Conservative Democrats were 15 to 20 percent more likely than liberal Democrats to think the national establishment was too big. By about the same margins, conservative Republicans were more anti–big government than liberal Republicans. At the same time, however, Republicans were more worried about big government than were Democrats of the same ideological proclivity. Usually, although not always, moderates fell somewhere in between the liberals and the conservatives.

The data from 1970 to 1976 are particularly interesting, for they bear most directly on the analysis of Nie et al. Initially, Johnson's replacement as president by Richard Nixon had no appreciable impact on Democrats' views of big government. At each level of ideology, Democrats in 1970 held identical views to those in 1968. On the other hand, there was a major change among the Republicans. (There may also have been some shifts in the opinions of liberal and moderate independents, but small numbers preclude any solid conclusions.) Regardless of ideological leaning, once one of their own became president, Republicans were about 25 percent less likely to fear big government. The drop is most noteworthy among conservative Republicans, for there are enough of them to lend credence to the magnitude of the shift between 1968 and 1970.

It would appear that in the first two years of Nixon's presidency, the chief consequence of his tenure was to reduce anti–big government opinions among Republicans of all ideological stripes while having no noticeable effect among Democrats. That is interesting because it was precisely the period between 1969 and late 1970 when many of the most dramatic events occurred that might have caused liberals to begin fearing big government. The invasion of Cambodia in the spring of 1970 generated the wave of student protests on university campuses that led to the deaths at Kent State and Jackson State, producing a fire storm of protests that forced many universities to close. There were the Days of Rage in 1969, when denizens of the New Left, especially the Weatherman faction of Students for a Democratic Society (SDS), reenacted, albeit on a much smaller scale, the violence at the 1968 Democratic national nominating convention in Chicago. This period also saw Vice President Spiro Agnew's highly visible and divisive campaign against the national news media and was the peak of the law-and-order issue (Bennett and Tuchfarber, 1975) that some analysts believed might be the fulcrum for a major partisan realignment (Scammon and Wattenberg, 1971). All of this, and more, had no apparent impact on Democrats' views.

But what a difference two years can make! In 1972, we see a totally different picture. These data appear initially to support the theory put forward by Nie et al. Liberal Democrats were almost 30 percent more likely to express anti–big government views now than in 1970, and there was almost as large an increase among liberal Republicans. Closer inspection, however, complicates things. With the exception of conservative Republicans, whose views were stable, there was an increase in anti–big government opinions among conservative Democrats, independents of all stripes, and moderate Republicans, although these increases are generally about half as large as among liberal Democrats and liberal Republicans. There was also a small increase among moderate Democrats, but it could have occurred just by chance. What seems to have happened between 1970 and 1972 was a general movement toward more negative opinions about Washington's power, a shift in sentiment felt most intensely by liberals of both parties but evidenced by all save conservative Republicans.

In fairness to the argument of Nie et al., we should point out that a number of events occurred between 1971 and 1972 that could have caused liberals much pause about the government's exercise of power for seemingly illiberal purposes. The major anti–war protest in Washington in the spring of 1971 led to massive arrests. This year also saw the national government try to prevent the *New York Times* from publishing *The Pentagon Papers,* secret government documents about American involvement in Vietnam that had been purloined by Daniel Ellsberg, a former minor governmental official. There were also a series of highly publicized arrests and trials of antiwar protesters, such as the Berrigans, as well as moves by government agencies against black militants. The Vietnam war went on with large-scale actions, usually as a result of attempts by the North Vietnamese high command to repeat the Tet offensive of 1968. During June 1972, a third-rate burglary of the Democratic party's national headquarters at the Watergate complex in Washington by minions of the Committee to Reelect the President (CREEP) was just a blip on the public opinion charts, but it only added to the left's image of Richard Nixon as the man who, next to the late Joseph R. McCarthy, they most loved to hate (Morris, 1984). With "that man" in the White House, and reelected by landslide proportions in 1972, was there any doubt that liberal Democrats might reexamine their historic views about Washington's power?

But, with Nixon in disgrace, the Vietnam war lost, and the inner cities quiescent, quiet settled on the nation's campuses as many younger Americans pursued the "me decade" (Wolfe, 1977). With Gerald Ford, perceived by many as an amiable if bungling president, might not liberal Democrats be expected to return to their former opinions about governmental power? This would be especially so since economic woes growing out of the 1973 OPEC oil cartel's sudden increase in energy prices had returned the economy to the forefront of the national psyche. By 1976, three-quarters of the public listed recession and unemployment or high prices as the country's most important problems (Abramson, Aldrich, and Rohde, 1983: 121).

As often happens with public opinion data, logic is one thing, reality something else. What we see from Table 3.1 is that liberal Democrats' views of big government remained unchanged from 1972 to 1976, while every other partisan and ideological grouping moved toward increased concern about too much power in Washington. Indeed, if one scans the table for the years after 1972, what seems to have happened by 1976 is a freezing of Democratic views about big government. Even with the Carter administration in power by 1980, Democrats of all ideological hues changed marginally or not at all from their 1972–1976 orientations. (Confirmation of this can be found in the 1978 NES. When the seven-point ideological self-placement scale introduced by the CPS in 1972 is recoded so that people picking categories 1–3 are classified as liberals, those choosing 4 are moderates, and those selecting 5–7 are conservatives, we find 63 percent of liberal Democrats saying Washington was too powerful, compared with 70 percent of moderate Democrats and 72 percent of conservative Democrats.)

The only meaningful shift in the pattern of the mid- to late 1970s to mid-1980s was for Republicans of all stripes to become especially wary of the central government when Ford and Carter were in office, although liberal and moderate Republicans relaxed a good deal at the height of Reagan's popularity (1984), while conservative Republicans tended to be wary even when one of their own was reelected by a landslide. The 1984 and 1988 data are worth a second look. The relationship between partisanship and ideology looks hauntingly similar to 1972 but is actually quite different in detail. As in 1972, the majority of Democrats in 1984 and 1988 with opinions about Washington's power were convinced that the central government was too big. However, unlike in 1972 (when ideology made virtually no difference in Democratic views), in 1984 and 1988, moderate and conservative Democrats were more likely than their liberal brethren to think that Washington was too strong. Ironically, despite Ronald Reagan's being considered by many to be the most conservative Republican president since Herbert Hoover, liberal and moderate members of his own party were less likely to be anti–big government than the GOP's conservative faithful.

Nor are the 1984 and 1988 NES data a fluke. Returning to NORC's 1985 GSS, when the big government question is broken down by ideology and party identification, the pattern looks virtually identical to 1984 and 1988. Fifty-three percent of liberal Democrats believed the federal government had too much power in 1985, while 42 percent said it had the right amount of power and only 5 percent thought it had too little. Among moderate Democrats, 63 percent said the government had too much power, 35 percent said it had the right amount, and only 2 percent said it had too little. Conservative Democrats divided as follows: 60 percent too much, 32 percent about right, and 8 percent too little. A small group of liberal Republicans divided almost evenly, with 53 percent saying the government had too much power and 47 percent saying it had about the right amount. Fifty-one percent of moderate Republicans said Washington was too strong, 44 percent thought it had about the right amount of power, and 5 percent said it had too little. Finally, 60 percent of conservative Republicans said

Washington had too much power, 38 percent said it had about the right amount, and only 2 percent said it did not have enough. (There are too few independents for an ideological breakdown to be meaningful.) Just as was true in 1984, early in the first year of Reagan's second term, differences between ideology and partisanship ceased to have much effect on opinions about big government. The 1988 pattern is identical.

To summarize Table 3.1, from 1964 to 1968, ideology and partisanship both affected big government opinions; thus liberal, moderate, and conservative positions can be identified among the adherents of both major parties and among independents. The transition year was 1970, with Democrats and, to a lesser degree, moderates unaffected by Nixon's rise to the presidency and Republicans of all ideological stripes becoming considerably less worried about Washington's power. From 1972 on, we see an entirely new pattern in which partisanship and ideology lose much of their capacity to help in differentiating big government opinions. The most notable aspect of the period from 1972 on is that majorities of liberals, moderates, and conservatives, whether Democrats, independents, or Republicans, consistently believed too much power was concentrated in the federal establishment. (We should point out that when blacks—who are overwhelmingly Democrats and highly unlikely to believe Washington has grown too big—are removed, from 52 to 56 percent of white liberal Democrats said government was too powerful.)

IDEOLOGY AND BIG GOVERNMENT OPINIONS: ONE LAST LOOK

By now it should be obvious that Nie and his associates both misread the reasons for changes in the relationship between ideology and big government opinions and missed the importance of partisanship. Still, there may be something to the argument that the vagueness of the SRC's big government item may have caused conservatives to respond to it from one perspective while liberals answered from another. Nie, Verba, and Petrocik claimed that a new question asked of a portion of the respondents to a late 1973 NORC survey seemed "to recapture the earlier New Deal component of the government size item" (1976: 127). Their new question was intended to focus "exclusively on domestic issues and on government as a 'solver' of our country's problems." Respondents were asked to select one of two options: "Some people think that the government in Washington is trying to do too many things that should be left to individuals and private business. Others think that the government should do even more to solve our country's problems."

Although it can be argued that the new NORC item had ambiguities of its own, Nie and his associates reported that in 1973 it was linearly related to a measure of ideology, whereas the SRC item, posed to a portion of the same

NORC survey, recapitulated the 1972 CPS pattern (1976: 127–128). With the new item, 47 percent of liberals said the national government was trying to do too much, compared with 63 percent of moderates and 72 percent of conservatives.

Even though we think the 1973 NORC data are consistent with the argument that the early 1970s saw the end of the old New Deal pattern of the relationship between ideology and big government opinions, the NORC item, ideally, should have been asked on more recent surveys. We have been unable to find an exact replication of the 1973 version. Although NORC has asked a version of the 1973 question on several of its General Social Surveys since 1975, the later versions differ from the 1973 question in three important ways: (1) the addition of a screen for nonsubstantive responses (NSRs); the provision of a midpoint; and the division of liberal and conservative options into two categories (NORC, 1987: 302). There are enough differences in the two versions to render any comparisons very risky (Schuman and Presser, 1981).

A few additional comments are in order. First, when opinions on the 1975 version are broken down by NORC's ideological self-placement item,[8] 49 percent of liberals said the central government should do even more to solve our problems, while the remainder were evenly divided between those saying it was already doing too much (27 percent) and those who agreed with both options (24 percent). Thirty percent of conservatives thought the government should do more, 29 percent agreed with both options, and 41 percent said the government was doing too much. Moderates were about evenly divided: Thirty-six percent thought the government should be doing more, 37 percent agreed with both options, and 28 percent said it was doing too much.

Some might be tempted to read these data as supporting the contention of Nie et al. that after 1972, ideology and big government opinions returned to the New Deal mold. It strikes us as more appropriate to interpret them differently. For one thing, liberals in 1976 were evenly divided between those who favored a more activist national government and those who thought it had overreached itself, or who at least saw merit in both positions. In addition, only two-fifths of conservatives in the mid-1970s still subscribed to the old fighting creed, while nearly one-third called for more activism in Washington.

Moreover, the General Social Surveys of the 1980s show liberals generally becoming even less enamored of greater governmental activism; at one point (1983), just over one-third of self-professed liberals called for greater governmental efforts. Although conservatives became slightly more likely to think government was doing too much already, over 50 percent usually either called for Washington to do more or were ambivalent on the question. In 1987, the year historians may some day say was the first of the post-Reagan era, 41 percent of liberals favored more federal activism, while 59 percent either called for less big government or were ambivalent. These figures compare with 47 percent of conservatives who held the orthodox belief, and 53 percent who either called for more governmental activism or at least saw merit in both positions. What the

GSS data from the 1970s and 1980s suggest is that ideology has come to play a smaller role in shaping opinions about whether or not Washington is involved too heavily in areas that should be left to the private sector. Unfortunately, the modifications introduced by NORC in 1975 make comparisons with the 1973 version very difficult.

On the other hand, the 1982 NES contains two forced-choice items that are similar to the 1973 NORC question in substance and format. The first reads: "Over the years, the government in Washington has taken on more and more responsibility for handling social and economic problems. In the future, should the government in Washington continue to have primary responsibility for the handling of social and economic problems, or should state and local governments be given most of that responsibility?" The second reads: "Do you agree or disagree with the following statement: Over the years, the government in Washington has gotten involved in handling and deciding issues which are not the federal government's business." Since the first item comes closer to the 1973 NORC question format, as well as captures the old New Deal battles between liberals and conservatives and Democrats and Republicans (Kessel, 1972: 463), we will focus on it. Table 3.2 presents the percentage of those who

Table 3.2 Opinions about Big Government, by Ideology and Party Identification, 1982

Question: Over the years, the government in Washington has taken on more and more responsibility for handling social and economic problems. In the future, should the government in Washington continue to have primary responsibility for the handling of social and economic problems, or should state and local governments be given most of that responsibility? (Percentage saying state and local governments should be given most of the responsibility for handling social and economic problems.)

Democrats			Independents			Republicans		
Lib.	Mod.	Cons.	Lib.	Mod.	Cons.	Lib.	Mod.	Cons.
49	61	69	80	93	88	74	88	90

Question: Do you agree or disagree with the following statement: Over the years, the government in Washington has gotten involved in handling and deciding issues which are not the federal government's business. (Percentage agreeing.)

Democrats			Independents			Republicans		
Lib.	Mod.	Cons.	Lib.	Mod.	Cons.	Lib.	Mod.	Cons.
69	77	84	73	96	83	81	87	90

Source: Adapted from the University of Michigan's Center for Political Studies' 1982 National Election Study.

Note: Democrats include strong and weak identifiers plus independent leaners. Independents include only those who do not lean toward either party. Republicans include strong and weak identifiers plus independents who lean toward the Republican party. Liberals are those who placed themselves at positions 1–3 on the CPS's seven-point self-anchoring scale. Moderates placed themselves at point 4. Conservatives placed themselves at points 5–7.

said that state and local governments should have primary responsibility for solving social and economic problems (controlled for ideology and partisanship).

The data in the table show that ideology and partisanship influence opinions about where social and economic problems are best solved. Republicans are still more likely than Democrats to opt for state and local governments, whereas liberals are more comfortable than conservatives with Washington. More important, these data suggest that Ladd's warning not to expect a return of the New Deal pattern is well taken (1978a). Granted, conservatives are more likely to favor stripping Washington of its responsibility for handling socioeconomic problems in favor of state and local governments, even when one of their own is president. But by 1982, liberal Democrats were evenly split on the question, and when the small number of liberal independents and liberal Republicans are added in, the tilt of liberal opinion was in favor of giving the power exercised in Washington to the states and localities. Moreover, when blacks, who continued to favor letting Washington have most of the responsibility for solving domestic problems, are excluded, 50 percent of white liberal Democrats preferred giving more power to state and local governments. We should also point out that 69 percent of all liberal Democrats agreed in 1982 that "Washington has gotten involved in handling and deciding issues which are not the federal government's business," compared with 84 percent of conservative Democrats and 90 percent of conservative Republicans. When 50 percent or more of liberal Democrats say that the national government is now too big, has gotten involved in issues that are not its business, and states and localities should have the primary responsibility for handling social and economic problems, the United States is clearly in a post–New Deal era.

CONCLUSION

The period from 1964 through 1989 has witnessed many profound changes in American society and politics. One of the more interesting is the breakdown of the New Deal era's ideological alignment, which saw liberals almost unanimously favoring an expansive federal establishment and conservatives adamantly calling for its curtailment. It is fortuitous that the Survey Research Center created its big government question in time for the Johnson-Goldwater presidential contest, for hindsight suggests that 1964 was the last time the old battle lines over big government would be so unequivocally drawn. Several factors would soon produce a situation in which liberal and conservative views of big government would be either indistinguishable or at least only minimally different.

First, after the 1964 defeat of Goldwater and dozens of conservative Republican legislators who, with their southern Democratic allies, had bottled up proposals to extend the welfare state since the late 1930s, Lyndon Johnson was able to put into place the Great Society programs. These programs not only carried the New Deal's reform impulse to fruition but also expanded federal powers far beyond anything anticipated by FDR. The Great Society was at once the apotheosis and the nemesis of traditional liberalism. It entailed a far greater economic redistributionist role for government and redefined relations between welfare recipients and their benefactors. Also, within a very brief time, the perceived failure of many of the Great Society programs, and the petty and sometimes not so petty corruption that accompanied others, led to a "crisis of the spirit for American liberalism and for the country as a whole" (Hamby, 1985: 261).

Second, American involvement in the Vietnam quagmire struck a deathblow to post–World War II liberal anticommunism. Although the dominant postwar policy of containment had been conceived and fashioned largely by liberals, a segment of the liberal community had never been totally comfortable with the anti-Soviet rhetoric that often accompanied it. Hence, when the bankruptcy of the Vietnam war, an undertaking initially associated with Democratic presidents, became inescapable, a sizable percentage of liberals withdrew into a quasi-isolationist stance, coupled with a desire to accommodate the Soviet Union whenever possible. Indeed, a small but vocal segment of liberalism in academe and the media drew the conclusion that the United States, rather than the Soviet Union, had been the primary source of East-West tensions since the end of World War II. At just about this time, Richard Nixon, once a major spokesman for militant anticommunism, chose to stake a substantial portion of his reputation on opening relations between the United States and the People's Republic of China.

Third, the rise of the New Class to influential positions in academe, the media, and government agencies, and even as nonentrepreneurial managers in business and industry, led to a profoundly different outlook in liberal circles. "Relatively rootless, highly mobile professionally and geographically, anticommercial by career choice and strong conviction, attracted instinctively to the novel and unconventional, and prone to depict itself as the protector of the oppressed, the New Class took liberalism well to the left—and well out of the mainstream of American politics" (Hamby, 1985: 346). Simultaneously, the left wing of the Democratic party expanded by incorporating what remained of the American socialist movement; it also embraced a revivified romanticism that called for a return to "power to the people" (Beer, 1978: 25–28). The New Left was created. The New Left's advocacy of participatory democracy, rooted in a deep-seated distrust of the institutions of representative government and of centralized power in general (Mauss, 1971: 14), represented a profound break with traditional liberalism's preference for an expansive federal establishment.

Fourth, conservative Republicans learned from Goldwater's experience the futility of attempts to dismantle the positive state. Instead, once they were in power after 1968, conservatives—or neo-conservatives, as they preferred to call themselves—left many of the Great Society programs essentially intact while proposing to shift power from Washington to states and local governments via the New Federalism, or through Nixon's proposed Family Assistance Plan, which would bypass the federal bureaucracy entirely by providing a guaranteed minimum income to every American family. In addition, conservatives such as Nixon and Ford either endorsed or accepted extensions of the positive state—for example, environmental regulation, occupational safety regulation, national health insurance, loans to lower-income and later to lower-middle- and upper-middle-income college students. It should also be pointed out that conservatives learned to use the power of the federal government for their own ends, either stupidly (such as Spiro Agnew's shrill crusade against the media establishment) or shrewdly (such as the Reagan administration's threat to withdraw federal highway funds from states that did not raise the legal minimum drinking age).

Thus from 1964 through 1989, there were major changes in ideology and governmental policies that were bound to have a wrenching effect on the New Deal relationship between ideology and opinions about big government. Sometime between 1964 and 1972, the clear-cut New Deal era pattern was swept away, and a new age emerged. It is difficult to say what this new period should be called. Its most defining characteristic is an uneasy acceptance by liberals, moderates, and even at times conservatives of a powerful national establishment. We are not foolish enough to label it a post-ideological era, for powerful divisions remain between liberals and conservatives. But we can say with confidence that ideological labels such as "liberalism" and "conservatism" have ceased to play a major role in the way most ordinary people react to questions about big government.

If ideology and partisanship are less reliable as mechanisms to organize people's attitudes about big government, then a closer look at specific governmental functions might help to clarify the increasingly complex relations between people and government. In the next chapter, we look at opinions about taxes, spending, and regulation and how they are related to views about big government.

4

Do We Really Want
Government off Our Backs?

The evidence in Chapter 2 strongly suggests that Americans do not perceive their federal government to be a "leviathan," a monster of immense size and power. This chapter also presents evidence that Americans have become accustomed to big government. Unlike Thomas Paine's view of government as inherently inimical to liberty (Paine, n.d.), Americans resemble Lane's common men of the 1950s, who did not fear government because they perceived it as a benevolent force working for them. There is ample evidence of similarly benign perceptions of government throughout today's public.

This chapter covers a wide range of topics, as it must, given the broad canvas upon which contemporary government works. Government can be perceived in many ways, some more sympathetically than others (see, for example, Parsons, 1969: 318; Easton, 1965: 19; and Weber, in Gerth and Mills, eds., 1958: 78). Bluntly put, no matter which definition one accepts, government comes down to four things: (1) it protects the sovereignty of the nation-state; (2) it extracts resources from society, including manpower and, by its taxation capacities, wealth; (3) it reallocates resources, again primarily wealth, through its abilities to spend on a panoply of programs; and (4) it regulates human behavior. To box the compass of American opinions about government, we focus on points 2 through 4 and plumb what the public thinks about taxation, spending, and regulation.

Americans have always been cranky about taxes. They consistently complain that too much of their tax money is wasted by government, and this belief in governmental wastefulness strongly correlates with their suspicion of big government. Not only do Americans perceive wastefulness in government, but also they believe taxes are usually unfair to people like themselves. Even with the much heralded Tax Reform Act of 1986, Americans remain suspicious of taxation policy.

This crankiness almost disappears when they are asked what they think government should be spending tax monies on. Across a host of domestic issues, Americans want more, not less, spending. Even those who say government is too big favor increased domestic spending. Support for budget cuts is limited to defense, foreign aid, and welfare, though if the latter is rephrased to ask for "aid to the poor," majority support for more spending returns.

Finally, opinions about governmental regulation and deregulation depend on what kind of activity government is attempting to check. People want government to enforce fairness in business profits, but they tend to believe governmental intervention can do more harm than good. Americans are most pessimistic about their ability to maintain their privacy from government or any other agency, and anger over regulation generally erupts in such areas. The recent realization by many politicians that there is not majority sentiment for government to forbid all access to abortion underscores this point. In the end, the American public has become increasingly comfortable with governmental activity across a wide range of areas, and they are not likely to change their minds about the appropriateness of governmental intervention. Americans may not love big government, but they most certainly have learned to live with it.

OPINIONS ABOUT TAXES

Any effort to deal with public opinion about taxes must begin with the understanding that a large percentage of Americans think of government as extravagant, inefficient, and wasteful of their tax monies. Belief that the central government is prone to boondoggling is probably innately American. Hence, we take up perceptions of governmental wastefulness first. For example, 1987 and 1988 Gallup polls reported that three-fifths of the public agreed that "when something is run by the government, it is usually inefficient and wasteful" (*Times Mirror*, 1987: 126, 1989: 13). The widespread perception of governmental wastefulness can be traced with public opinion data to the late 1950s. In 1958, the Survey Research Center included the following item as part of a battery of questions tapping public trust in the central government: "Do you think that people in the government waste a lot of the money we pay in taxes, waste some of it, or don't waste very much of it?" Figure 4.1 depicts responses to this question from 1958 to 1988.

Four things stand out in this figure. First, only a tiny fragment of the public did not have an opinion when asked about government wasting tax monies. Questions about governmental waste are not, in short, irrelevant to most Americans. Second, over the thirty years covered by the data, only a small portion believed government did not waste very much of its tax revenues. Moreover, from the late 1950s to the early 1970s, that percentage fell, from one-tenth of the public to barely a trace element, where it has remained since. Third, and most important, there have been even bigger changes in the distributions

Figure 4.1 Public Perception of the Federal Government's Wastefulness, for various years, 1958–1988

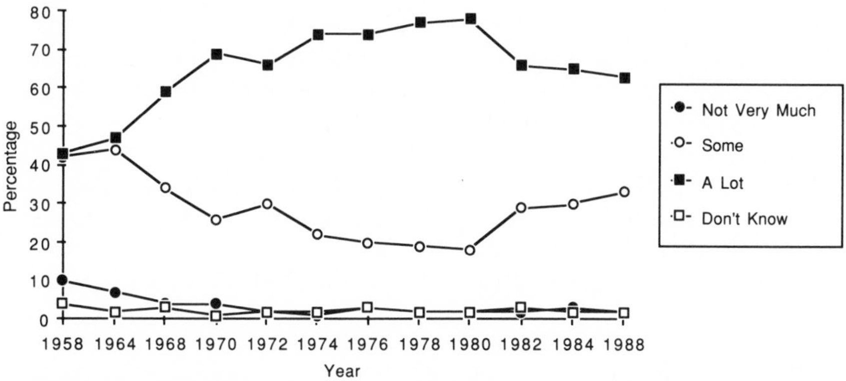

Source: University of Michigan's Survey Research Center–Center for Political Studies' National Election Studies

selecting "some" versus "a lot." Opinions were about evenly divided between 1958 and 1964. By 1968, in the midst of Vietnam and revelations of extravagance and corruption in some Great Society programs, opinion shifted to the belief that a lot of tax monies were being wasted. The proportion of the public thinking a lot of their taxes were wasted grew steadily throughout the 1970s, reaching slightly over three-quarters in 1980. The changing perceptions of governmental wastefulness moved in lockstep with other items making up the SRC's scale measuring the public's trust in government (Miller, Miller, and Schneider, 1980: 257–259).

There is a final point to make about Figure 4.1. Between 1980 and 1982, the proportion believing government was very wasteful fell to two-thirds, where it remained two years later. Simultaneously, the proportion believing only some of the public's taxes were wasted rose by an almost identical amount. Whether the 12 percent decline in perceptions of governmental wastefulness can be traced to the 1981 tax cut, or to the belief that the Reagan administration's highly publicized spending reductions had trimmed much of the budgetary flab, cannot be answered here. Suffice it to say that even when the public was most likely to think that the administration had had some success in reducing the size of the federal government (Gallup, 1982: 198), two-thirds still believed most of what they paid in taxes was wasted. Moreover, belief in governmental wastage was soon on the rise. In polls for CBS News–*New York Times* and the *New York Times* in early and late 1985, the percentage saying most of the federal government's tax revenues were wasted rose to 71 and again to 76 (*Public Opinion*, 1987: 27). Increased belief that governmental wastefulness was on the increase stemmed at least in part from the waning expectation that the Reagan administration would be able to reduce the federal government's size (*Gallup Report*, 1985b). However, the 1988 NES indicates that the proportion believing the federal government was very wasteful of its tax revenues fell to just over three-fifths, slightly less than what the figure had been during the early years of the Reagan administration. Reagan was basking in the bright light of strong public approval near the end of his second term, and it is possible that some of the glow contributed to a slight diminution in the public's perception of governmental extravagance.

Nevertheless, 1987 and 1988 Gallup polls for ACIR show that the public thinks the federal establishment is much more wasteful than either state or local governments (ACIR, 1987: 5, 22, 1988: 4–5). When the public in 1987 was asked which government it thought wasted the most tax money, two-thirds picked the federal government, one-seventh selected state governments, and one-twelfth chose local governments. The 1988 poll shows that the public thinks local governments are the most cost efficient, and the central establishment is by far the least efficient. (Whites are much more likely than nonwhites to perceive Washington as the most wasteful. In addition, the well-educated, the well-to-do, and those in professional and business occupations are more likely than those from the lower social orders to believe the central government was most likely to waste tax dollars.)

Are perceptions that the government wastes taxpayers' monies related to beliefs about Washington's power? Yes, and generally the relationship is quite robust. With but a few exceptions, the small percentage that said the central establishment was not particularly wasteful is 25 to 35 percent less likely to think that Washington was too powerful than was the large proportion that thought federal personnel were very wasteful. Usually, those who believe a lot of tax revenues are wasted are 15 to 25 percent more likely to think Washington is too big than those who say only some tax monies are wasted. Generally, there is a clear, linear relationship between the two variables.

Tax policy is the single most important way government signals who is favored and who is not. As Leff (1984) explained and as the Tax Reform Act of 1986 showed, because taxes are so important they are very likely to be wrapped in symbolic rhetoric when any changes are contemplated (Murray and Birnbaum, 1987). According to Murray Edelman (1985), symbolic discourse marks democratic politics as elites seek to satisfy restive masses and individuals in the mass public seek reassurance from government. What results is not an elite conspiracy but, rather, an exchange of roles and a tendency for political elites to say one thing even while they are really doing something quite different. Ginsberg more pointedly states that "a successful regime caters more to the interests of its elites and more to the emotions of its masses" (1986: 46).

Leff (1984) focused on FDR's rhetoric about taxation during the New Deal years, when there was strong feeling among the public that wealth gained by greedy industrialists during the Depression and early war years should be confiscated by the government. Even as FDR excoriated the "economic royalists," he maintained a regressive workhorse tax system of excise taxes and fees from the Hoover years. He lauded increases in a federal income tax system that, in the late 1930s, affected only 5 percent of the public. The continuation of the Depression even in the face of New Deal programs made such proclamations an important part of FDR's appeal that everyone, from the top on down, would be forced to sacrifice for the common good. By pleading tax fairness, FDR and all those who have labored in his shadow participated in the attempt to assuage public fears that taxes were levied unfairly.

A symbolic element in understanding American opinions about taxation is whether the tax system is perceived as fair or unfair. Opposition to taxes has been part of American culture and political folklore since the Revolutionary War cry, "No taxation without representation!" During the 1970s, in the wake of California's Proposition 13 property tax revolt, many public officials feared that the new cry would be "No taxation even with representation!" No other endeavor of government is likely to stir the passions of as wide a variety of groups as taxation, in part because "taxation has always lacked a certain legitimacy in this country" (Leff, 1984: 5). Polls from the 1940s through the 1970s showed from three-fifths to three-quarters of the public dissatisfied with what they believed were overly high rates of taxation (Ladd et al., 1979: 127). In addition, at least since the late 1960s, from two-thirds to four-fifths of the public have thought that taxes in this country are unreasonable, and nearly identical percentages have said that as far as they and their families are concerned, they "have reached the breaking point on the amount of taxes" they pay (Ladd et al., 1979: 127). When, in 1980, the CPS asked, "Do you feel you are asked to pay much more than you should in federal income taxes, somewhat more than you should, about the right amount, or less than you should," the results confirmed widespread public discontent. Just over a third of the public claimed they paid much more than they should and only a tiny fragment admitted to paying less than they should. Many national legislators cite the public's aversion to paying higher taxes as the primary reason for their reluctance to propose higher levies to reduce the burgeoning federal deficit (Haas, 1989).

As the central government has grown, its appetite for more revenues has grown as well. Most research suggests that opinions about taxation are tied to perceptions of governmental activity, a rough "cost-benefit" analysis based on usually impressionistic evidence of the return the taxpayer is getting for his or her tax contribution (Beck, Rainey, Nicholls, and Traut, 1987). When economic times take a downturn, middle-class groups begin to feel unfairly overburdened by the cost of governmental programs that appear to benefit the very wealthy and the very poor. Wilensky eloquently describes the frustration of the "American middle mass":

Looking up, the citizen of the American middle mass sees the overprivileged, college-educated upper middle class and the rich, who seem to evade taxes, live well, let their children run wild at expensive colleges—or worse, at state universities, at his expense. Moreover, the overprivileged seem often to be in alliance with the poor, with the blacks from whom he has escaped to a middle-mass suburb.

In short, he sees an unholy alliance of the immoral poor, despised minorities, lazy, undisciplined, unpatriotic youth and their friends among the libertarian educated. When the coalition tells him that the poverty he happily escaped must be wiped out at his expense and that racial minorities must take over his job, his neighborhood, his children's school, he is understandably indignant (1975: 117).

Wilensky's depiction of the "middle-mass" reaction to the welfare state and its costs appears consistent with what some researchers have described as a "self-interest" response, particularly during times of economic hardship, when taxes are viewed as taking a burdensome chunk out of their living wages (Hansen, 1983; Beck, Rainey, Nicholls, and Traut, 1987). Ironically, even though the income tax is the most progressive if it is laced with minimal deductions, it has emerged as the least favored of the taxes, in no small part because of long, arcane tax forms for filing. In addition, most people recognize that long forms permit wealthier individuals to escape taxation more readily than those in lower-income brackets.

A wide variety of polls from the 1960s, 1970s, and 1980s indicates that attempts to persuade the public that the tax system is equitable have fallen on almost deaf ears. Although it is difficult to determine what people sometimes have had in mind when framing their responses, a CBS News–*New York Times* poll in April 1978 found that a majority believed the tax system was unfair (Ladd et al., 1979: 128). Polls taken in 1984 and 1985, after the tax cuts enacted during Reagan's first year, showed little change in views of the tax system's fairness (*Public Opinion*, 1985: 22–23). Depending on when and how the question is asked, perception of the system's unfairness consistently overwhelms belief that it is equitable. Moreover, surveys in the mid-1980s indicate that the well-to-do, who are often said to have profited disproportionately from the 1981–1983 tax cuts (Ferguson and Rogers, 1986), are somewhat more likely to perceive unfairness in the tax system than are those in the lower- and middle-income brackets (*Public Opinion*, 1985: 22).

It is not difficult to discover why many view the tax system as inequitable. They believe people like themselves bear a disproportionate share of the tax burden, whereas corporations and the very rich shirk their load. Louis Harris polls from 1969 through the late 1970s consistently found that 90 percent agreed that "the big tax burden falls on the little man in this country" (Ladd et al., 1979: 128). Two-thirds of those responding to a January 1985 ABC News–*Washington Post* survey agreed that "the present tax system benefits the rich and is unfair to the ordinary working man or woman" (*Public Opinion*, 1985: 23). A survey by the Roper Organization in January 1985 found that four-fifths of the public believed that "large business corporations" and "high-income families" paid too little in income taxes, whereas only 5 percent thought big business and the wealthy paid too much. The same survey, on the other hand, found that slightly over two-thirds believed "middle-income families" paid too much; three-fifths thought "people whose income all comes from salary or wages" were overtaxed and nearly the same proportion thought "lower-income families" were overtaxed. In each of the latter three cases, only tiny percentages thought they were undertaxed, whereas somewhere from a quarter to a third said they paid about the right amount (*Public Opinion*, 1985: 23). Furthermore, Americans have a firm view of how the rich evade taxation. A November 1984 Harris poll found that 92 percent agreed that the rich used tax accountants and lawyers to show them how to use loopholes in the tax laws to evade taxation (*Public Opinion*, 1985: 23).

Adding to the pain is that it is not just a federal income tax any longer. In the late 1930s, as the *Fortune* poll described in Chapter 2 indicated, only a twelfth of the public selected the federal income tax as the "most unfair" tax, whereas a third picked state sales taxes and one-sixth chose local real estate levies (Cantril, with Strunk, 1978: 325). States and cities found the income tax to be a useful revenue source that would grow as incomes grew in the prosperous 1960s and early 1970s.

Data from the Advisory Commission on Intergovernmental Relations (ACIR, 1986: 19–20, 1987: 3–5) show that in the aftermath of the property tax revolt that swept from California across the nation in the late 1970s (Kuttner, 1980; Sears and Citrin, 1985), the federal income tax emerged as the most unpopular tax of those levied at the federal, state, and local levels. In 1972, well before the tax revolt had crystallized, slightly over two-fifths of the public said the local property tax was "the worst tax, that is, the least fair," while one-fifth picked the federal income tax. In 1977, a third of those queried said the property tax was the most unfair tax, compared with just over a quarter who named the federal income tax. In May 1978, at the peak of the tax revolt, the federal income tax and the local property tax were tied, with about a third of the public identifying each as the least fair tax.

In retrospect, 1978 was the critical year for the campaign to reduce the local property tax burden, although even in that year, referenda in other states would have a checkered outcome (Kuttner, 1980). But the California movement was well known nationally, as data from the CPS's 1978 National Election Study attest. Asked whether they had heard or read about the June property tax vote in California, three-quarters said they had. When the CPS followed up by asking, "If you had the chance, would you vote for or against a measure similar to Proposition 13 in your state," over a majority said they would favor such a measure.

Even though the impact of the tax revolt varied considerably from state to state, the furor over the local property tax had a significant impact on subsequent responses to the ACIR's question about which was the fairest tax. Beginning in 1979, just under two-fifths said the federal income tax was the worst, or least fair, tax, compared with a quarter who named the property tax. Those numbers would remain almost identical in 1980. There is little wonder that candidate Reagan could fire public imagination with his 1980 campaign pledge to lower federal income taxes by 30 percent.

Data from the 1980 NES indicate that his plan to curtail federal income taxes had substantial popular backing, although less than half the public would have cut as deeply as he wished. When the public was asked what it would like to see happen to federal income taxes over the next three years, 13 percent opposed any cuts, 18 percent said the federal tax should be cut by 10 percent, 12 percent favored a 20 percent reduction, 16 percent backed Reagan's call for a 30 percent cut, 8 percent wanted even deeper reductions, while two-fifths either had no opinion or did not know what their opinion was. Among those with opinions, proponents of some degree of reduction in the federal income tax outnumbered opponents of any curtailment by slightly better than three to one. As the ACIR data cited above indicate, even with the three-year 23 percent income tax cut achieved in the early months of Reagan's first term, there was no lessening of unhappiness with the federal income tax. From 1981 through 1986, a steady 36 to 38 percent picked the federal income tax as the worst tax, whereas a quarter to a third chose the local property tax.

This continued public pressure helped convince Congress to pass a Tax Reform Act in 1986. Heralded for its "equity, fairness, and simplicity," the act was said to represent a major change in the tax system, as the burden was to be shifted somewhat from individuals to corporations. Congress and the Reagan administration emphasized that eliminating many of the deductions from individual schedules and increasing the corporate share would help to remove over six million working poor from the tax rolls.

Public response to the bill was less than enthusiastic, however. An October 1986 Gallup poll showed two-fifths of the public approving of the new tax bill and a third disapproving of it (*Gallup Report*, 1986: 15). Tempering the public's response to this historic reform of the old tax code was the people's expectation of higher taxes under the new law (*Gallup Report*, 1986: 16). Splitting fairly evenly on whether the tax reform was more fair (27 percent) or less fair (20 percent), over a third did not think the new bill enhanced the equity of the tax system (*Gallup Report*, 1986: 17). Half of the respondents did not think the process of filing their taxes would be any simpler (*Gallup Report*, 1986: 18). As if fulfilling a taxpayer's worst fear and a tax accountant's most fervent hope, the Internal Revenue Service unveiled a new, longer W-4 in November 1986. The form's complexity resulted in its withdrawal in early 1987 and the release of an easier form to complete. Still, public officials continued to laud the new tax bill's fairness and simplicity compared with the old system. Perhaps some of those assertions had an impact, as there was a slight reduction in the public's perception of the federal income tax as the least fair tax (ACIR, 1987: 5, 1988: 3). Nonetheless, a Gallup poll in early 1989 showed that a plurality of the public (39 percent) had concluded that the 1986 tax reform bill had made the tax burden less fair for all taxpayers, while only 13 percent believed it had made taxes more equitable and a third thought the 1986 act had had no impact on tax equity (*Gallup Report,* 1989: 22).

We should also note that the percentage saying, "Don't know," to the ACIR's question increased in 1987, suggesting a heightened uncertainty about what the new tax structure might achieve. When the CPS asked respondents to its 1986 NES whether or not they had an opinion about the new tax code, about three-fifths replied that they either had no opinion or did not know what opinion to give. The tendency for large segments of the populace to offer nonsubstantive responses to survey questions about federal income taxes, coupled with widespread ignorance about taxation at all levels (Murray and Birnbaum, 1987; *Times Mirror,* 1989), means that public opinion about taxes in general, and federal taxes in particular, can vary greatly according to the broader context within which such questions are asked.

Therefore, a symbolic explanation for tax opinions allows that people will succumb to government's need for taxes so long as there is a *perceived* fairness in their collection and no *perceived* wastage in their disbursement. The self-interest explanation for tax opinions holds against governmental confiscation of middle-class wealth and would appear to constrain government more than the symbolic explanation. In reality, there is no reason to think of the two explanations as mutually exclusive. As the example from the New Deal years indicates, those likely to think they are unable to pay any more for governmental services can be appealed to with symbolic rhetoric emphasizing that the pain is being diffused and that the well-to-do in particular will bear a disproportionate burden, whether the wealthy do in fact bear a heavier burden or not.

Hence, public opinions toward taxation are affected by the complexity of a multi-layered tax system about which Americans have only the most basic information: what they see going out of their own pockets and how they view those hard-earned tax dollars being used. Everett Carll Ladd, Jr., characterized public opinions toward the service state as "splendidly ambivalent" (1979b: 132, 1983, 1985: 8–9). A public simultaneously demanding services and lower taxes may help to explain why politicians have sounded increasingly schizo-phrenic on the subjects of governmental taxing and spending. Their polls tell them to "reduce taxes, maintain 'big government'; end the waste and ineffi-ciency of big government" (Ladd et al., 1979: 135; Haas, 1989). Some might find it difficult to feel too sorry for these officials since many who hold seats in Congress or who recently occupied the White House campaigned on anti-Washington platforms while simultaneously promising groups special consideration or largess once their race is won. Jack Citrin (1979) noted that the tendency of politicians to separate their political appeals for costly programs from their election-year opposition to higher taxes causes some of the confusion in tapping people's opinions about the juxtaposition of taxing and spending. In an attempt to remind the public that there are no free lunches from government, Walter Mondale set the theme of his 1984 campaign by promising higher taxes to pay for the services. He met with a landslide vote for his incumbent opponent. Americans, some charged, wanted "something for nothing."

OPINIONS ABOUT SPENDING

On the debit side of the ledger, public opinion concerning how much the national government should spend on various functions is often interpreted as signals of ideological shifts (Davis, 1980; T. Smith, 1981, 1985a). Chapter 3 outlines the dangers of relying on too simplistic a formulation of ideology among the public. It is particularly risky to use spending items as ideological indicators because of the fuzziness of the spending items. When people are asked whether the government "is spending too much money on [defense, welfare, health care, and so on], too little money, or about the right amount," it is doubtful that they respond with real federal budgetary figures in mind (Citrin, 1979). Data from the SRC's 1970 National Election Study show that when asked if they knew what percentage of the tax dollar was being spent for defense, three-quarters of the public admitted they did not know. Only one-tenth of the public could place the figure within plus or minus ten cents of the forty-three cents of the federal tax dollar consumed by defense in 1970 (U.S. Department of Commerce, 1986: 311). Similar ignorance of how much of the federal budget went for military and defense purposes was revealed in a Gallup poll taken early in 1976 (Gallup, 1978: 666). People respond to the function named rather than to a specific notion of fiscal allotments. A 1989 Gallup poll shows that "the public has only limited knowledge about how their federal tax dollars are spent" (*Times Mirror,* 1989: 11). Although four-fifths of today's public is aware that defense is one of the largest components of the federal budget, only one-quarter know that Social Security is also one of the largest line items in Washington's budget, and half of the public incorrectly believe foreign aid consumes a large portion of federal outlays (*Times Mirror,* 1989: 11).

Does ignorance about the amount being spent on a particular function render people's spending opinions meaningless? Not if it is realized that many opinions are formed without reference to and sometimes in spite of specific information. This does not make those opinions any less significant to those expressing them, but it does suggest the possibility of great volatility. Analyses of the National Opinion Research Center's (NORC) spending items from 1973 to 1989 reflect this volatility, as different items combine in each year to form factors that usually reflect changing domestic and foreign policy concerns. Those changing concerns are undoubtedly affected by the amount and tenor of media coverage given at any time to specific issues. Hence, spending priorities are generally tied closely to changing perceptions of the important issues confronting the nation (T. Smith, 1985b) and serve as a very general barometer of public concerns. Furthermore, the spending items are usually worded to favor the "increase spending" response. NORC and the CPS in 1980 and 1982, for example, prefaced their spending questions with, "We are faced with many problems in this country, none of which can be solved easily or inexpensively." With that as an introduction, you can forget bargain-basement prices.

Tom Smith (1987a) warned that some of the spending items used words with negative connotations (such as "welfare"), and that the substitution of some phrases (such as "aid to the poor") would result in even greater willingness to favor increased spending (see also Rasinski, 1989). Also, if ideology is a less than satisfactory organizing principle for understanding American politics, using inexact indicators to tap a fuzzy concept does not take us far into the realm of how people view big government. What people think should be government's spending priorities is only one part of the larger puzzle involving their opinions about a growing public sector.

With these caveats in mind, it is still worthwhile to take a brief look at trends in opinions about federal spending for fifteen domestic and international programs since NORC introduced its series of spending items on the 1973 GSS (for earlier reports, see Davis, 1980; T. Smith, 1981, 1985b, 1987a). Table 4.1 presents the needed information. To facilitate comprehension, the years from 1973 to 1989 are broken into six periods, each corresponding to a presidential term: 1973–1974, the last two years of Nixon's presidency; 1975–1976, when Gerald Ford was president; 1977–1978 and 1980, when Jimmy Carter occupied the White House; 1982–1984, Ronald Reagan's first term; 1985–1988, Reagan's second term; and 1989, the first year of George Bush's presidency. Others have written about these data from several perspectives (Davis, 1980; T. Smith, 1981, 1985a, 1987a, 1987b; Shapiro, Patterson, Russell, and Young, 1987), thus we need to cover only the essential points. We concentrate on the Reagan era (1981–1988), since some have heralded these as years when Americans became more conservative, while others have detected a leftward tendency in public opinion.

Most evident is the basic stability of opinions about federal spending for the eleven problems addressed by NORC between 1973 and 1989. With but few exceptions—one of them being spending to protect and improve the environment—the percentages vary so little over time that any differences could be due simply to sampling variability. The period from 1973 to 1989 saw major changes in the political fortunes of the two major political parties, of individual personalities, and even trends in opinions on economic and social issues (Davis, 1980; T. Smith, 1981, 1985a; Robinson and Fleishman, 1984). But when it

Table 4.1 Public Opinion about Eleven Governmental Spending Programs, by Presidential Administration, 1973–1989 (in percentages)

Question: We are faced with many problems in this country, none of which can be solved easily or inexpensively. I'm going to name some of these problems, and for each one I'd like you to tell me whether you think we're spending too much money on it, too little money, or about the right amount.

	Nixon (1973–74)	Ford (1975–76)	Carter (1977–78, 1980)	Reagan I (1982–84)	Reagan II (1985–88)	Bush (1989)
Space Exploration						
Too little	8	8	13	12	14	15
About right	28	29	35	39	41	44
Too much	60	59	45	43	40	35
Don't know	4	3	7	6	5	6
Environmental Protection						
Too little	60	54	49	54	61	72
About right	26	31	33	31	28	20
Too much	8	10	12	9	6	4
Don't know	6	5	6	6	5	4
Health Care						
Too little	62	61	55	58	63	68
About right	30	30	33	32	30	25
Too much	5	5	7	6	4	3
Don't know	3	4	4	4	3	4
Big Cities' Problems						
Too little	49	45	40	44	43	46
About right	26	25	27	26	31	29
Too much	12	16	20	16	14	11
Don't know	13	14	13	13	12	14
Fighting Crime						
Too little	66	66	66	70	66	72
About right	24	22	23	21	25	20
Too much	4	7	6	5	5	5
Don't know	6	5	5	4	4	3
Drug Addiction						
Too little	63	57	57	60	64	71
About right	25	28	28	27	27	19
Too much	6	8	8	7	5	6
Don't know	6	7	7	6	4	4
Education						
Too little	50	50	51	61	62	67
About right	37	36	35	30	31	27
Too much	9	10	10	6	4	3
Don't know	4	4	4	3	3	3

	Nixon	Ford	Carter	Reagan I	Reagan II	Bush
Blacks'						
Conditions						
Too little	32	27	24	35	35	32
About right	41	41	43	40	41	41
Too much	21	25	25	17	16	16
Don't know	7	7	8	8	7	10
Defense						
Too little	14	20	35	24	15	15
About right	45	44	38	37	40	41
Too much	35	29	19	33	40	39
Don't know	6	7	7	6	5	5
Foreign Aid						
Too little	3	4	4	5	6	4
About right	19	17	22	18	21	22
Too much	73	74	68	72	68	68
Don't know	5	4	6	5	4	6
Welfare						
Too little	21	18	13	24	22	23
About right	28	26	25	28	32	30
Too much	47	51	58	44	42	42
Don't know	4	5	4	4	4	5

Source: University of Chicago's National Opinion Research Center's General Social Surveys.

comes to public opinion about the national government's spending on these key domestic and foreign problems, very little movement occurred.

Granted, there were some notable changes, such as the 15 percent jump in opinion (greatest during 1980) that defense spending was too little under the Carter administration. This increase was quickly followed by a decline of similar magnitude during Reagan's first term. (CPS data from the 1980 Major Panel Study and the 1980 NES confirm that there was a dramatic decline in the percentage thinking too little was being spent on defense.) In retrospect, it is easy to understand public concern in 1980 about a weak national defense: The Soviet invasion of Afghanistan, the seizure of the American embassy in Teheran, Iran, and the holding of fifty-three U.S. diplomats as hostages were fresh in everyone's mind. As if to underscore the country's military weakness, an attempt by U.S. armed forces to free the hostages ended tragically.

There is at least one other interesting change in the table: a long-term growth in the belief that the federal government was not spending enough for "improving the nation's education system." Sixty-seven percent of the public in 1989 said that America was spending "too little" on improving the nation's education system, compared with 49 percent in 1973, when NORC initiated its series of spending items.

Since the mid-1970s, evidence has accumulated that American public education has fallen into serious disrepair (see Boyer, 1983; Ravitch, 1983, 1985), and countless media stories on the "crisis" in American education have driven that message home. The result has been an 18 percent increase in the belief that Washington was spending too little for education, despite repeated statements by Presidents Reagan and Bush and their education secretaries, particularly William Bennett, that more money is not the solution. The attention given to education by presidential candidates Dukakis and Bush in 1988 reflected the continuing importance of education in public opinion polls. A May 1988 Gallup poll found that almost half of the public favored government action to improve the quality of public schools, even if more taxes were needed (*Times Mirror,* 1988: 37). In an attempt to live up to his campaign promise to be the "education president," Bush convened a two-day meeting in September 1989, attended by members of his administration and all fifty state governors, to draw the nation's attention to the need for improvement in public education (Weinraub, 1989). Although largely heralded as a success, it is not surprising that one controversial aspect of the meeting was how to improve the schools while holding the line on federal spending for education and keeping a pledge not to increase taxes.

We should also note that unlike the case with many survey questions about taxes, NORC's spending items seldom elicit high rates of "don't know" responses. Except for the question on big cities, which generally elicits 12 to 15 percent don't know responses, the spending items find that roughly 95 percent of the public are willing to express some opinion. Thus, the most important message in the table is that with but few exceptions, the public of the 1970s and 1980s was much more likely to think Washington was spending too little rather than too much. Most of the exceptions deal with international affairs (for example, foreign aid and defense) and space exploration. The only domestic problem on which the public has consistently believed too much was being spent is welfare. When NORC asked about "assistance to the poor," three-fifths to two-thirds of the public think too little is being spent, about one-quarter think Washington is spending about the right amount, and roughly one-tenth believe spending is too high (T. Smith, 1987a; NORC, 1987: 102; Rasinski, 1989). The 1989 GSS illustrates Tom Smith's point nicely. When asked about spending for "welfare," 24 percent thought too little was being spent, 32 percent thought it was about right, and 44 percent believed too much was being spent. When NORC asked about spending for "assistance to the poor," however, only 9 percent believed too much was being spent, whereas 23 percent said about the right amount was being spent and 67 percent said too little was being spent (NORC, 1989: 106, 110).

It should also be pointed out that beginning with the 1984 GSS, NORC added questions about spending for highways and bridges, Social Security, mass transportation, and parks and recreation. In each instance, the percentage that thought too little was being spent far outnumbered the percentage that believed government was spending too much (NORC, 1987: 98–99, 1988: 104–105, 1989: 107). In short, Americans have a healthy appetite for governmental spending, one that remained unsatiated throughout the Reagan era. Possible exceptions to the public's tendency to favor more domestic spending are for programs perceived to benefit only a specific clientele group rather than the populace as a whole (Citrin, 1979; Sears and Citrin, 1985; Ippolito, 1981). For example, when the CPS asked about federal spending for food stamps on its 1982, 1984, 1986, and 1988 National Election Studies, more people thought too much was being spent than too little.

However, it is possible to find examples of programs that benefit specialized clienteles but still draw widespread backing. In 1982, for example, when the CPS asked about governmental spending for aid to the handicapped, half of the public said too little was being spent and only 3 percent believed too much was being laid out. Similarly, CPS data in 1982, 1986, and 1988 show support for more federal spending for student loans. In addition, NORC and CPS data show widespread support for more spending on behalf of the elderly, and a 1988 Gallup poll showed that more than half of the public (56 percent) backed governmental action to provide "a decent standard of living for the elderly" even if it requires new taxes (*Times Mirror,* 1988: 37).

Even more interesting, the October 1989 Yankelovich-Clancy-Shulman poll for *Time*-CNN found majorities willing to pay more in federal taxes if the additional monies were earmarked for several specific purposes. Overwhelming majorities were willing to lay out more taxes if the funds went for "feeding and providing medical care for very poor children" (86 percent), "fighting the war on drugs" (79 percent), "increasing benefits for retired people" (75 percent), and "improving public schools in communities like yours" (72 percent). Almost three-fifths agreed to heightened taxation if the new funds were used for "reducing the federal budget deficit" (57 percent), and half would agree if the money were used to "ensur[e] modern weapons and equipment for the armed forces" (Barrett, 1989).

A better appreciation of the public's willingness to support more federal spending on domestic issues can be gained by combining several individual items into an overall spending index. The 1982, 1984, 1986, and 1988 National Election Studies provide useful vehicles for determining relative support for greater or lesser spending. The 1982 index is an additive combination of nine spending items: improving and protecting the nation's health, the nation's education system, the conditions of blacks, welfare, Social Security, food stamps, government-guaranteed student loans, unemployment compensation, and aid to the handicapped. In 1984, six items were combined: public schools, Social Security, food stamps, Medicare, government jobs for the unemployed, and assistance to blacks. In 1986, five items were included: financial aid for college students, Social Security, food stamps, government assistance for the unemployed, and programs that assist blacks. In 1988, eight items were used:

Social Security, food stamps, government assistance for the unemployed, programs that assist blacks, child care, public schools, care for the elderly, and aid to the homeless. The items selected represent a wide range of spending programs that compose the modern welfare state, the essence of which "is government-protected minimum standards of income, nutrition, health, housing, and education, assured to every citizen as a political right, not as charity" (Wilensky, 1975: 1).

What the data show is far greater support for increased federal spending than for budgetary cutting. Depending on the mixture of items included in the spending index, 45 to 61 percent of the public in the 1980s favored more federal spending, whereas only 6 to 21 percent supported reduced outlays. In 1988, for example, 61 percent of the public favored additional spending, and 6 percent were opposed. At that, these figures tend to understate the numerical advantage of those who favor more federal outlays. If we look just at the two most extreme categories in the spending index, that is, those who were most in favor of increased spending versus those who were most supportive of reduced spending, 11 to 26 percent composed the first group, and only 1 to 4 percent made up the latter. Again using the 1988 NES, 26 percent of the electorate fell into the "very pro-spending" category, while only 1 percent were "very anti-spending." In short, what these data suggest is that in the 1980s, there was virtually no constituency favoring large cuts in federal spending for domestic programs. We shall return to this point shortly.

Although some have been tempted to equate support for increased federal spending on domestic problems with liberalism (Davis, 1980; T. Smith, 1981, 1985a; Robinson and Fleishman, 1984), that is not necessarily so. Note in Table 4.1 that the problems that drew the most support for increased federal outlays were for halting the rising crime rate and dealing with drug addiction, issues backed more by conservatives than by liberals (Scammon and Wattenberg, 1971; Sears and Citrin, 1985). Indeed, what seems to have occurred during the 1970s and 1980s has been for ideology to play a limited role in shaping people's responses to many of the spending items. Data from the National Election Studies show correlations between the spending indexes described above and a seven-point ideological self-identification item of $r = .38$ in 1982, $r = .35$ in 1984, $r = .11$ in 1986, and $r = .34$ in 1988. In short, ideology and the spending indexes share, on average, only 9 percent of common variance (as estimated by r^2). The upshot is that treatment of shifts in public opinion about spending as indicators of movement right or left should be taken with a very large grain of salt (see, for example, Ferguson and Rogers, 1986).

Even more important, there appears to be only a slight relationship between opinions about big government in the abstract and opinions about spending for specific programs. The 1988 NES, for example, indicates that 55 percent of those who said Washington had become too big nonetheless favored increased spending for eight domestic programs. Only 9 percent of those who thought the national establishment had become too strong were in favor of reduced spending on these problems. Even worse, when only the most extreme views on spending for these programs are concerned, only 2 percent of those who thought government was too big in 1988 were very much in favor of reduced spending, whereas 21 percent were very much in favor of increased federal outlays.

Does increased support for greater federal spending for most of the domestic problems probed by NORC and CPS mean that Americans have become a nation of wastrels, profligate with the national treasury? Not really. Scholars such as Ippolito (1981: 225–230) and Wildavsky (1985: 59) have pointed out that even though Americans favor more spending on the specific programs that constitute activist government, they believe governmental spending as a whole is much too large. They are worried about government deficits and, as Gallup polls since the 1970s have shown, are likely to favor a constitutional amendment or a law mandating a balanced national budget (Gallup, 1978: 679; Ippolito, 1981: 227; *Gallup Report,* 1987: 28). Moreover, Gallup data from the 1970s on consistently show that three-fifths to two-thirds of the public say it is very important to them that the federal budget is in balance (Gallup, 1978: 105, 680, 1176). Finally, there is no doubt that Americans are aware when the national budget is imbalanced (Gallup, 1978: 681, 1178), although they are fuzzy on the details about how big the deficits are (Gallup, 1978: 1179). A 1989 Gallup poll shows that "the deficit has emerged as the public's chief economic concern as other problems, such as unemployment, have receded in importance" (*Times Mirror,* 1989: 4). This finding was heralded by the 1988 NES, which found that three-fifths of the public thought the deficit was a very serious national problem.

Data from the 1980s, however, reveal a public at once in favor of deficit reduction and supportive of programs that could only lead to increased budgetary outlays. For example, the 1985 GSS included the following: "Here are some things the government might do for the economy" (*Public Opinion,* 1987: 23). Although the public was overwhelmingly supportive of "cuts in government spending," with four-fifths in favor, Americans were just about as likely to endorse "government financing of projects to create new jobs" (69 percent). In addition, nearly three-quarters (72 percent) favored governmental "support for industry to develop new products and technology," and half said the government should "support declining industries to protect jobs." Presumably, the latter two activities would entail either more governmental spending or, at the very least, tax abatements. Neither, however, would do much to reduce the deficit.

The 1988 NES reinforces the public's inconsistent opinions about taxes, spending, and budgetary deficits. When opinions about the seriousness of the federal deficit are cross-tabulated with the eight-item spending index described earlier, there is virtually no relationship between the two variables. Among the three-fifths of the public who said they believed the federal deficit was a very serious problem, one-quarter nonetheless were very much in favor of increased outlays for domestic programs, and nearly two-fifths (37 percent) wanted at least some increase in spending. Only 6 percent of those who said that the federal deficit was a very serious problem favored curtailment of federal outlays for domestic programs.

Moreover, the 1988 NES indicates that those who say they are not willing to pay more in federal taxes to reduce the deficit are just as likely to favor increased spending for domestic programs as those who are willing to see their tax burden go up in order to reduce the deficit. When the CPS asked, "In order to reduce the size of the federal budget deficit, are you willing or not willing to pay more in taxes," two-thirds of the public adamantly refused, and only one-fifth said they were willing. Nevertheless, half of those who refused to pay more taxes wanted domestic spending increased in 1988, only a little less than the 54 percent who were willing to pay more taxes and favored more domestic outlays.

In responding to survey questions like these, Americans manifest inconsistencies of opinion that would have driven to distraction a generation of social psychologists who theorized that people strive to achieve cognitive consistency (see Abelson et al., 1968). If they were to be confronted by the seeming inconsistencies between their support for more spending on a multitude of specific programs and their belief that governmental spending in general is too high, most people would argue that government is wasteful and that reducing inefficiencies would bring the budget down while leaving most programs intact (Ladd et al., 1979: 133–135).

A key question, of course, is what the public would like to have done to reduce budget deficits. Gallup data from 1983 to 1987 offer some useful evidence (*Gallup Report,* 1987: 23–27). When Gallup offered the options "cut defense spending," "cut government spending for social programs such as health and education," "raise income taxes," and "cut 'entitlement' programs such as social security, medicare, and the like," public support for trimming the military was overwhelming. Moreover, the disparity in support for cuts in defense spending (58 percent), reductions in social programs (21 percent), higher income taxes (16 percent), and reductions in entitlements (9 percent) was greatest in 1987. As far as John Q. or Jane Q. Public is concerned, if Uncle Sam is to get his budgetary house in order, it will have to be borne on the back of the military and not by the civilian portion of the federal budget. Moreover, a June 1988 Gallup poll shows that only one-quarter were willing to pay higher personal income taxes to balance the federal budget (*Gallup Report,* 1988: 14).

Some have interpreted American disinclination to support higher taxes or curtailed social-entitlement programs to reduce deficits as a "something for nothing" mentality (Sears and Citrin, 1985). Contrary to the notion that most Americans are out for a "free lunch," there is evidence that Americans are quite willing to pay for the governmental services they have grown to expect. Wilson (1983) relied on specially constructed telephone surveys of two cities (Eugene, Oregon, and Tempe, Arizona) to juxtapose spending and taxing choices.

Respondents were asked if they favored increased spending for specific local services; those who favored more spending were then asked if they would support tax hikes to pay for the increased services. Wilson found that "free ridership" was characteristic of a very small group of respondents. Most respondents expressed a willingness to increase their taxes in exchange for more services. Welch (1985) conducted a telephone interview within one state to tap people's willingness to pay for increased services and found similar low levels of "free lunchers." Although differences in question wording complicate comparisons, similar sentiments can be found in nationwide data, even at the height of the tax revolt. In 1978, the CPS asked whether people agreed or disagreed with the following item: "Federal income taxes should be cut by at least one-third even if it means reducing military spending and cutting down on government services such as health and education." Although we wish the item had not been double-barreled, it is interesting that only one-quarter of the public agreed with the item, while three-fifths disagreed.

Similarly, a May 1988 Gallup poll showed that a substantial proportion of the public favored a number of governmental programs even if they required new taxes. Two-thirds said they would pay higher taxes to stop drug smuggling. Over half said they favored more taxes to provide a decent standard of living for the elderly and to provide "adequate health care for all who need it but can't afford it." Nearly half (45 percent) said they supported increased taxation to improve the quality of education in the public school system and to provide "health insurance for major illnesses." Two-fifths would support more taxes to ensure that "every American can read and write" and that "every American has food and shelter." It is only for such programs as providing jobs for everyone, ensuring equal job opportunities, protecting against sudden layoffs, and seeing that everyone can send his or her children to college that most people would balk at new taxes (*Times Mirror*, 1988: 37–38).

There is some evidence that this pattern is only slightly different from that in the 1950s. In 1956, the SRC asked its respondents to agree or disagree that "the government ought to cut taxes even if it means putting off some important things that need to be done." Only one-quarter of the Eisenhower era public agreed, whereas slightly over two-fifths (45 percent) disagreed. When the CPS asked the same question in 1988, the public appeared slightly more polarized. Agreement had risen somewhat (29 percent) but so had disagreement (52 percent). Despite Reagan's crusade to curtail the federal tax bite, Americans were slightly more likely to oppose cutting taxes if important programs would be postponed than they had been midway through Ike's presidency. The only significant difference between the public of the 1950s and that of the 1980s was a substantial decline in "no opinion" responses (from 19 percent to 1 percent), which indicates that questions about taxes and spending were more remote in Eisenhower's time than they are today.

After looking at the 1956 data showing massive inconsistencies in public support for increased spending on social welfare programs and unwillingness to support higher taxes to pay for them, V. O. Key was driven to "melancholy thoughts" about the implications for taxation policies (1961: 168). Many public officials contend that things remain the same today (Haas, 1989). We shall return to this issue in Chapter 6. At any rate, these studies indicate two important points. First, the complexity of opinions on taxing and spending are not tapped by measuring opinion on only one side of the budget ledger. Second, taxing and spending opinions need to be anchored in specific, meaningful contexts rather than framed on broad-gauged policy areas if one wants to get a true sense of the extent to which "self-interest" may affect fiscal preferences.

There is another more subtle aspect to the charge that Americans demand more from the service state than they are willing to pay for. Sniderman and Brody (1977) asserted that Americans still believe firmly in the ethic of self-reliance and are reluctant to turn to government to solve problems, particularly those of a personal nature (either economic or quality of life). Far from being greedy, stingy complainers, Americans—whether black or white, young or old, rich or poor—generally hold to the belief that they are responsible for their own problems. The intriguing difference exists among "middle-income" Americans (with a family income in 1972 of eight thousand dollars to fourteen thousand dollars), who tend to blame government more for their economic ("cost-of-living") problems than do the poor, who see it as their responsibility to "make ends meet" for their families, or the wealthy, who tend to be concerned with "quality-of-life" problems rather than economic ones. Does this mean that three years after the publication of Sniderman and Brody's article, candidate Ronald Reagan was prescient in his exhortation to "get government off the backs of the people," to let people handle their own problems without governmental interference? Sniderman and Brody warned that such a conclusion would be wrong: "It would surely be a mistake to jump from our finding that most Americans feel they ought to take care of their personal problems on their own to the conclusion that they similarly oppose policies to deal with many of these problems. So far as we can tell many feel quite comfortable believing at one and the same time that they should cope with such problems themselves and that political leaders and public officials should put forward policies which would have the government help too" (1977: 518–519).

Clearly, Ronald Reagan's rhetoric appealed to the value of self-reliance held by so many in this country, but moving from rhetoric to specific programs brought the Reagan administration up against the political reality that many conceive of such programs as a "helping hand, not a handout." A couple with a disabled breadwinner drawing Social Security and veteran's disability pensions, along with SSI (supplemental security income) and food stamps, may see these governmental programs as essential support that permits them to maintain their sense of "self-reliance" and independence from other family members or social agencies. President Reagan's rhetoric changed in 1984 to reflect this reality.

Keep in mind that political candidates rarely present election-year "trade-off" choices that tie the cost of proposed programs to real revenue increases. Even in 1988, presidential candidates proposed increased social spending based on nebulous changes in interest rates (not controlled by fiscal policymakers) or other equally vague ideas, such as "windfalls" that would result from an even more diligent Internal Revenue Service. Republican candidate George Bush flatly denied that he would institute new taxes, while Democrat Michael Dukakis preferred to say that "only as a last resort" would he favor increasing taxes. Both knew that the last thing a politician wants to promise is higher taxes. Can the American public be blamed for echoing this failure of politicians to make connections between taxing and spending?

What do opinions about fiscal policies have to do with opinions about the power of the central government? Sniderman and Brody once again offered a useful observation: "A personal problem becomes translated into a political demand when a citizen feels that the government ought to take care of the problem" (1977: 520). If most Americans see themselves as responsible for their own problems and yet accept the legitimacy of governmental involvement, what is the source of government's growing agenda? How much does government's agenda grow from political demand and how much from the state's tendency to generate demand by developing more programs to define and address those problems as appropriate for public action? As government grows, does its agenda become increasingly "state-centric" or self-generating (Peters, 1986)? Is part of the "domestication" of public opinion by government the use of public opinion technology to convince citizens of the appropriateness of governmental intervention? Furthermore, once government moves in to address a problem, how does it then legitimate its withdrawal to citizens? Such is the problem with deregulation.

REGULATION AND DEREGULATION

Where government has been able to have the most (though not complete) success in legitimating its withdrawal to citizens has been in regulatory policy. The countervailing power of government has been sought by many groups since the Interstate Commerce Act was passed in 1887. Although early Progressive Era efforts at regulation were intended to target business-corporate interests in order to protect a larger public interest, government has since moved beyond the realm of economic regulation to social regulation. Even within the context of economic regulation, government's efforts expanded to include consumer and environmental protection. The regulatory "binge" of the 1960s and early 1970s saw the *Federal Register*'s listings of new regulations burgeon, as rapidly under Republican as under Democratic administrations.

When economic hard times came on the heels of an oil embargo by a cartel of primarily Arab oil states seeking to capture the attention of the Western world and particularly the strongly pro-Israeli United States, increasing numbers of political observers began to comment on the high cost of regulation and the need to reinforce free markets and support open competition. Derthick and Quirk (1985) suggested that the move toward deregulation was brought about by an unusual combination of factors, including mass sentiment and the ability of policy experts to project that such changes would be in the national interest.

Lipset and Schneider (1987) provided a brief outline of public opinion toward economic regulation from the New Deal era to the beginning of the Reagan years. Most striking in that half-century was the ambivalence with which most Americans approached government's countervailing potential to big business. Consistent with what had been traditional feelings about governmental power, Americans called on government to ensure that business interests were held responsible for more than just the bottom line on their profit statements; they were quite hesitant, however, to support wholesale governmental intervention into business practices in the marketplace. This was particularly evident during a period of crisis, such as a war, when the potential for destabilization of wages and prices added to public fear of inflation and support for governmental control on not only business but also labor.

In a review of several public opinion polls tapping responses to economic regulation, Shapiro and Gillroy (1984a: 532) summarized the main characteristics of American opinions about regulation as, first, a stable ambivalence that reflected fundamental creedal values of free enterprise and protection of citizen rights, and, second, very slow changes in those opinions in response to perceived changes in political reality. Hence, after a period of crisis, things do not return to a pre-crisis state. Indeed, Higgs's (1987) notion of the growth of government in "ratchets" is somewhat reflected in public opinion toward government regulation as well.

The stable ambivalence noted by Shapiro and Gillroy is evident in looking at what seem to be a range of inconsistent responses by the public to questions about regulation. On closer inspection of the items, it becomes evident that question wording has an important impact on responses to governmental regulations. For example, Gallup asked the following question at least three times in 1940: "During the next four years do you think there should be more regulation or less regulation of business by the federal government than at present?" Answers that year did not vary much from the distributions of October 1940, which showed a plurality favoring less regulation (41 percent) and slightly over one-fifth of the sample (22 percent) favoring more regulation of business (Shapiro and Gillroy, 1984a: 536). In June 1978, the Opinion Research Council asked, "In general, what is your attitude toward the federal government's regulation of business? Do you think there is a need for more government regulation of business, is the present amount about right, or do you think there should be less government regulation of business?" After thirty-eight years, the percentages were close to the 1940 distribution, with 43 percent favoring less regulation and 25 percent supporting more regulation. Lest you come to the conclusion that the public tends to balk at governmental regulation of business, a Harris poll item in 1973 and 1975 asking for an agree/disagree/not sure response to, "All government regulation of business should be based on what is best for the country and not on what is best for business," elicited an overwhelming proportion (91 percent and 88 percent, respectively) who believed regulation should be based on a national interest (Shapiro and Gillroy, 1984b: 667).

None of this information is particularly surprising. How a question is framed and which themes it stresses (free competition, national interest, consumer safety) can result in public opinion shifts that reflect more about commonly held values relating to competition, the national interest, and citizen rights than to regulation in an absolute sense. Lipset and Schneider (1987) stated that even Americans who support increasing regulation are not as enthusiastic about government intervention as they are concerned about business being a "responsible" citizen. Again, as in taxing and spending questions, we see the importance of contextual factors in survey items tapping knowledge and preferences about specific governmental actions.

What can help us in understanding the public's changing opinions is the conceptual distinction between economic and social regulation, which also encompasses two historical periods. Government moved into the private economic realm in an unprecedented fashion during the New Deal years, though the Supreme Court rebuffed executive and legislative regulatory enthusiasms until the famous "decision in time that saved nine" in 1937. What is missed by many accounts of the Roosevelt years before World War II is that there was not unanimous or even majority support for many of the now-revered New Deal alphabet soup programs (see Chapter 2). Even given the limited support for FDR's New Deal programs, many of them were given the veneer of permanence and continued through subsequent presidencies and Congresses.

By the early 1960s, attention was increasingly focused on the societal sources of poverty and racism, and the only force seen as significant enough to tackle those problems was the federal government. Michael Reagan described social regulation as the effort "to provide personal protection against the physical hazards of modern industry and technology, and the moral hazards of discrimination" (1987:85). The scope of social regulation reached far beyond that attempted by economic regulation and hence much of social regulation has generated intense controversy. Whereas economic regulation generated debate among the political elite, struggling over whether the public philosophy would reflect laissez-faire or positive-state values, social regulation brought the controversy of government's expanding role to the general public in a far more direct and palpable fashion.

The 1970s brought oil embargoes, high inflation, high interest rates, high levels of unemployment, and low levels of confidence in private and political institutions. Although there was a small rebound of public confidence in the leadership of key national institutions during Reagan's first term, the "confidence gap" closed only slightly (A. Miller, 1983; Lipset and Schneider, 1987). Revelations of secret dealings between the Reagan administration and Iranian mullahs in late 1986 and early 1987 precipitated another decline in confidence. The 1988 NES shows trust in governmental leaders was somewhat higher than at the nadir of the late 1970s but far below the halcyon days of the late 1950s and early 1960s (A. Miller, 1974a).

It is small wonder, therefore, when Gallup's 1987 *Times Mirror* poll reported that majorities were concerned about governmental regulation of business and people's daily lives. Just over half of the public (53 percent) agreed that "government regulation of business usually does more harm than good," and nearly three-fifths (58 percent) concurred that "the federal government controls too much of our daily lives." Still, as discussed in the next section, cries for further deregulation and for less governmental activism fell largely on deaf ears.

DO AMERICANS REALLY WANT
GOVERNMENT OFF THEIR BACKS?

Chapter 1 outlines the wide range of American views about governmental power. Huntington (1981) contended that a pervasive "anti-government" orientation lurks just beneath the surface of the American psyche. This tendency interacts periodically with perceptions that government is failing to live up to idyllic conceptions of the good society, thereby producing convulsive attempts to bring reality into line with ideals. Lowi (1979), however, argued that Americans of all political stripes have come to grips with bigness in government and that the battle to limit governmental powers has essentially been stilled. Still others, such as Ladd (1983), believed Americans are ambivalent—worried about big government in the abstract but wedded to the benefits that activist government provides in the specific (see also Free and Cantril, 1968).

Clearly, we have differences of opinion that are not easily resolved. If one looks either at general items, such as the SRC's question about big government, or at almost any item tapping opinions about taxes, the public appears anti-big government. The same can be said when survey researchers ask about federal spending in the abstract or about governmental inefficiency or budgetary deficits. But this tells only part of the story and perhaps the least revealing portion at that. When asked about spending for specific programs, the bulk of the public is for more spending, not less. Sen. Robert Byrd's (D., W.Va.) admonition in 1981, "Don't cut you, don't cut me, cut that fellow behind the tree," appeals to a large percentage of his fellow citizens. The truth is that a large proportion of Americans—white and black, rich and poor, young and old— have grown used to activist government and can think of a wide variety of things for it to do. Data from three nationwide surveys underscore this point. One is the CPS's 1976 NES; another is NORC's 1985 GSS; the third is Gallup's 1987 *Times Mirror* poll.

The 1976 NES offers two sets of questions tapping different aspects of the public's perceptions of government's powers and responsibilities. At one point, the CPS posed the following to its respondents: "Some people say the federal government has to have certain powers to protect the interests of the country as a whole whereas others say the rights of the individual come first. Which of the following do you think the government in Washington should be able to do and which do you think it should not do?" Six powers were mentioned: "Limit the amount of gas you can use during an energy crisis"; "require everyone to carry a national identification card"; "regulate local business to meet job safety standards"; "look into your background if you were to apply for such things as unemployment benefits, welfare, or a passport"; "require pollution equipment on new cars even if it increases the price you will have to pay"; and "wiretap phones for national security reasons." The six items are a mixture of economic and personal privacy issues.

Essentially, what the 1976 data show is a public willing to grant fairly sweeping powers to the national establishment. Large majorities thought Washington should be empowered to investigate personal backgrounds when people apply for unemployment or welfare benefits (71 percent), to regulate businesses on behalf of employee safety (69 percent), and to limit gas usage during energy shortages (63 percent). A majority would also allow the federal government to require pollution equipment on autos, even if that were to increase the cost to consumers (59 percent).

However, when it comes to personal privacy issues, the public is leery of big brother. Americans were evenly divided over allowing Washington to wiretap phones (43 percent for, 49 percent against), and they were opposed to the notion that government could require everyone to carry a national identification card (37 percent for, 56 percent opposed). Polls in the 1970s and 1980s show Americans concerned about potential and actual threats from government to personal liberty (McClosky and Brill, 1983: 173).

In Chapter 2, we mentioned the 1983 Gallup poll that asked about George Orwell's prediction of an anti-utopian police state. Although Americans discounted most of his predictions, they believed he was on the mark when it came to personal privacy. When Gallup asked, "There is no real privacy because the government can learn anything it wants about you," 47 percent of the public said this was already happening in the United States (*Gallup Report,* 1984: 46). Hence, we should not be surprised when people balk at the idea of national identification cards and wiretapping. Most surprising, perhaps, are the percentages who are willing to allow these kinds of powers to be undertaken by the central government. McClosky and Brill (1983) reported that American views on privacy issues are, at best, inconsistent and equivocal, except on issues involving confidential personal records. The 1976 NES data are consistent with their evidence.

In short, when it comes to grants of broad powers to Washington, Americans are willing to be quite expansive. The 1976 NES also shows that Americans think the federal government should have a great deal of responsibility for handling the wide variety of issues that confront American society. The CPS gave its respondents ten cards depicting various issues confronting the United States; respondents were first asked to note the issues that were "not at all important to you." When a respondent replied that an issue was important, the interviewer asked, "How much responsibility do you think the government in Washington has toward solving the problem?" Figure 4.2 depicts the distributions on the ten issues, which range from obvious national government functions, such as "U.S. relations with foreign countries," to symbolic issues unlikely to elicit much controversy, such as "honesty in government," to the highly controversial and unpopular, such as "racial issues, including busing."

Overwhelming majorities expect Washington to have major responsibilities in dealing with foreign relations and such "valence" issues (Stokes, 1966) as honesty in government, high taxes, and inflation. Indeed, as one scans the graph, it is difficult to find even one issue of which a sizable proportion of the public would absolve Washington of any responsibility. The possible exception is race, which may not be surprising since busing has been one of the most unpopular issues during the past twenty years. At that, 70 percent of the public thought the federal government should have at least some role in solving racial issues.

The public's insistence upon governmental activism becomes even more apparent when six of the ten issues depicted in Figure 4.2 are summed to create a governmental responsibility index. These issues—energy shortages, unemployment, racial issues, combating crime and drugs, consumer protection, and pollution—were found to load on the same underlying dimension by a confirmatory factor analysis with maximum likelihood (ML) extraction and a varimax rotation.[1] The index identified 40 percent of the public as very much in favor of the government having broad responsibilities in solving contemporary issues, 24 percent slightly in favor of it, 23 percent fell into a neutral category, 11 percent were slightly opposed to government taking broad responsibilities, and only 2 percent were very much opposed to an activist government.

Moreover, people's willingness to assign major responsibilities to the national government to deal with domestic issues has but little relation to their opinions on the SRC's big government question. As you would expect, 88 percent of the small group who were very opposed to giving Washington major responsibilities thought the federal government had gotten too strong already, as did 80 percent of those who were slightly opposed to giving it broad responsibilities and 72 percent of those who fell into the neutral category on the index. But 63 percent of those who were slightly in favor of granting broad responsibilities to the national establishment were nonetheless of the opinion that Washington had already

Figure 4.2 Public Opinion about the Federal Government's Responsibility for Solving Problems, 1976

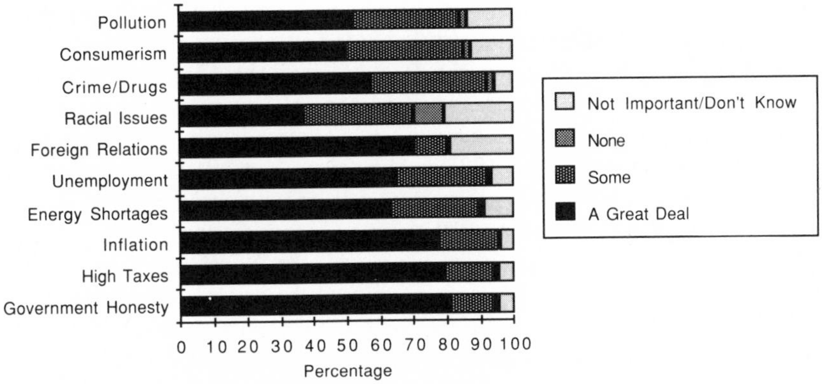

Source: University of Michigan's Center for Political Studies' 1976 National Election Study

become too powerful for the good of the country and the individual. Of those most in favor of having Washington take on major responsibilities in dealing with problems, 68 percent said it was already too big! The relationship between the government responsibilities index and the SRC's big government question is very weak (r = .09). People compartmentalize their answers to a general item such as the SRC's big government question and their replies to questions asking about Washington's responsibilities for dealing with important domestic problems.

The 1976 data are confirmed by a series of questions asked of a portion of the respondents to the 1985 GSS. NORC asked, "On the whole, do you think it should or should not be the government's responsibility" to deal with these seven economic functions: "provide a job for everyone who wants one," "keep prices under control," "provide health care for the sick," "provide a decent standard of living for the old," "provide industry with the help it needs to grow," "provide a decent standard of living for the unemployed," and "reduce income differences between the rich and poor" (*Public Opinion*, 1987: 23). These seven activities constitute much of what makes up the welfare state (Wilensky, 1975: 1). In some ways, the NORC items provide a better test than the CPS questions, because they ask about more issues that have been at the heart of controversies between liberals and conservatives, and Democrats and Republicans since the New Deal era.

Although the NORC data show more diversity of opinion, they also indicate a public quite willing for government to assume major economic responsibilities. Consensus exists on three issues: Government should provide a decent standard of living for older people (88 percent agree); provide health care for the ill (83 percent agree); and keep prices under control (75 percent agree). Just over three-fifths (63 percent) would also have government help industry to grow. On the other hand, Americans were evenly split over whether or not government should provide decent living standards for the unemployed, and only minorities thought Washington should reduce income differences between the rich and poor (39 percent agreed and 61 percent disagreed) or thought it should provide jobs for all who wanted one (35 percent agreed and 64 percent disagreed).

When the seven items were combined into a second government responsibilities index, 39 percent of the 1985 public favored granting broad economic responsibilities to Washington, 37 percent fell into a neutral category, and 24 percent were opposed to granting Washington more responsibilities. In short, although the two indexes cannot be compared, the NORC data also show a public disposed to grant broad responsibilities to the national establishment for economic issues. The NORC data reinforce the CPS survey in another sense. Scores on the NORC government responsibilities index are unrelated to opinions on the NORC big government question (r = .01). Forty-two percent of those who said the federal government was too powerful were nonetheless very much in favor of granting broad economic responsibilities to Washington.

Gallup's 1987 *Times Mirror* poll provides additional confirmation. At the same time that majorities said government controls too much of people's daily lives, majorities—sometimes overwhelming majorities—called for more governmental activism. Nearly three-quarters of the public (71 percent) agreed that government has a responsibility "to take care of people who can't take care of themselves." Three-fifths agreed that "government should guarantee every citizen enough to eat and a place to sleep." Moreover, slightly over half of the public (53 percent) said "the government should help more needy people *even if it means going deeper into debt*." What is more, the percentage completely agreeing with these three statements is two to four times the proportion completely disagreeing.

There are, of course, limits to what Americans are willing to see the national government undertake and they are hinted at by the 1985 GSS questions asking what people thought government's role should be in regulating five industries: electric power, local mass transportation, the steel industry, banking and insurance, and the automobile industry. Three options were provided: Government could "own it"; government could "control prices and profits but not own it"; or government could "neither own it nor control its prices and profits."

Basically, the NORC data show Americans are very unwilling to back governmental ownership of basic industries and banking. Only 9 percent favored government ownership of local mass transportation, and only 6 percent would have government own electric power plants. When it comes to banking and insurance, steel, and car companies, only 2 to 3 percent favor outright governmental ownership. There is also majority opposition to having government control the prices and profits of the steel and automobile industries.

Americans are badly split when it comes to governmental control of the prices and profits of banking and insurance and even local mass transportation. It is only the electrical power industry that finds a majority (59 percent) in favor of governmental regulation of prices and profits. When opinions on the five questions were combined into a composite governmental ownership-control index, only 6 percent of the public were very much in favor of governmental regulation of key industries. McClosky and Zaller (1984) reported that Americans are still strongly committed to the capitalist economic system, and the NORC data corroborate their findings.

PUTTING IT ALL TOGETHER

Gallup's 1987 *Times Mirror* poll enables us to understand how the public can maintain their inconsistent opinions about big government and such topics as taxation, regulation, and spending for specific programs. A total of twenty-seven items covering virtually every aspect of government in society was entered into an ML factor analysis rotated to a varimax solution.[2] Using the criterion advocated by Wheaton and his associates (1977), the best factor solution identified four underlying dimensions. The first comprised items tapping various aspects of civil libertarianism: banning books containing dangerous ideas, denying free speech to groups such as the KKK or the Communist party, permitting governmental censorship of press reports, permitting school boards to fire teachers who are homosexuals, and so on. The second dimension comprised items tapping welfare state issues: governmental help for those who cannot help themselves, preferential treatment of blacks and minorities, a guarantee of food and shelter to the needy, and so on. The third underlying dimension consisted of five items tapping opinions about governmental power: the federal government is inefficient, federal regulation of business usually makes things worse, dealing with a federal agency is not worth the trouble, and the federal government controls too much of our daily lives. The final, and by far the weakest, dimension contained items tapping trust in government and external political efficacy.

For our purposes, the most important conclusion from the 1987 Gallup data is that the "big government" dimension is not related to the other three identified factors. When the maximum likelihood factor analysis was rerotated to an oblique solution, the "big government" dimension was modestly related to the "welfare state" and "trust-efficacy" dimensions ($r = .30$ and $.24$) but essentially independent of the "civil libertarianism" factor ($r = -.08$). American opinions about big government share only 9 percent of variance with views on welfare state issues, and 6 percent with trust-efficacy opinions.[3] Opinions about big government, in short, exist in "splendid isolation" from views on more specific aspects of governmental involvement in our society. As Lane (1962) pointed out, people "morselize" their views about government. In that morselization, people's opinions about big government are not only isolated, they are also less intensely felt than their preferences on taxes and even their vague notions of where government should be spending their tax monies. This, as much as any other factor, accounts for the inconsistencies we have uncovered in this chapter.

Even with the antagonism that remains toward big government, there is clear evidence that people have growing expectations for what government should be doing. But what do people expect of themselves in relation to government? Democratic theorists warn that citizens must monitor governmental power to keep the bases of politics democratic. Do modern citizens continue to feel that sense of responsibility? Chapter 5 reveals that fewer citizens, particularly the young, feel a strong sense of responsibility toward the state. If feelings about big government are becoming more abstract, the sense of what it is to be a citizen in a democratic state is also becoming more indistinct.

5

Young People, Old Questions

As we noted in Chapter 2, in 1984 and 1988 more than a majority of young people (under the age of thirty) had no opinion on the power of the central government. This is not just an indication of youthful ignorance or indifference that will be swept away as these young men and women mature and take on adult roles and responsibilities. Rather, it is a sharp departure from previous generations of young people, such as those polled in the 1960s. In this chapter, respondents to the SRC-CPS National Election Studies from 1964 to 1988 are divided into seven birth cohorts, beginning with those who came of age before the New Deal was implemented and ending with those born after the baby boom years. Clear attitudinal differences exist between the older and younger citizens. Among those born after World War II, there is only slight movement toward the Republican party, although Ronald Reagan was very popular among those born after 1954. Younger Americans differ among themselves on ideology, and education increases liberalism as well as conservatism. The young want government to spend more on a series of domestic issues, but they are less enthusiastic about the welfare state than their New Deal and World War II elders. Finally, measures tapping egalitarian opinions show the young to be more in favor of expanding equality than older cohorts.

Too infrequently asked in the relations between people and democratic government is what obligations do people have regarding government. Combining the rights and duties of democratic citizenship was essential to John Locke, the democratic theorist most often cited as central to the framing of the Constitution (Pennock, 1979: 191–198). Furthermore, some understanding of what people think about obligation, beyond what we have already outlined in the previous chapter's section on paying taxes, is an essential part of understanding how comfortable some might be with the governmental leviathan.

Recalling Ginsberg's (1986) warning that modern Western governments have "domesticated" public opinion, or learned how to manipulate opinion for their survival and expansion, one critical reality remains about a citizen's sense of obligation: It empowers a citizen to monitor what government is doing. If Ginsberg's thesis about the intent of Western governments is correct, then confronting an attentive public could be one of the last things the modern leviathan would welcome. If public opinion has been tamed to the extent that more and more of the public see little point or have little interest in following what government does, then the people release government from accountability for its actions. When citizens expect more of government, they must expect more of themselves to maintain a democratic polity.

Using the seven cohorts defined below, we find that younger people feel less obliged to serve their country (either in the military or through more general national service), to follow what is going on in politics, to vote, to serve on juries, or to serve a community. Younger Americans have lower levels of civic obligation across the board, and many are unwilling to feel guilty about it. In sum, among the youngest, best-educated segments of our society, the concept of democratic citizenship is in serious decline. Before focusing on these issues, we turn to a discussion of the largest group (which we divided into two separate cohorts), what many have called the baby boom "generation."

GENERATIONAL GENERALIZATIONS

The explosion of births after World War II baffled demographers and made ridiculous Census Bureau predictions of a slowing birthrate once the country had moved a few years beyond the war. Landon Jones (1980: 2) referred to the "army of babies" that now constitutes almost one-third (seventy-eight million) of this nation's population. Publications such as *American Demographics* refer to the baby boom "generation," as do many others, but we will refer to two baby boom "birth cohorts." The difference between "cohort" and "generation" is that the former denotes an age grouping without the presumption of shared values and common experiences that the latter denotes. Sociologist Karl Mannheim warned against the inexact use of "generation," stating that "individuals of the same age . . . are . . . only united as an actual generation insofar as they participate in the characteristic social and intellectual currents of their society and period" (1972: 119). He defined an even more cohesive "generation unit" that introduces the bonding element of a *concrete* experience that cements a group in conscious identification. Perhaps some observers of post–World War II population trends can be forgiven for their use of the generation concept, because certainly the sheer numbers represented by the baby boom formed one common experience as those babies matured: overcrowding.

Efforts to describe the characteristics and explain the opinions of this large population group have resulted in the inevitable generalizations. From "yippies" (referring to the 1960s Youth International party) to "yuppies," boomers have found themselves described as the hope for a new age, a "greening of America" in the 1960s, to the epitome of selfishness in the 1980s. As the more fortunate of those born in the years immediately after World War II reached their late thirties, they pondered—as does one character in the popular movie *The Big Chill*—whether their youthful enthusiasms and ideals were "just fashion." The baby boom birth cohort is simply too large, too complex, and too wide a spread in years (nineteen) to allow for simple description.

In a demographic profile of baby boomers, an *American Demographics* article warned, "No business should treat the baby boom as a single market when it is, in fact, a multitude of markets" (1985: 23). In reality, baby boomers are poor, middle class, and wealthy (see also Light, 1988). A 1984 U.S. Census Bureau Current Population Survey indicated that almost one-fifth of boomer households have incomes under ten thousand dollars a year, compared with 15 percent with household incomes of forty thousand dollars a year or more (1986: 25). About an equal proportion (13 percent) are at the two extremes of the education spectrum—high school dropouts or recipients of advanced graduate degrees. A bare majority are married, though that percentage rises to two-thirds among older boomers. Although an equal percentage of men and women are "professionals" (18 to 19 percent), one-fourth of female boomers have never worked (compared with 9 percent of males), and a similar proportion of women provide "administrative support," generally as secretaries (1986: 25, 27). For all the attention they garner from the media, "yuppies" are a small percentage (5 percent) of the boom cohort. Research into their distinctiveness as a political force indicates that yuppies are more a media creation than a reality (Delli Carpini, 1986; Delli Carpini and Sigelman, 1986; Hammond, 1986). Hammond blamed the term's popularity on the "pack mentality" of journalists, who, he believed, were more interested in "journalistic storytelling" than in accurately describing social groupings.

Our fascination with the baby boom cohort, which for many of us in academe and journalism translates into an absorption with ourselves, has usually led us to ignore those born in 1965 and after. These are the young people in the wake of the largest birth cohort in American history, and they have yet to make their mark.

DEFINING THE COHORTS

Although our primary focus is on those born after World War II, we present data on seven birth cohorts. As Norval Glenn (1977: 8) explained, the boundaries of a cohort can be somewhat arbitrary, but they "usually consist of people who experienced a common significant life event within a period of from one to 10 years." Some of the seven birth cohorts we define are longer than ten years, because the "significant life event" had sufficient impact to incorporate more years (for example, the New Deal era). There is the inevitable simplification that occurs when creating such groupings. However, to keep this study focused on changing perceptions of the size and power of the central government in American political culture, we have attempted to delimit our cohort boundaries on the basis of important periods in the relations between people and government. Although some events have an impact on more than one cohort (for example, the Great Depression would still have been very significant to the World War II cohort), we have attempted to define cohorts as those who "came of age" during a period. "Coming of age" is an admittedly vague concept, but our intent is to include the impact of a period on young adults, sometimes as young as sixteen or seventeen, who, although they would not have been eligible to vote, would have felt the impact of the times on their young lives. We tracked the opinions of the following cohorts from 1964 to 1989.

Pre–New Dealers (born in 1908 or earlier). These individuals came of political age (twenty-one) before the "Black Thursday" stock market crash of October 1929. Although the New Deal years no doubt had a tremendous impact on their lives, they entered the adult world and were eligible to participate in the public arena (particularly if they were white males) before the tremendous expansion of government during this period. If they were attentive to politics, these individuals would remember the last time the Republican party was a majority party. Blacks in this cohort could have had living relatives who remembered the Emancipation Proclamation and might even have recalled when Republicans were called "radical." The men in this cohort would have been of draft age for the brief American turn in World War I and would have remembered when the United States was not a superpower. By the early 1980s, the youngest members of this cohort were in their early seventies.

New Dealers (born from 1909 to 1921). The oldest of this cohort would have been twenty-two years old when Franklin Delano Roosevelt ran his 1932 campaign promising a "new deal" for the American people. Their young adult lives would have been dominated by FDR's thirteen-year presidential tenure. Probably no other group, even those who remembered where they were on November 23, 1963, were as profoundly affected by the death of a president. As one member of this cohort commented, "I was one of that generation who really could remember no other President. Now he was gone; and I sensed even then that this was more than the inevitable passing of a mortal man" (Wolfskill, 1962: vii). As the analysis in Chapter 2 warned, FDR's imprint on these years did not result in unanimous acceptance of his New Deal programs, or even enthusiasm among a sizable proportion of the populace. Still, whether in agreement or disagreement, the New Deal was the focus of debate. Older men in this cohort would be the first wave of draftees and volunteers in World War II, the war that would keep FDR in office and see him reelected for an unprecedented fourth term in 1944. (This is no longer possible since ratification of the

Twenty-second Amendment in 1951.) By the time Ronald Reagan entered the White House, members of this cohort were on the cusp of their retirement years, from sixty to seventy-two years old.

World War II cohort (born from 1922 to 1929). We grant some overlap between this cohort and the New Dealer cohort, yet the youngest of this group would have been twelve when the Japanese bombed Pearl Harbor and their adolescence would have been strongly affected by the more than four and a half years of U.S. involvement in that war. Unlike the World War I years, the early 1940s saw a mobilization of the American public for the war effort, and that mobilization had a profound impact on this cohort's opinions, particularly those about civic obligation. Young women were encouraged to take their cue from "Rosie the Riveter" and help the war effort by taking positions on defense-plant assembly lines left empty by the exodus of young men to the military. FDR's executive order forbidding discrimination in hiring at defense plants meant that black women would share in some of the benefits of increased opportunity. As one black woman reflected on her experiences during those years, "The war made me live better, it really did. My sister always said that Hitler was the one that got us out of the white folks' kitchen" (Gluck, 1987: 23). The war cohort would begin trends that would shake the foundation of cultural values. In large part, these are the parents of the baby boom's first wave and their worldviews would shape the expectations of the boomers. Members of this cohort were in their fifties at the beginning of Reagan's presidency.

Cold Warriors (born from 1930 to 1945). The oldest of these individuals came of political age (eighteen to twenty-one) in the wake of World War II, when tensions between the United States and the Soviet Union affected not only foreign policy but also domestic relations. Even before Republican Senator Joseph McCarthy began his anticommunist crusade in the early 1950s, President Truman had instituted loyalty checks for federal government workers, with the result that thousands lost their jobs (O'Neill, 1986). The furor surrounding the investigation and trial of Alger Hiss came to a head in 1950 when a jury was convinced that he had perjured himself on his espionage activities for the Soviet Union while testifying before the House Committee on Un-American Activities. In the same year, Ethel and Julius Rosenberg were accused of passing atomic secrets to the Soviets. The 1950s and early 1960s were dominated by cold war politics that affected the political rhetoric of Republicans and Democrats alike. No politician desirous of being elected dared be thought of as "soft" on communism. The youngest of this cohort were sixteen years old when newly elected president John F. Kennedy delivered an inaugural address replete with cold war references. Even before they reached their twenty-first birthday, they experienced that week of late October 1962, when the United States and the Soviet Union stood "eyeball to eyeball" over Russian missiles in Cuba, surely one of the most dramatic and chilling events of the cold war era. The heavy doses of cold war rhetoric in Ronald Reagan's 1980 campaign speeches were probably quite familiar to these individuals in the "prime" of their lives from their late thirties to their early fifties.

Early Boomers (born from 1946 to 1954). We have chosen to divide the baby boom birth cohort into two cohorts of roughly equal time length. The choice is not just an arbitrary one but, rather, is supported by what those born in the first nine years of the boom would have experienced in their young adult lives compared with what those born after 1955 experienced. The coming of age of this wave generated considerable concern about the rise in juvenile delinquency and provided fuel for the Great Society. Daniel P. Moynihan's *Maximum Feasible Misunderstanding,* first published in 1969, outlined the urgency with which Great Society programs (specifically the Community Action Program) were generated, and why they were doomed to fall far short of their goals. Landon Jones asserted that "for [those] . . . born between 1946 and 1954, Vietnam and the draft were the most cauterizing events of their young lives" (1980: 106). Baskir and Strauss, in their 1978 study of the Vietnam "generation" limited the cohort to those born before 1954 yet agreed that the Vietnam war profoundly changed the lives of those who fought, those who evaded the draft, and those who protested the draft on college campuses. But Vietnam was only part of the social activism of the period. Upon the heels of presidential executive orders barring discrimination in defense plants and the military came the first monumental decision of the young Warren Court, *Brown v. the Board of Education of Topeka, Kansas,* in 1954.

The civil rights movement, still based in the South, benefited tremendously from the egalitarian energies of the young, white and black. From the civil rights movement would come some of the organizers for the student movement in the late 1960s and the feminist movement of the early 1970s. It was this first wave of the boom that would be buffeted by a series of political and social events, from war to assassinations, from the walk on the moon to Woodstock, from Camelot to a presidential resignation in disgrace. In the Reagan years, these individuals would have to dig out an old Bob Dylan tune to stay "forever young" as the youngest among them faced the "passage" of turning thirty while the oldest savored their mid-thirties. Perhaps only those over fifty could not be trusted.

Late Boomers (born from 1955 to 1964). Though the oldest of this cohort should have been cognizant of Vietnam, most of these individuals would come of age (again, from sixteen to eighteen) during one of the most difficult economic decades, the 1970s. The economic, social, and political landscapes were permanently changed by the dislocations resulting from oil embargoes by a newly organized Middle East–dominated cartel and double-digit figures for inflation, interest rates, and unemployment. In the face of economic calamity, the federal government offered little solace and fewer solutions other than to wage a war with buttons that said, "Whip Inflation Now" or "WIN," or to counsel people to "expect less" from their government. The halcyon days of economic prosperity appeared to be over and the presidency was an office diminished by scandal and the inability of two men to project legitimate leadership. Young people in this cohort were said to be more concerned about grades than politics or social issues. Contrasting the high school senior classes of 1965 (made up of Early Boomers) and 1973 (consisting of Late Boomers), Jennings and Niemi stated that "we can categorize the 1973 cohort as distinctly less imbued with the traditional virtues associated with civic training. Politics was less central in their lives and the participant culture was less valued. Indeed, one sees signs of a withdrawal, of a turning inward" (1981: 225). Those tracking popular subjects in college watched as more filed into business and economics than political science and sociology. These young people were being told to "get serious" sooner, because their world would not be the comfortable, tolerant cocoon experienced by the older baby boomers. Candidate Reagan's optimistic message in his 1980 and 1984 campaigns would play particularly well with these folks in their late teens to mid-twenties who had not, *in their lifetimes*, experienced a president able to project confidence and leadership.

Post-Boomers (born in 1965 and after). Although these individuals are not considered part of the official baby boom cohort, they have much in common with the Late Boomers. They are part of what Susan Littwin (1986) called the "postponed generation." In a world of decreased expectations and what appears to be enfeebled government, young people are taking longer to "grow up" and leave the parental nest. Census Bureau statistics track the trend for young people to stay at home into their twenties (53 percent of those eighteen to twenty-four years old in 1986, according to the 1988 *Statistical Abstract of the United States*: 47) or to return home in the course of a life crisis, such as a divorce. In interviewing several young people, Littwin found a confused mixture of entitlement and frustration. Her conclusion was that parents shared no small part of the blame for preventing their children from taking on adult responsibilities, yet she acknowledged that the world these young people were entering was a less hospitable one (at least economically) than that confronted by the Early Boomers. Little wonder that a candidate could come along in 1980, when the oldest of this cohort was fifteen, and preach the gospel of great expectations again, of a rosier future that could be had if obstacles (such as government) were removed, and receive a wave of appreciation from a portion of the young. By 1984, when Ronald Reagan would run for reelection, the most enthusiastic Reagan supporters among whites would be the Late and Post-Boomers.

THE BASIC POLITICAL DISPOSITIONS
OF THESE COHORTS

A reexamination of the item measuring opinions toward the power of the central government using our seven birth cohorts reveals some interesting cohort and period effects. First, by 1988 it is evident that Late and Post-Boomers are the most uninterested in the issue of the federal government's power, though a plurality of all the cohorts also exhibit apathy. Pre–New Dealers share similar levels of uninterest in the federal government's power, but by the beginning of Reagan's second term (1984), they are also the most likely to say the government in Washington has gotten too powerful. Older cohorts (the Pre–New Dealers to the Cold Warriors) were less likely to say government was too

Table 5.1 Public Opinion about the Power of the Federal Government, by Cohort, for various years, 1964–1988 (in percentages)

	Pre–New Dealers (up to 1908)[a]	New Dealers (1909–21)	World War II (1922–29)	Cold Warriors (1930–45)	Early Boomers (1946–54)	Late Boomers (1955–64)	Post-Boomers (1965 on)
No Opinion							
1964	31	32	30	31	—	—	—
1968	31	21	29	27	20	—	—
1972	32	28	22	28	30	—	—
1976	43	26	22	24	26	39	—
1980	36	29	26	29	34	55	—
1984	49	41	41	39	46	50	76
1988	48	47	40	42	41	52	66
Not Too Powerful							
1964	36	38	36	44	—	—	—
1968	29	38	31	32	44	—	—
1972	31	30	36	30	29	—	—
1976	19	25	21	21	24	24	—
1980	21	19	15	17	17	15	—
1984	10	21	20	24	28	27	9
1988	25	17	31	38	22	16	13
Too Powerful							
1964	34	30	34	25	—	—	—
1968	39	41	40	41	36	—	—
1972	38	42	41	43	41	100	—
1976	38	49	56	55	50	38	—
1980	43	53	59	55	50	30	—
1984	41	38	39	38	27	24	15
1988	28	36	29	20	37	32	21
Number of Cases							
1964	435	410	271	448	—	—	—
1968	371	356	266	481	59	—	—
1972	225	243	174	392	280	1	—
1976	400	532	325	731	665	198	—
1980	117	242	164	345	307	228	—
1984	51	150	93	223	230	188	33
1988	65	225	167	381	406	393	134

Source: Adapted from the University of Michigan's Survey Research Center–Center for Political Studies' National Election Studies.
[a]Years of birth.

powerful by the end of President Reagan's second term. The slight increase in the percentages of Early, Late, and Post-Boomers who said that the federal government had gotten too powerful are inside the range of sampling error and do not change the reality that most boomers could not care less about the issue.

There are clear differences in Early and Late Boomer opinions in 1976 and 1980, suggesting a range of different forces at work on the two cohorts. Treating the entire boom cohort as a monolith would disguise these differences. Someone born in the early throes of the baby boom—anywhere from 1946 to 1950—would have experienced a very different world from someone born between 1960 and 1964. The decade separating those birth years contained turmoil that only the older boomer would have been old enough to experience, or at least remember. Note that half (50 percent) of Early Boomers are concerned about too much power in Washington during the Carter years, compared with 38 percent of similarly disposed Late Boomers. Further unraveling of these data would probably reveal combined life-cycle and period effects.

The small number of Post-Boomers included in the 1984 and 1988 surveys makes generalizations tenuous, but those included, from the oldest to the youngest cohorts, certainly reflect a declining likelihood to say government is too powerful. Would the gulf in experience between Late and Post-Boomers be as wide as between Early and Late Boomers? Would someone born in the late 1950s have experienced so different a world from someone born in the late 1960s? We think so.

One charge made about the young in the 1980s is that they flocked to the Republican party out of their enthusiasm for Ronald Reagan. After combining data from the 1985, 1986, 1987, 1988, and 1989 NORC General Social Surveys, we found that the Reagan years generated fewer young Republicans than many might suspect. If partisanship is measured by a seven-point scale from "strong Democrat" to "strong Republican," we find only 8 to 9 percent of the Early, Late, and Post-Boomers willing to declare themselves as fervent Republicans, while at least 13 percent of the boom cohorts and 10 percent of the Post-Boomers ally themselves decidedly in the Democratic corner. This underscores Paul Light's warning that "Reagan's success in courting the baby boom does not mean the Republicans have a permanent lock" (1988: 241). The Early, Late, and Post-Boomer cohorts are distinguished from their elders in their diminished enthusiasm for intense partisanship. Those declaring themselves as independent, for example, range from 8 percent of the Pre–New Dealers to a linear increase across the cohorts of 14 percent of the Post-Boomers.

When ranges of partisanship are included to allow respondents to declare "weak" or "independent" affiliation and the percentages for the two parties are summed, trends are evident. The New Deal and World War II cohorts made Democrats the majority party in the 1930s and 1940s, and no other cohort exhibits their strong enthusiasm for the party of FDR. In fact, the jump in Democratic affiliation marked in the transition from Pre–New Dealers to New

Figure 5.1 Party Identification among Cohorts, 1985–1989

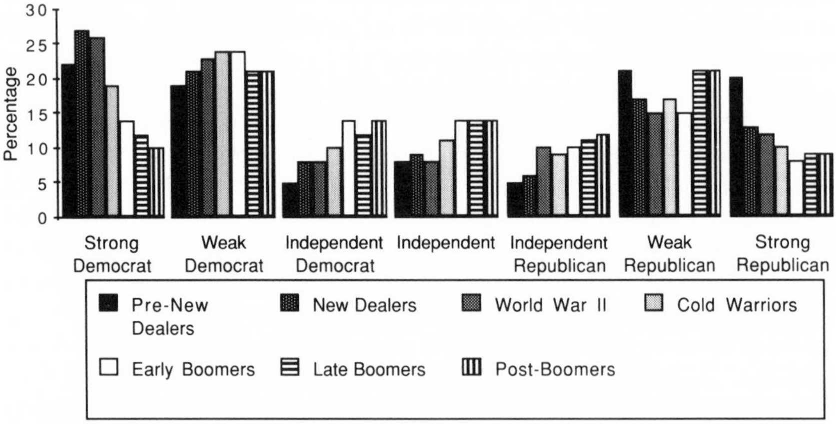

Source: University of Chicago's National Opinion Research Center's Pooled 1985–1989
General Social Surveys

Dealers (46 percent compared with 56 percent, respectively) begins to slide in
intensity as younger cohorts are brought into the picture. Although Early, Late,
and Post-Boomers are still more likely to be Democratic than Republican, they
are less enthusiastic than New Dealers by half. Early Boomers retain the
Democratic preferences of their parents' and grandparents' generations (though
not as strongly), but Late Boomers begin the defection from the fold. These
partisan leanings aside, when it came time to register their preference for
president in the 1984 election, a majority of all cohorts reported they voted for
Republican incumbent Ronald Reagan.

Because of the close relationship between partisanship and ideology, some
sense of ideological identifications among the cohorts is in order. Relying on the
same 1985, 1986, 1987, 1988, and 1989 NORC GSS, we found that Early
Boomers are equally attracted to the positions of "liberal," "moderate," and
"conservative," with roughly one-third identifying with each ideological
position. Late Boomers are more likely to say they are moderate (38 percent)
rather than liberal (30 percent) or conservative (32 percent). Post-Boomers, in
their early twenties when these NORC data were being collected, generally
preferred to think of themselves as moderate (41 percent) while exhibiting
somewhat less enthusiasm for the liberal label (33 percent) and even less
willingness to accept the conservative tag (26 percent).

Before drawing any firm conclusions from these distributions, keep in mind
that among those willing to stray from the plurality at the ideological middle, in
Late and Post-Boomer cohorts, very few (under 5 percent) chose the extreme

liberal or conservative positions. Most of those willing to take a liberal or conservative position do so by hovering close to the safety of moderation. This echoes the younger cohorts' diminished enthusiasm for strong party affiliation in comparison with the older cohorts. There is a volatility among younger citizens in partisan and ideological identifications.

Education enhances liberal as well as conservative identification, with a slight edge to liberalism among Early Boomers. Late Boomer college graduates are evenly divided between liberalism (38 percent) and conservatism (37 percent). Only a small number of Post-Boomers were old enough to have completed college, and the split between liberals (35 percent) and conservatives (41 percent) should not be marked as a trend until more data are available at a later time. The college-educated among the pre–New Deal, New Deal, World War II, and cold war cohorts consistently found conservatism a more attractive option.

Why would the impact of college on ideological identification have changed over time? Certainly, the older cohorts are more removed from their college days and have had a wider range of experiences that may have affected their views. It would not be correct, however, to assume that as the Early and Late Boomers age, they will become more conservative. Norval Glenn (1974) asserted that there is no clear empirical evidence for the assumption that as one moves through the life cycle, one will become more conservative. What he did find is evidence that political opinions are less volatile as one ages. In their early to late thirties when the NORC data were collected, Early Boomers' ideological identifications are less likely to change than those of their younger Late and Post-Boomer counterparts.

Liberal Early Boomer college graduates are undoubtedly a product of the particular time they spent in college. Many campuses were scenes of tremendous disruptions and even violence as the first of the Early Boomers arrived on campuses in the fall of 1964 and as their younger siblings arrived in the late 1960s. Although only a small proportion took an active part in demonstrations, many campus climates were dominated by the most vocal of the New Left's partisans. Some view the changes resulting from the disturbances as the dawning of a new age of freedom and consciousness-raising, whereas others see the grim devastation of true believers (Bloom, 1987). Whatever final judgment is rendered, the intensity of the period left its impression. Higher education does not exist in some distant ivory tower. It reflects political and social reality, and the 1960s were years of liberal, even radical, reform.

In comparison, the 1980s marked the first time in the United States that conservatism could claim intellectual respectability, particularly in economic issues. Perhaps it is not surprising that liberal and conservative identification should show an increase among Late Boomers who attained higher levels of education during the late 1970s and early 1980s, when social issues favoring liberalism and economic issues favoring conservatism competed for the public agenda. Education's impact appears to tilt toward liberalism, as Post-Boomers with "some college" declared themselves liberal (41 percent) compared with Post-Boomers who had not completed high school (29 percent).

Young people in college during the late 1980s experienced a political climate in which Democrats used the term "progressive" to mean "liberal," and Republicans teased their opponents about the "L word." To be liberal took on something of a negative connotation, and among young impressionable minds, the point was not lost. But political climates can change, and the stormy divisions that marked the 1980s may not continue into the 1990s. In fact, the absence of Ronald Reagan from the national scene has already brought in gentler winds that have swept away clear distinctions between liberal and conservative fronts, even Democratic and Republican fronts. Like the weather, the only constant in political imagery is change.

The tendency for younger baby boom cohorts to prefer the weaker levels of partisan attachments means that their partisan preferences are volatile. The same can be said for their ideological preferences. No searing event has sealed their loyalty to one party or the other that could begin to compare with the advantage Democrats gained from FDR's tenure during the Great Depression and World War II. Patterns among the younger cohorts show that not even Vietnam was a mobilizer for the party system. Presidents of both parties administered the war, and both parties moved toward disengagement after the Tet offensive by North Vietnam (Sundquist, 1983).

By the end of President Reagan's second term in 1988, more than two-thirds of Early, Late, and Post-Boomers either declared that the federal government in Washington was not too powerful or did not consider the question sufficiently consequential even to attempt an answer. As these younger cohorts replace older cohorts in the electorate (baby boomers are already 40 percent of the eligible electorate), their expectations of what government should be doing and what their obligations are to government will change government's agenda.

EXPANSIVE EXPECTATIONS

Young adults expect more from government today than any previous cohort or generation, and that includes those who experienced the Great Depression and New Deal years. Landon Jones (1980: 300) discussed their feelings of "entitlement"—because many of their lives began in comfort, they have come to expect of government what they once expected as children from their parents. Baby boom lifestyles build in greater expectations of government. As divorce rates are higher for boomers than for older cohorts, and more boomers in general delay or opt out of having children, the resource of the nuclear family for coping is not one that many boomers are counting on. Barbara Price's summary of baby boom opinions gleaned from an American Council of Life Insurance's (ACLI) analysis of Census Bureau data points to the expectation of Early and

Late Boomers that women should "expand beyond the traditional roles of wife and mother" (1984: 31).

This expectation for women provides support for government-funded or -sponsored day care for working mothers. Not surprisingly, pollsters for both presidential candidates in 1988 advised their clients to be sensitive to the day care issue. An August 1989 ABC News–*Washington Post* poll found that three-fifths of a nationwide survey wanted governmental action on day care programs for working parents unable to afford the high cost of day care.

Movement by the government to expand health care coverage for and accessibility to the elderly is likely to find many supporters among boomers since ACLI–Census Bureau data indicate that 73 percent of boomers feel a "great deal" of responsibility to see that their parents receive good health care (Price, 1984: 32). Once the bills for that health care arrive, demands for governmental help are inevitable and are already being heard. In addition, over a third (36 percent) said they had the responsibility to make certain their parents had an adequate income. It should not be surprising that some of the strongest support for Social Security comes from younger citizens, many years from being eligible themselves to collect retirement benefits.

To get some sense of how much or to whom the younger cohorts believe government should be giving a helping hand, we combined responses to four items in the 1985, 1986, and 1987 NORC GSS. The four items tapped respondents' opinions about whether government should help the poor, the sick, and blacks and whether government in general should leave more of these types of concerns to the private sector.[1] It is an additive index intended to give a rough sense of the willingness of the different cohorts to consider a role for government in helping those suffering from the misfortunes of life and discrimination. What we found was that the tendency to be more in favor of governmental help than against it shows up first among those in the cold war cohort (44 percent for government help; 42 percent against). The gap in favor of governmental help widens slightly with Early Boomers (45 percent for government help; 36 percent against), even more with Late Boomers (50 percent in favor; 32 percent against), and becomes a chasm as more than a majority (61 percent) of Post-Boomers say they favor governmental help over the private sector in issues relating to the sick, the poor, and blacks (23 percent were against governmental help).

When considering the impact of race, we found that three-quarters of blacks in all cohorts favor governmental help. Whites in the younger cohorts are slowly narrowing the gap that approaches 50 percent between whites and blacks in the older cohorts. Among Post-Boomers, 76 percent of blacks and 54 percent of whites favor governmental help of some kind. Compare that difference with the 74 percent of New Deal blacks favoring governmental help and the 27 percent of New Deal whites, and you get a sense of the movement among whites. Keep in mind that this index does not begin to tell us what kind of help those favoring governmental action would prefer and consensus can break down quickly when policy specifics are advanced. Still, the increasing openness to a role for government and a declining sense that the private sector is willing or able to help signals a transformation in expectations of the appropriate role for government. A *Times Mirror* survey from April and May of 1987 echoes the pro-government stance adopted by the younger cohorts. Post-Boomers in the survey were two and a half times more likely than New Dealers to express confidence in governmental regulation of business. They were also less worried about governmental waste, more uncertain about trading national for local control, and less concerned that government was too involved in their daily lives.

Of course, there are a variety of ways government can help to resolve problems, but one of the first ways many think of is by spending money. Public willingness to support more or less spending on a function is often used to justify candidate promises and the direction of federal policymaking. We have already discussed in Chapter 4 some of the hazards of putting too much emphasis on vague spending items that are rarely juxtaposed with questions asking where the additional revenue should be found. Also, single items can register a tremendous volatility in public opinion, depending upon the political climate of the times.

To get at least some picture of the political times up to President Bush's first year in office, we returned to the 1985, 1986, 1987, and 1989 NORC GSS and combined several domestic spending items[2] into an index that would give a sense of whether there was more or less support for more spending on a range of domestic policies among all or just a few cohorts. In general, the younger cohorts, beginning with Early Boomers, are more in favor of increasing domestic governmental spending than are their elders. Although 37 percent of Pre–New Dealers say they would like to see spending increased, 58 percent of Early Boomers, 66 percent of Late Boomers, and 62 percent of Post-Boomers favor increased spending on a series of domestic issues. As with the desire for governmental help, racial differences are narrowing, though Late Boomer blacks are still more likely than Late Boomer whites to favor more domestic spending (84 percent and 62 percent, respectively).

Before getting out the government's checkbook, a word of caution is in order. Even while favoring more governmental help and being readier to favor increasing governmental spending than their elders, the Early, Late, and Post-Boomer cohorts are far from cozying up to the welfare state, at least if it is called welfare. A series of items in the 1986 NORC GSS tapping opinions about the impact of welfare on individual motivations was combined into a welfare index[3] to see if Early, Late, and Post-Boomers would continue to evidence patterns favoring government's role in this area. As it turns out, the two most supportive cohorts of welfare are the New Dealer (36 percent) and the World War II cohort (45 percent). Among Early, Late, and Post-Boomers, roughly one in four are favorably disposed toward welfare, and these same cohorts evidence the highest levels of "anti-welfare" sentiment (41 percent, 49 percent, and 42 percent, respectively). Clearly, support that is perceived as "welfare" does not warm the hearts of those who otherwise say they favor more domestic spending and more governmental help.

Even more interesting, black as well as white baby boomers are unenthused about the impact of welfare on individuals. Among Early Boomers, only 14 percent of blacks and 27 percent of whites and only 19 percent of blacks and 22 percent of whites among Late Boomers have favorable opinions about welfare. Higher levels of education do not significantly change these percentages. Higher levels of income increase the favorable opinions of older cohorts (pre–New Deal to Cold War cohorts), but there is no such impact for higher levels of income among the Early and Late Boomer and Post-Boomer cohorts.

We believe that the anti-welfare opinions displayed by the Early, Late, and Post-Boomer cohorts are not inconsistent with their opinions about spending and governmental help for some groups. The index tapping willingness to entertain governmental help to certain groups included an item that asked about government's "helping the poor." Tom Smith (1987a) noted the importance of semantics when asking about "the poor" as opposed to asking about those "on welfare." The latter term carries a far more negative connotation and is likely to stir a higher level of opposition than items that ask about help for the poor. What the cohort analysis reveals is that the negative connotation attached to the term "welfare" is one that has its greatest impact on those who remember a time when the federal government's welfare role was almost nonexistent (Pre–New Dealers) and those who matured during the Great Society and its aftermath (Early to Post-Boomers). We surmise that the younger baby boom cohorts see no inconsistency in their expectations that government should be a resource on which to draw to permit them and others to live in a fashion to which they are *entitled*, but that whatever help they would like to have from government, be it day care, health care for their parents and grandparents, or help for the poor, it is "a helping hand, *not* a handout."

Finally, we wondered if the younger cohorts would display more egalitarian opinions than older cohorts. This would be one indicator of what Chapter 1 described as the shift from the "rage for liberty," which characterizes most of the American republic's first century, to the "rage for equality," which appears to dominate American political debate from the nineteenth century to the present. Changes in the dominance of these values signal an important shift in the relations between people and government and are fundamental to the expectations people have of government's appropriate role in their lives. Paul Light (1988) asserted that baby boomers are committed to self-reliance and individualism but also to a "level playing field." These opinions are in conflict, and the tension could lead to a lessened commitment to egalitarianism and the governmental action that has made increasing equality a reality.

It is possible to get a general sense of egalitarianism by relying on data from the University of Michigan's CPS National Election Surveys in 1984, 1986, and 1988. In all three years, a series of questions were asked concerning equal opportunity, the extent to which equality is possible in American society, the amount of inequality people are willing to tolerate, and how much we should worry about equality.[4] The items were identically worded in each year, hence we do not have the problem of comparability.

As Figures 5.2, 5.3, and 5.4 indicate, in 1984 Late Boomers were most likely to express more "egalitarian" than "individualistic" opinions. By 1988 they had been joined by the older Early Boomers and surpassed by Post-Boomers, who expressed the most egalitarian opinions. Higher levels of education enhance egalitarian opinions, with the most impact on Cold Warriors and Early Boomers. Late Boomers did not show a significant increase in egalitarianism as a result of education in 1984 and 1986 and only a slight increase in 1988. Although the case numbers are few, preliminary evidence indicates that education slightly enhances egalitarianism among the youngest cohort. Blacks consistently expressed more egalitarianism than whites, though, again, the gap between blacks and whites is narrowed among the younger cohorts. Interestingly, the gap narrowed in part because whites in the cold war to boomer cohorts began expressing more egalitarian opinions, but also because Cold Warrior blacks began a declining trend in egalitarianism that continued into the younger cohorts. Still, overall, the gradual trend from the oldest to the youngest cohorts and from 1984 to 1988 favored gradually increasing levels of egalitarianism.

As noted in Chapter 1, Alexis de Tocqueville warned that the quest for equality inevitably generates growth in the central government and, in his opinion, a diminution of individual liberty. His view of the quest for equality was undoubtedly affected by his status as a minor aristocrat, wistfully pondering the

Figure 5.2 Pro-Egalitarian on Egalitarianism Index, by Cohort, 1984, 1986, and 1988

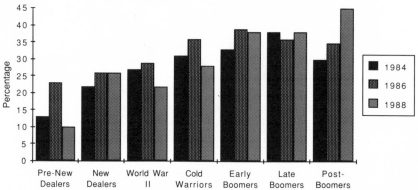

Source: University of Michigan's Center for Political Studies' 1984, 1986, and 1988 National Election Studies

Figure 5.3 Neutral on Egalitarianism Index, by Cohort, 1984, 1986, and 1988

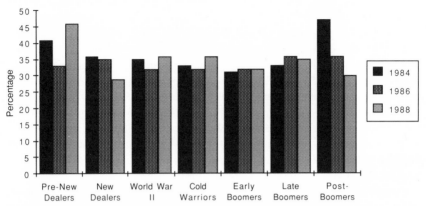

Source: University of Michigan's Center for Political Studies' 1984, 1986, and 1988 National Election Studies

Figure 5.4 Pro-Individualism on Egalitarianism Index, by Cohort, 1984, 1986, and 1988

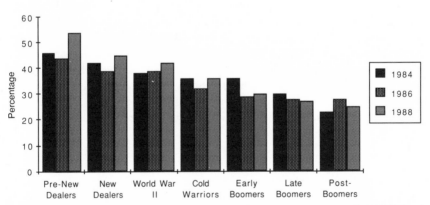

Source: University of Michigan's Center for Political Studies' 1984, 1986, and 1988 National Election Studies

end of an era for the European aristocracy. There can be no question that the focus on egalitarian values helped the United States to absorb an unprecedented range of ethnic, religious, and racial groups, though rarely peacefully or with immediate tolerance and acceptance. The theory of pluralism even allows for a certain form of egalitarian individualism ("Don't bother me and I won't bother you"). Yet Tocqueville was prescient in his prediction that the quest for egalitarianism would result in a larger central government. If rudiments of the values inherent in a democratic republic are to be maintained amid the growth of national power, the increasingly complex relations between people and government require consideration not only of what people expect from government but also what they perceive to be their obligations to that government.

In a final word on our findings regarding egalitarianism, we note that if those finishing high school, entering the work force, or graduating from college are supposed to be the most "selfish" of any previous age group, they certainly do not show the enthusiasm for pure individualism exhibited by older cohorts (if individualism must be equated with selfishness, which some commentators assume). The data from 1984 and 1986 are from the middle Reagan years, when, according to Irving Howe, "we are living in a moment of moral smallness, a curdling of generosity, a collapse of idealism" (1986: 419). Much was made of the selfishness of the Reagan years, of the mean-spirited tone the Reagan administration allegedly encouraged (Block, Cloward, Ehrenreich, and Piven, 1987), yet even though many younger Americans supported Reagan, it did not seem to enhance the individualistic impulse. The expansive expectations these young adults have of government apply not only to their welfare but to the welfare of others as well. What boomers do not like is to have the governmental involvement they expect called welfare. We also note that somewhere between a quarter to a third of the boomer cohorts express strong individualistic sentiments and that higher education does not affect this. Hence, the tension between egalitarian and individualistic forces will continue to be on the political agenda for a long time to come.

COHORTS AND *CIVITAS*

One sign of the predominance of egalitarian values is the extent to which college textbooks on American government discuss the right of all citizens to equality. The thirteenth edition of one of the most popular volumes, by James MacGregor Burns, Jack Peltason, and Thomas Cronin, devotes three chapters (over eighty pages) to civil rights and liberties. The authors bluntly state, "Americans are committed to equality" (1987: 94). They explain the complexity inherent in the concept of equality and the history of the American quest for equality, but at no point do they express any concomitant concern with the notion of civic obligation. Lest it be thought that a review of one textbook is unrepresentative of the larger body of American government textbooks, we would suggest a quick review of the books currently being used in any college introductory American government course.

The concept *civitas* (Latin pronunciation, kee-wee-tas) incorporates the rights as well as the obligations of citizenship. Since such short shrift is given to civic obligation in college textbooks, it is not surprising, perhaps, that a 1979 survey by Morris Janowitz asking more than fifteen hundred undergraduates their opinions about a variety of rights and accompanying obligations (for example, the right to a trial by a jury of one's peers juxtaposed with the obligation to serve on juries) should find that students regularly rate rights as more important than obligations. The three duties rated the highest were "to educate one's children to civic responsibility, the duty to vote, and the duty to pay taxes" (Janowitz, 1983: 7–8). Even here, the right to vote was considered more important by the students than the obligation to vote.

Given our earlier findings on the expansive expectations of younger cohorts, we wanted to get a sense of what the different cohorts saw as their responsibilities as citizens. Fortunately, the 1984 NORC GSS included a cluster of ten questions on civic obligation. Two of those questions ("Should young men/ Should young women serve the nation for one year?") were asked in the 1982 NORC GSS, and those responses were included in our analysis. The other questions asked about the obligation to serve one's community, to serve on juries, to serve in the military during peacetime and wartime (both men and women), to vote, and to be politically informed. Table 5.2 displays the percentages in each cohort saying that each obligation is "very important." The most striking observation is that with the exception of opinions about whether women should serve in the military during peacetime or wartime, there is a consistent diminution of feelings of obligation as one moves from the older to the younger cohorts.

Whether women should serve in the military at any time appears to get the highest level of support among the World War II cohort, a majority of whom favor women serving during wartime. Close behind in strong support for wartime military service for women are the other two cohorts to experience a war period, Early Boomers (50 percent) and New Dealers (49 percent). Exhibiting the norms of sex role socialization from an earlier era, those who came of age before the New Deal are the most likely to say women do not have the obligation for military service even during wartime (23 percent). Although the Pre–New Dealers exhibit strong gender differences, with women far more likely to say they do not have the obligation for wartime military service, Vietnam-era Early Boomers exhibit no gender differences and are less likely (17 percent) to excuse women entirely from this obligation.

Changing the wording of the "service" obligation to omit reference to the military and asking whether young women "should serve the nation for one year," increases the feelings of obligation among older cohorts but does not

Table 5.2 Cohort View of Political Obligations as "Very Important" (in percentages)

	Pre-New Dealers (up to 1908)[a]	New Dealers (1909–21)	World War II (1922–29)	Cold Warriors (1930–45)	Early Boomers (1946–54)	Late Boomers (1955–64)	Post-Boomers (1965 on)
Women's duty to serve in military during peacetime	12	19	22	21	18	15	9
Women's duty to serve in military during wartime	37	49	54	47	50	41	46
Duty of young women to serve nation 1 year[b]	34	34	29	28	22	15	14
Men's duty to serve in military during peacetime	35	42	43	38	34	20	14
Men's duty to serve in military during wartime	85	94	94	90	81	73	71
Duty of young men to serve nation 1 year[b]	46	50	42	39	30	20	14
Obligation to be politically informed	62	71	63	61	57	41	41
Obligation to vote	93	91	87	83	78	67	73
Obligation for jury duty	74	76	70	70	64	54	64
Obligation to serve the community	44	40	43	32	31	19	18

Source: University of Chicago's National Opinion Research Center's 1984 General Social Survey.

[a]Years of birth.

[b]These items were from the University of Chicago's National Opinion Research Center's 1982 and 1984 General Social Surveys.

sway the Early, Late, and Post-Boomer cohorts. There is a more consistent willingness to believe that young men should serve, particularly during wartime, though even under such extreme conditions, the boomer cohorts are harder to convince that wartime military service is not to be questioned.

Interestingly, among Early and particularly Late Boomer cohorts, higher levels of education suppress both men's and women's feelings of obligation to serve in the military during wartime. For example, 86 percent of Early Boomers with less than a high school education and 78 percent of similarly educated Late Boomers said it is very important for men to serve during wartime. Among college graduates for both cohorts, 77 percent of Early Boomers and 67 percent of Late Boomers feel that obligation to be very important. Higher levels of education have a similarly depressing effect on service obligation, whether for men or women, during war- or peacetime and that depressing effect is generally greater for Late Boomers than for Early Boomers. For example, when asked about peacetime military service for men, 47 percent of Early Boomers with less than a high school education and 30 percent of their Late Boomer counterparts believe strongly that men have a military obligation even during peacetime. Their college-educated peers are less enthused, as only 27 percent of Early Boomers and 7 percent of Late Boomers agree with their lesser educated contemporaries.

Moving on to the other obligations included in the 1984 NORC GSS, declining levels of obligation from older to younger cohorts are evident. Essential to every civics class' conception of the "good" citizen are the obligations to be politically informed and to vote. The small number of Post-Boomer cases limit our ability to discuss trends in that cohort, but their cues from immediately older cohorts seem clear. Not even a majority of Late Boomers believe that it is very important that they stay informed politically, and 9 percent say that it is not an obligation at all! Across all the cohorts, except among the least educated (less than high school), women are more likely to say it is very important to be politically informed, though when questions tapping political knowledge are posed, women exhibit lower levels of political knowledge than men (S. E. Bennett, 1986). Education appears to make little difference for the older cohorts (pre–New Deal to cold war) and enhances only slightly the percentage of Early and Late Boomers who say being politically informed is very important (among the college-educated, 59 percent of Early Boomers and 47 percent of Late Boomers). Not even a college education appears to convince Late Boomers (in their twenties when these data were collected) of the importance of being politically informed.

If being politically informed wanes in importance among boomer cohorts, what about the activity that is supposed to be the culmination of keeping politically informed: voting? Again, we see a diminution in the percentages among younger cohorts saying that this obligation is very important. Early Boomers in their thirties were less convinced of the importance of voting in 1984 than are older cohorts, and Late and Post-Boomers appear to continue the declining trend. Higher levels of education have some impact on the college-educated Early Boomers, with 83 percent saying the obligation to vote is very important, and an even stronger impact on Late Boomers, with 80 percent saying it is important. Before younger cohorts can be as participative in elections as the older cohorts they will replace, something will have to change to enhance their perception of voting as the fundamental obligation of democratic citizenship. In fact, there is an increase in the percentage of those who flatly state that voting is *not* an obligation—1 percent among Pre–New Dealers, New Dealers, and those in the World War II cohort; 4 percent of Cold Warriors; 5 percent of Early Boomers; and 9 percent of Late Boomers.

Although these data are cross-sectional (from a single survey), they do suggest that the decrease in turnout for national elections has yet to "bottom out." Attitude theorists are careful to warn that behavior does not necessarily follow attitude, yet voting turnout data confirm that not only are the Boomer cohorts less likely to perceive voting as an obligation but also they are even less likely to vote. CPS data from 1984, 1986, and 1988 of "validated vote" (confirmed voters in the survey, not just those who said they voted) offer dismal evidence. Turnout by the cohorts in the 1984 presidential election ranged from 62 percent of Pre–New Dealers, 78 percent of New Dealers, 77 percent of the World War II cohort, and 75 percent of Cold Warriors, to 69 percent of Early Boomers, 52 percent of Late Boomers, and 44 percent of Post-Boomers. Without a presidential race on the ballot in 1986, the turnout figures dropped to 53 percent of Pre–New Dealers, 65 percent of New Dealers, 61 percent of the World War II cohort, and 53 percent of Cold Warriors, to 39 percent of Early Boomers, 25 percent of Late Boomers, and 16 percent of Post-Boomers. By 1988, with Ronald Reagan no longer on the ticket, validated turnout dropped further among all cohorts but most sharply among the youngest (60 percent of Pre–New Dealers, 72 percent of New Dealers, 65 percent of the World War II cohort, 66 percent of Cold Warriors, 60 percent of Early Boomers, 43 percent of Late Boomers, and 30 percent of Post-Boomers).

Many in the older cohorts probably know that guilt can be a powerful motivator to encourage actions that might not otherwise take place. What is happening among the younger cohorts is less feeling of obligation to vote as well as less guilt. Three-quarters of all cohorts *except* the Late and Post-Boomers agreed to a survey item stating, "I feel guilty when I don't get a chance to vote." Two-thirds of Late Boomers agreed with the item. Post-Boomers were split fifty-fifty and the most likely to disagree that any guilt should be felt. These are the individuals supposedly closest to the socializing experience of civics classes in high school and preachments by college professors. The message of voting as a civic obligation either is being discussed less in the educational system or the audience has become decidedly less receptive.

The last two obligations presented in Table 5.2 are jury duty and serving one's community. The trend of a declining sense of obligation is evident in both items. Higher levels of education usually increase the feeling that both obligations are very important, but that impact is not consistent across all the cohorts. For example, education has little or no impact on Early Boomers for either obligation, whereas college seems to enhance the feeling of obligation for both jury duty and community service for Late Boomers. Perhaps it is because the younger cohorts, particularly the Late and Post-Boomers, are taking so long to establish independent adult lives that the levels of obligation among them are relatively low. However, if they continue the trend of the Early Boomers into their thirties, not much of an enhancement in a sense of obligation can be expected.

In the end, we must ponder what responses to somewhat vague survey questions really mean. Given that respondents were not asked to give proof of the extent of their feelings of obligation, one could assume that even the percentages saying the various obligations are very important are probably inflated. With deflated levels of obligation evident on almost all the items in Table 5.2, the first impulse is to shake one's head, cluck the tongue, and despair about young people. Yet that has never been very productive. Declining levels of obligation are built into what has become a balkanized political and social environment and not much will change in the foreseeable future.

In a study that echoes many of this chapter's findings, a Washington-based special interest group urged increased effort by parents, teachers, and governmental leaders to educate the young and enhance their connectedness to the political system (see People for the American Way, 1989). One of the remarkable observations by the study is that many of the young people surveyed and interviewed in person by Peter D. Hart Research Associates commented that they were apathetic because *no one asked anything of them.*

Of great concern to us is that among the Early, Late, and Post-Boomer cohorts, expectations of government are higher than for any of the older cohorts, yet they do not appear to recognize the implications for democratic governance that increased expectations in combination with decreased feelings of obligation present. They do not feel as compelled to stay politically informed, to vote, or to serve the nation either generally or in the military. Furthermore, education has no consistent impact on these feelings. Indeed, for the service obligation, the college-educated Vietnam "generation" within the Early Boomer cohort and their younger Late Boomer siblings have come to believe they are less "obligated" than others. Perhaps the most lasting remnant of the Vietnam era's draft deferments for those in college, particularly in graduate school (until 1967 when violent protests erupted over ending of this practice), is a continuing feeling of exclusivity among some of the beneficiaries.

Baskir and Strauss recorded the responses of some who boasted of their right to exclusion during Vietnam: "A Rhodes scholar, now a corporate lawyer, observed that 'there are certain people who can do more good in a lifetime in politics or academics or medicine than by getting killed in a trench.' A University of Michigan student commented that 'if I lost a couple of years, it would mean $16,000 to me. I know I sound selfish, but, by God, I paid $10,000 to get this education' '' (1978: 7). A devaluation of military service by the college-educated calls into serious question the maintenance of what Janowitz (1983) referred to as the "citizen-soldier" concept. In the United States, civilian control of the military has been a cornerstone of the guarantee that the military will not become a threat to democracy.

The inability of education to enhance feelings of obligation toward the nation-state is viewed by some as a sign that many have escaped narrow-minded patriotic brainwashing. Yet the data in this chapter, the data offered by Peter Hart Associates to People for the American Way (1989), and our practical experiences as college teachers tell us that most college students have not replaced simplistic patriotism with a more sophisticated understanding of the increasingly powerful national government from which they expect so much.

There are also signs that the younger cohorts respond differently than their elders to national symbols. The Supreme Court's 1989 decision that burning the American flag is a protected form of political speech so long as it does not incite violence is more likely to stir the impassioned anger of the older cohorts than baby boomers. In response to a question from the 1988 CPS National Election Study asking how the American flag "made the respondent feel," there was almost a twenty percentage point decline from the New Dealer to Post-Boomer cohorts in saying extremely or very good (92 percent to 74 percent). Those 1988 data also show that boomer cohorts, while still expressing pride in their country, are more tempered in saying they love their country and less emotionally stirred by the National Anthem.

To balance the picture, and frustrate those who prefer simpler answers, keep in mind that the higher levels of obligation evidenced by the older cohorts did not spring just from the education system. Most in the pre–New Deal, New Deal, and World War II cohorts received fewer years of schooling than the younger cohorts. They did, however, experience periods of national crises, when government worked overtime to exhort feelings of personal obligation for the good of the country; the most important of these was World War II. John Morton Blum described the creation in 1942 of the Office of War Information (OWI), which was charged with the "dissemination of war information by all federal agencies" (1976: 31). Considerable effort was put into not only the dissemination of information but also the mobilization of public support behind governmental actions. For those who say, "There's no school like real life," the values emphasized by the media at that time certainly reinforced the maintenance of civic obligation in a fashion that no classroom could imitate.

The gradual trend (and we emphasize gradual) toward indifference about the power of the central government and the concomitant decline in obligation may be signaling a shift in American political culture. Ambivalence is still visible, but in the absence of any demands (in terms of service, national or military) from government short of paying taxes and consuming for the good of the economy, the younger cohorts do not realize that their increased demands of government necessarily require additional effort from them as citizens to follow government. The danger is that such high expectations of government, and particularly of the person at the head of government, will inevitably generate disappointment and cynicism as expectations are not met and as some governmental officials choose to abuse their access to the tremendous resources entrusted to government. In this instance, ignorance, not familiarity, breeds contempt for government and undermines its legitimacy.

6

Coming to Terms

The character of American ambivalence toward big government has changed in the last two decades. The increasing belief in egalitarianism, particularly among younger Americans, means that there will be no constituency for smaller government in the foreseeable future. The presence of growing expectations, however, does not mean these young people feel any increasing sense of responsibility as citizens to monitor government. Partisanship and ideology have become enmeshed in their impact on big government opinions and now the party, or the person, in the White House is the most important. For this reason, we look at the relationships between trust in government, approval of the president, and big government opinions. These findings have implications for the quality of democratic citizenship and political leadership in the United States. Benjamin Ginsberg may be quite correct to say that Western governments have deliberately set about, with the aid of public opinion polls, to tame or domesticate public opinion. There is evidence as well that in the process of taming the public, the ability of our political institutions to offer policy leadership has also been domesticated. The accepted dictum in Washington that "all politics is local" is enervating policy leadership.

Chapters 2 through 5 used a wide range of data to chart subtle shifts in a tenet of American political culture: opinions about the central government's power. Slowly, sometimes in fits and starts, Americans are coming to terms with the leviathan they have helped to create. So elemental has their attachment to government become that even an immensely popular president pledged to trim the size of the national establishment was forced to concede to a nation that has come to terms with big government.

There continues to be some ambivalence in Americans' opinions about big government. Many Americans will offer that the national government is involved in too many issues and yet expect it to do more. Gallup polls for the

Times Mirror found in 1987 and 1988 that slightly over half of the public agreed that "the federal government controls too much of our daily lives." The 1987 poll found, however, that many of those who complained about too much federal control of their lives nonetheless favored increased federal involvement in a wide range of domestic issues. Cranky about taxes, even in the face of a huge cut in the national income tax, citizens still have a "wish list" they want the national government to spend on, particularly domestic programs. Convinced that government wastes too much and that increased efficiency (and honesty) would pay for their policy preferences, they do not see that their attitudes are in any way inconsistent.

Whether the public perceives the inconsistency or not, the latter's impact on policy is what we have witnessed in the late 1980s and is the source of V. O. Key's "melancholy thoughts" about the effect of public opinion on tax policy in American democracy: "The balance of forces drives policymakers back toward concealed and indirect taxation, which may be regressive in its incidence. Such an approach may have strategic advantage in that it may be safely assumed that most of those persons who both take the simple-minded position on taxes and support expansion of welfare activities have no impressive comprehension of the theory of the incidence of taxation" (1961: 168). These thoughts take on an eerie prescience more than two decades later. Anyone interested can watch the political contortions of the executive and legislative branches as they attempt to satisfy the public's demand for more spending in domestic problems such as drug control and simultaneously play "chicken" to see which will be the first to find the revenues to pay the bill.

Many of us believe that government should be there if needed, but its presence should not be burdensome or too obtrusive or make us think too much. Americans still express belief in "individualism," and many hold to their personal responsibility to surmount the obstacles they confront in life. But belief in individualism does not preclude the possibility of a helping hand from government. Furthermore, there is little fear that the power emanating from Washington will result in a sterile, authoritarian, Orwellian world of big brother.

Another major continuity among late-twentieth-century American citizens is the belief in increasing equality. Tocqueville predicted that the quest for equality would create a large, centralized state capable of trampling the individual liberties he admired among the Jacksonian Americans. But the tension between liberty and equality has been changed by the rise of the egalitarian service state. Although there will undoubtedly be controversy over the achievement of equality rooted in differing definitions of "opportunity" and "results," there has been and will continue to be strong support for a continuing public emphasis on equality. The stronger support for egalitarianism among those who came of age after World War II compared with their parents or grandparents underscores the extent to which the concept has been linked to a sense of fundamental

fairness. Evidently, those educated to awareness of rights without a corresponding sensitivity to obligations have less concern for issues centering on big
government's place in our society.

But even these continuities have germinated seeds of discontinuity. Although
many Americans still fear "bigness" and remain testy about too much
governmental power, fewer and fewer really care enough to offer an opinion
when asked whether the power of the national government is getting "too big for
the good of the country and the individual person." Most uninterested are the
young, particularly baby boomers and those born after the baby boom years.
Lacking any fundamental orientation toward government, their opinions reflect
the volatile swings of the political moment. As Paul Light commented, "At least
for now, [baby boomer] political brand loyalty appears to be based on inertia,
easily shakable by the latest scandal or newest promise" (1988: 157).

Contrary to Light's belief that the better-educated boomers are able to think
on several political dimensions and "keep track of multiple cuts of information"
(1988: 237–238), it is more likely that boomers have blocked out or ignored
some of the more confusing tracks, such as politics, and convinced themselves
that they have no obligation to do otherwise. Many younger Americans think that
government is remote to their lives, not because government is so in reality, but
because they do not care to think about it. As they have become a larger
proportion of the eligible electorate, turnout has dwindled. Although observers
of the 1988 campaign charged that the "dirty campaign" tactics turned people
off, in truth politicians were dealing with people who had little interest in
political campaigns even under the best conditions. Sadly, some of the dirtiness,
such as sexual peccadilloes, probably held interest longer than any discussion of
the issues. If a discussion of the issues was what most Americans really wanted,
the Public Broadcasting System would have a much larger share of the market.

Partisan and ideological identifications used to guide and be guided by one's
feelings about Washington's power, but even those factors are less and less
important in understanding orientations toward the central government today,
particularly among younger citizens. Discussions about whether this nation is
continuing a "liberal" tradition or preserving "conservative" values miss the
fundamental point that the standard distinction between liberal and conservative
has lost much of its meaning. We showed in Chapter 3 that the traditional, New
Deal–style division over big government that liberals and conservatives continued to manifest in the mid-1960s had begun to break down by the early 1970s.
Today, those who call themselves liberals and conservatives no longer dispute
whether the government should or should not be involved in almost every aspect
of life; rather, they now dispute *which* aspects merit governmental involvement.
The debate following the Supreme Court's abortion ruling in 1989 clearly
reflects this point, as many liberals found themselves arguing for the invio-
lability of judicial precedent while conservatives heralded change.

Ambivalence as a theme in American political culture has allowed many observers to explain some of the contradictions evident in attitudes about government and what it does or does not do. Our analyses have noted the contradictions in simultaneous concern about government's power amid a desire for it to do more; a hope that it will check the worst vagaries of big business as well as a concern that it could go too far; a belief in domestic programs to help the poor but disdain for welfare; a firm conviction that much of government's largess is entitlements with little or no concomitant obligation on the part of the citizen. Some believe that Americans "embraced" big government in 1936 and provided the leverage that pushed the reluctant Supreme Court into swallowing FDR's "alphabet soup" of New Deal programs (Lowi, 1985). The data we presented in Chapter 2 show that the assignation between people and government developed gradually and that after World War II the surviving New Deal programs were accepted even more slowly until finally they were legitimized by President Eisenhower.

Today, the ambivalence expressed by many Americans has become increasingly hollow. Ambivalence, or difficulty in choosing between conflicting options, makes sense in a nation with truly limited government, where citizens might be struggling with the choice of whether or not to extend government's hold on their daily lives. But when that government has grown to extend its regulations into all reaches of the private sector, economic and social, and supports a complex that generates trillion-dollar budgets and a multitrillion-dollar debt, we are no longer talking about ambivalence but rather a distant angst. Americans are no longer struggling with a choice. They have made a choice, and it is in favor of big government. The degree to which they are comfortable with the centralization of government may vary at times. But when that concern does arise, government does not withdraw from providing its many services and benefits; instead, it shifts service provision to another level, most recently to that of the state. Inevitably, the widespread belief in equality will generate concern about the unequal distribution of services and/or benefits that states provide, and a centralization of authority will occur again. As time passes, and as the younger cohorts replace older citizens, even the angst may pass, particularly if government continues to ask only what public opinion will tolerate.

Lessened concern about government's power and lower levels of civic obligation serve as tentative indicators of the "domestication" of public opinion (Ginsberg, 1986). Even as government expanded to do more, Americans saw less reason to be concerned about that expansion. Younger citizens evidence this quiescence to the greatest degree. If public opinion polling is the instrument of governmental manipulation, then perhaps the polls show the extent to which government has been successful in quelling public intrusiveness into the care and maintenance of big government. If the young stay disconnected, they will continue to encourage trends (such as political corruption) they claim are the cause of their apathy. To an important degree, however, these trends can also be seen to enervate government. Tied to frequent popularity polls, presidents can become wary of the bold policy initiative. Members of Congress, hoarding campaign contributions to scare away competitors, are not immune to these forces and wait for some other signal that policy leadership is electorally safe. Thus, along with domesticating public opinion, the trends outlined in previous chapters also point to the domestication of leadership in government.

Although we argue that the lessening of ambivalence is a major discontinuity from the historical pattern of American political culture, Aaron Wildavsky (1982) argued that it was not. He described the rise of three cultures in Western countries. The one that is relevant to this analysis is "egalitarian sectarianism." Many have labeled this culture the "New Class," and we have used this term to describe a modern educated elite, simultaneously dependent upon and suspicious of government and determined to eliminate invidious distinctions among groups of people, usually with the help of government. The placement in society of those in the New Class or "sectarian culture" is strategic: the mass media, education institutions, and the public sector. Hence, their influence spreads far beyond the card-carrying members of their sect. As Wildavsky noted, "Sectarians impose contradictory demands on government and society" (1982: 57).

Wildavsky also described two other cultural strains, "hierarchical collectivism" and "competitive individualism." The former accepts a stratified society and control by an elite. The elite's control is buttressed by the formal power of church or state. Competitive individualism is a more fluid system that selects leadership through a bidding or bargaining process. Both are said to shape the older institutional structure to varying degrees in different countries, with individualism slightly stronger in the United States than in Europe (Wildavsky, 1982: 47).

Wildavsky argued that egalitarian sectarians want small government, but we think he was closer to the mark when he outlined their hostility toward hierarchical authority. This hostility is directed even toward those institutions from which the group expects the most, such as the presidency. Most citizens, and we would argue that this includes the sectarians, have accepted bigger government. The sectarians Wildavsky described may grouse about governmental authority, but they do so while simultaneously demanding governmental action, usually in the form of regulating behavior.

As noted in Chapter 1, rising expectations of what government could and should be doing in the post–World War II world greatly increased presidential power. No other institution was as closely identified with overseeing greater equality than the presidency, unless it was the courts, but even they must rely upon the "executor of the laws" for the enforcement of case decisions. The primacy of the president's position has become more important in shaping how people respond to the national government. For this reason, a brief discussion of the impact of one of the most popular presidents in the last generation, Ronald Wilson Reagan, is in order. Although many commentators believe that presidential popularity serves as an effective tool in providing leverage with Congress, there remains an enervating dimension to popularity. In its cultivation, it limits action by both branches.

PUTTING A FRIENDLY FACE ON BIG GOVERNMENT

We began this book discussing Reagan's first inauguration to the presidency after a long drought of weak, unpopular presidents. Trust and confidence in all institutions, which had been in decline since the early 1960s, took a sharp nosedive as race relations, Vietnam, and Watergate became national obsessions (A. H. Miller, 1974a; Abramson, 1983; Hill and Luttbeg, 1983; Lipset and Schneider, 1987). Was this downward spiral of confidence linked to attitudes about the power of the national government? Figure 6.1 gives the clear answer— "Yes." It shows the relationship between opinions about Washington's power and a four-item trust in government index.[1] The figure charts the percentage of each category on the index stating that Washington had become too powerful. Clearly, people who trust the government are much less likely to think Washington is too powerful than those who do not trust it, and this remains true over twenty-four years.

Just as other scholars have shown, there was a massive decline in trust in government between 1964 and 1980, a loss only partially recovered by 1988. More than any other single factor, the decline in trust after 1964 accounts for the concomitant increase in opinion that the federal government had become too strong. Multivariate analyses (see the appendix) show that the trust in government index is consistently one of the best predictors of opinions about Washington's power. From 1970 until 1984, it was the most powerful predictor in every year except 1980, and usually it was by far the strongest factor. Trends in trust go a long way toward explaining why fear of big government rose between 1964 and 1980 and fell thereafter.

Although Jimmy Carter may have believed that the answer to the "national malaise" was not in the White House, the eyes of many Americans were turned toward the president. Approval or disapproval of presidential job performance is known to shape confidence and trust in government (Citrin and Green, 1986). If the way people feel about how an incumbent president is doing his job has an impact on their trust in government, does it also shape their views about big government? Our analysis of SRC-CPS data indicate it does and, at least since the late 1970s, in some important ways.

People who approved of LBJ's actions as president in 1968 were much less likely than those who disapproved to say Washington was not too strong. Even once other factors (party identification, trust, race, and ideology) were taken into account, presidential performance ratings still had a significant bearing on attitudes about big government. However, in 1976, ratings of Ford's job as

Figure 6.1 Opinion That the Federal Government Is Too Powerful, by Trust in Government, for various years, 1964–1988

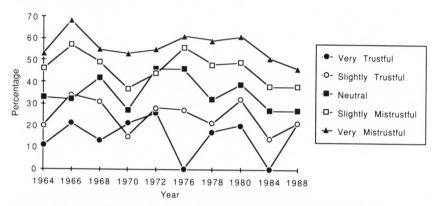

Source: University of Michigan's Survey Research Center–Center for Political Studies' National Election Studies

president were unrelated to views about the federal government's power. Ford's unique position—he had been elected to the House of Representatives from Grand Rapids, Michigan, but elevated to the presidency because first the vice president and then the president resigned—could account for this departure.

By 1978, 1980, and 1984, not only were people who approved of Carter's or Reagan's job performance less likely to think Washington was too strong than those who disapproved, but also assessment of the chief executive's job performance was a strong predictor of big government opinions even when partisanship, trust, ideology, race, and socioeconomic class were taken into account. Thus as the public's approval rating of Reagan increased between late 1982 and late 1984, one consequence was a slight diminution in the perception that Washington was too powerful. Approval of Reagan's job performance remained a significant predictor of opinions about big government in 1988.

In his revisionist analysis of Eisenhower's presidency, Greenstein (1982: 4–5) asserted that modern presidents have come to personify government. If this is the case, then Ronald Reagan, whose only rival for popularity when leaving the Oval Office (though under very different circumstances) was FDR, put a very personable face on government for many people. Before it was revealed that his administration had traded arms to Iran for the release of American hostages in Lebanon, which led to a precipitous drop in his approval ratings, Reagan, who came to Washington to trim big government, may have made it safer for a powerful central establishment. Sixty-eight percent of a CBS News–*New York Times* poll taken January 12–15, 1989, approved of his performance as president (Roberts, 1989) and said he had probably contributed to increased confidence in government. All this without an appreciable diminution in the public's appetite for more governmental programs and services. The same poll showed an increase of sixteen percentage points in Americans' trust in government since 1980 and a similar increase in preferences for bigger government. Forty-eight percent of the public favored big government on the eve of Reagan's departure from the White House, compared with 32 percent immediately before he took office in 1980.

Reagan's personal style kept his approval ratings high for most of his two terms, though the Iran-Contra scandal exposed the importance of stagehands to his presidency and caused a serious wave of doubt among Americans who had supported him. Although none of his four immediate predecessors—LBJ, Nixon, Ford, and Carter—was able to recover public esteem once it had been lost, Reagan showed an amazing resiliency. What his avuncular style may have accomplished was to help most people to worry less about what the central government was doing. In the end, the most important and ironic Reagan legacy may be that he managed to put a friendly face, one that more people felt they could trust, on national power.

Ronald Wilson Reagan may be the last American presidential candidate to win office by echoing the "limited government" thinking of political philosophers from more than two centuries ago. Once the president began his "Reagan Revolution," his political support began to evaporate, and observers charged that his administration would represent only a "detour" from the path the United States had taken toward active, interventionist national government (Reeves, 1985). What Reagan discovered was that the maintenance of popularity has its price. Whatever policy leadership he could have offered, for good or for ill, had to be blunted in the face of growing opposition to further budget cuts.

Congress, divided in the first six years of the Reagan tenure between a Democratic House and a Republican Senate, fared no better in policy leadership. Just as sensitive to the public's appetite for programs and distaste for taxes, both chambers wrestled with the desire to forward new proposals, including increased taxation, without seeming to attack a personally popular president. In the end, both institutions collapsed into a series of "no tax" feints and revelations of scandal.

Although judgments of the Reagan legacy will need more time for more balanced assessment, it is a fact that much of the New Deal–Great Society remains intact, though battered in places. Indeed, President Reagan showed willingness to use big government's muscle to cow state governments (something he chided President Carter for doing) when it came to raising the nationwide drinking age to twenty-one. He even increased the size of the institution he had sought to trim by two departments, the Cabinet. Finding the elimination of the Departments of Energy and Education more politically difficult than he had bargained in 1980, he championed the addition of a Department of Veterans' Affairs as one of his last administrative acts in office.

Ronald Reagan may have learned what his post–Great Society predecessors learned: A powerful central government is here to stay, and its beneficiaries, many of whom approved of Reagan, want it that way. As we stated in Chapter 4, there is no longer any sizable constituency in the United States committed to major, across-the-board cuts in governmental spending for a host of domestic programs. In fact, at the end of the 1980s, there is a growing public cry for more spending to address domestic problems, particularly drugs. As we showed in Chapter 5, the disinclination of baby boomers and those born after the baby boom years to be exercised by the big government question makes it highly unlikely that the immediate future will see a hue and cry for cutting the national establishment down to size.

And it is not only in domestic programs that tremendous resistance to cutting the size of government has been and will continue to be seen. Although our data analyses point to the public's preference for cuts in the military budget to address budgetary deficits, getting to specific cuts will be as difficult as in domestic spending. Most people ignore the simple fact that a large portion of the defense budget is not hardware but personnel. Every military base has its constituency, including civilian workers, retailers, and small businesses that attach themselves to the needs of those on military bases. Every weapons program has its contracts with a variety of small businesses and large factories, and the politics of local economies and jobs is a major preoccupation of any member of Congress who wants to be reelected. Many members of Congress are willing to give eloquent disquisitions on the bloated military establishment . . . until the base or weapons program in their district or state is targeted. "All politics is local," declared former Speaker of the House Tip O'Neill, and that certainly includes the military industrial complex. So long as politics remains local, no national leadership can be expected and the country will continue to drift into what a recent issue of *Time* described as "paralysis" (October 23, 1989: 27–33).

Furthermore, aside from specific benefit programs and services, enthusiasm for deregulation seems to be waning. Arguments in favor of a free market economy where competition is supposed to drive prices down and quality up, begin to lose their force in the face of higher fifteen page telephone bills, collapsing savings and loan companies, and concerns about the safety of various industries, for example, commercial airlines. The 1990s will see increasing pressure for re-regulation of particular industries and sharper criticism of the unevenness of state regulatory efforts.

CONCLUSION

The 1988 presidential election campaign underscored that the "limited government" theme had its boundaries. Both major party candidates promised a more attentive national government to a host of concerns. George Bush, the vice president who by being elected achieved what no sitting vice president since Martin Van Buren in 1836 had achieved, peppered his campaign rhetoric with promises of a "kinder, gentler nation." Bush and the Democratic candidate, Michael Dukakis, sparred over who would lead the national government to do more for the environment, day care, drug abuse, and crime. In a campaign over "valence" or consensus issues, the details of how they would accomplish their proposed programs got lost in a race to see who would develop a presidential personality that could withstand the glare of the klieg lights.

As the candidates waged a personality battle, a myriad of economic problems including the national debt, trade deficits, and a looming savings and loan crisis, all of which have the potential to limit a president's ability to deliver on campaign promises, were left orphaned. During 1988, congressional leaders averred that despite their constitutionally granted control over the purse strings, the president sets the budgetary agenda and it would take presidential action to address the host of economic woes. It is not only the public that has become fixated on presidential action. Years of divided national government, with Democrats ensconced on Capitol Hill and Republicans jealously protecting their Electoral College lock on the White House, do not promise much happiness for those banking on vigorous policy leadership.

Aaron Wildavsky asked, "Is the presidency the institution of first resort, and are presidents responsible for redressing every evil? Or is the presidency the institution of last resort, and should presidents only step in when other institutions fail to do their duty?" (1982: 52). The latter notion is related to the theory of limited presidential governance, usually associated with William Howard Taft, and has long been relegated to the pages of history. The eighteenth-, nineteenth-, and twentieth-century presidencies of Washington, Jefferson, Jackson, Polk, Lincoln, Teddy Roosevelt, and Wilson established a series of precedents that set up the vortex of power centered in the White House. Franklin Delano Roosevelt built on those precedents, expanded the presidential complex, and used what his distant cousin called the "bully pulpit" to reach out to the public, to encourage them to think of him as a friendly ear in their living rooms, no farther away than their radios. Presidents after FDR have had to live "in his shadow," as one historian notes (Leuchtenburg, 1983), and Republicans have been as sensitive to his legacy as Democrats, lest they be labeled "another Hoover." No president since 1945 has been as adept or as enthusiastic about enhancing the iconography of FDR as Reagan, though many would take issue with the accuracy of his historical knowledge (Leuchtenburg, 1983: 209–235).

If historians have pondered the long shadow cast by FDR, many observers were wondering how George Bush would handle filling the shoes of popular Ronald Reagan. Sensing that anti-governmental rhetoric will not suffice in the 1990s, George Bush has announced, "I do not hate government. . . . A government that serves the people effectively and economically, and remembers the people are its master, is a good and needed thing'' (Hoffman, 1988: 31). Even Democratic congressional leaders sense that Bush does not share the Reagan philosophy of government. One commented, ''Carter and Reagan ran against the federal system and when elected, acted opposed to the federal system. Neither really understood it. You now have a man who is the product of the federal system . . . and enjoys governing in it'' (Hoffman, 1988: 31). Not only is the forty-first president a product of the federal system, the American public and its expectations of government are as well.

President Bush accepted the centrality of presidential leadership that has become the hallmark of the modern positive state. After his election, he acknowledged, ''I know I have to take the initiative [on pressing economic problems]'' (Hoffman, 1988: 32). Bush confronts the range of public attitudes described in this book. Large portions of the public can still muster some outrage at the idea of big government, though younger citizens are far less likely to understand what all the bluster is about. Bush must deal with a public that feels less obligation to pay attention to political events and is listening to fewer news broadcasts and reading fewer newspapers. Many are even turning away from the most fundamental task of selecting the nation's leader. George Bush could not have missed that his election to the White House was the result of the lowest voter turnout since 1924. What the first year of the Bush presidency suggests is that action is not necessarily needed to heighten presidential popularity. So long as most folks feel they can trust the man in the White House, they can return safely to their daily concerns and tune Washington out. Given the trends in opinion outlined in previous chapters, it should not surprise anyone that President Bush could be charged with timidity in policy leadership and still maintain high levels of personal popularity.

The notion of being against big government has become part of a myth that political leaders will find less and less useful in rousing public sentiment to their side. Only in the face of tremendous wastefulness or perniciousness on the part of public officials might preachments against big government find a sympathetic ear among the populace. In the late 1980s, congressional hearings exposing such ethical lapses ousted a Speaker of the House and tainted officials employed by the Reagan administration's Department of Housing and Urban Development. Since these scandals touched both political parties, they are more likely to reinforce the decision many have made to ignore Washington and its inhabitants as much as possible. Politicians with their eyes on the next election and their poll results in hand know that railing against the services and benefits of big government will garner little more than suspicion from groups arguing for their entitled status.

Although big government may make all Americans queasy some of the time, it now makes only a tiny fragment nervous all of the time. With fewer and fewer exceptions, Americans have come to terms with a powerful central establishment. It may be telling that when they are informed that they have become quite comfortable "living with leviathan," most Americans today cannot begin to fathom what that means. In all likelihood, future office seekers and their public opinion advisers will quickly take into account America's willingness to accept a permanent service state. Hence, we may well have seen the last campaign centered on the theme of vastly curtailing big government. That might be yet another ironic feat historians accord to Ronald Wilson Reagan.

Appendix: Multivariate Analyses of Opinions about Big Government

This appendix has two purposes. The first section identifies the factors that discriminate between those who have opinions about Washington's power and those who do not. The second differentiates between those with opinions who think that the central establishment has not gotten too big and those who believe it is too powerful. To achieve each task, we use a statistical technique that can discriminate between two groups on several independent variables at once: multiple discriminant analysis. Originally developed for the calibration of biological classification instruments, discriminant analysis has been adopted by political scientists to assess the relations between a dichotomous dependent variable and several independent variables (Aldrich and Cnudde, 1975; Klecka, 1980; Daniels and Darcy, 1983; Sigelman, 1984; Norusis, 1985). Discriminant analysis provides two types of information: the relative strengths of the relationships between the dependent (that is, the "grouping") variable and each of the independent (that is, "discriminating" or "predictor") variables; and the overall fit of the model (Klecka, 1980; Sigelman, 1984; Norusis, 1985).

By learning which independent variables have the strongest impact on the dependent variable, even when the effects of other predictors are controlled, we can determine which factors to stress and which to ignore when discussing the dependent variable. It is also important to know how much of the variation in a dependent variable can be attributed to a relatively small set of independent variables, because that suggests the possibility that other variables need to be added to the analysis if we are to understand better all the factors influencing the dependent variable.

The data base we use is the University of Michigan's Survey Research Center–Center for Political Studies' National Election Studies between 1964 and 1988. Our findings are fairly easily summarized. Interest in public affairs, gender, education, and strength of ideological commitment are the strongest predictors in discriminating between those who have opinions about big government and those who do not. That finding pretty well confirms the conclusions of other studies of factors influencing whether or not people have opinions about public policy questions.

In discriminating between those with opinions, we found that several factors shape whether or not people think the federal government is too big. The best predictors over much of the period from 1964 to 1988 are trust in government, evaluation of the president's job performance, race, and ideology. Although important during the 1960s, when elements of the New Deal agenda still had an impact on public opinion, partisanship and socioeconomic status (SES) gradually lost their predictive power. Age, on the other hand, grew in importance during the 1980s.

These findings are basic. They tell us that if we wish to understand what molds American views about big government, we need to know whether people think an incumbent president is doing a good job or not, and whether they think the federal establishment can be trusted to do the right thing. The decline of partisanship as a predictor shows that as the GOP has come to occupy the White House more and more since the late 1960s, older partisan battles over big government have lost much of their meaning. Sometime between 1964 and the early 1970s, the New Deal era ended, and the standard factors shaping battle lines over big government eroded as well. The growing importance of age as a predictor of big government opinions also points to the necessity of looking at different birth cohorts and how they feel about a host of issues relating to government and to citizens' responsibilities toward the public sphere.

SEPARATING THOSE WITH AND WITHOUT OPINIONS

Scholars have learned much during the past fifteen years about survey respondents' no opinion/don't know answers to public policy questions (Francis and Busch, 1975; J. M. Converse, 1976–77; Schuman and Presser, 1981; Rapoport, 1979; Bishop, Oldendick, and Tuchfarber, 1980, 1982, 1983; Bishop, Tuchfarber, and Oldendick, 1986). Personal factors known to affect the likelihood of giving a no opinion/don't know response include education, age, gender, race, income, and psychological involvement in politics. Survey designers can also heighten the incidence of don't know/no opinion responses by including filters to policy questions, although the rate of increase varies with the wording of the filter, the subject of the policy question (domestic versus foreign), and the respondent's level of familiarity with and emotional involvement in the issue. In addition, Bishop and his associates (1983) claimed that filtering out don't know/no opinion responses can also alter the seeming distribution of public opinion on an issue (however, see Schuman and Presser, 1981). Adding a filter, particularly on such issues as cutting federal taxes and governmental versus private solutions to national problems, increases "the percentage in favor of the more 'conservative' alternative" (Bishop, Oldendick, and Tuchfarber, 1983: 539).

Since the item on Washington's power is not focused on any particular program, it is not surprising that the question has elicited a high rate of nonsubstantive replies. Although the issue of a powerful central government can hardly be said to be "remote" given American political culture, ideology, and partisan politics, the unspecificity of the SRC-CPS question evidently screens out some who might otherwise express an opinion. For example, even though 31 percent of the public gave nonsubstantive responses to the question of Washington's power in 1964, only 13 percent had no interest in the responsibility of government to guarantee every person a job and a good standard of living and 2 percent did not know. In 1984, although over two-fifths expressed nonsubstantive responses on Washington's power, only 12 percent had not "thought much about" government's responsibility to provide people with a job and a good living standard, and 2 percent did not know what to think. The much lower rate of nonsubstantive responses is fairly common on items dealing with specific facets of domestic policies, even when they contain rather rigorous filters.

Not only is the SRC-CPS item unfocused, the presence of a filter seems to present an especially high hurdle for some. When similarly general questions are posed without filters, a much lower percentage gives nonsubstantive responses. In addition to the question depicted in Figure 2.3, consider this item asked by Gallup in September 1981:

"Which theory of government do you favor—concentration of power in the federal government or concentration of power in the state government?" (Gallup, 1982: 235–236). One might expect that this query, which presupposes some familiarity with the theory of federalism, would elicit a high percentage of nonsubstantive responses. However, only 16 percent had no opinion. That a filter on a general question about the central government's power screens out so many people above and beyond those who volunteer no opinion when the filter is absent is testimony to the big government subject's low salience to a large and growing portion of the American public.

The goal, then, is to differentiate those giving nonsubstantive responses to the item about Washington's power from those with opinions. Although much of the research on nonsubstantive responses has relied on percentage analysis, Francis and Busch (1975) use ordinary least squares (OLS) regression, and Jean Converse (1976–77) employs multiple classification analysis (MCA). Multiple discriminant analysis is appropriate since we wish to discover those factors that determine whether or not people hold opinions on the central government's power.

In this section and the next, we report standardized canonical coefficients (r^*), as well as the unstandardized discriminant function coefficients for each discriminator. We also report the final value of Wilks's *lambda* (also called the U statistic), which can be used to determine the proportion of the total variance in the discriminant scores not accounted for by differences among groups (Norusis, 1985). Although Wilks's *lambda* tells little about the effectiveness of the discriminant function in classifying cases, it does test the null hypothesis that the population means are identical. To test the model's overall goodness-of-fit, we report the percentage of grouped cases correctly classified by the discriminant function, although this statistic must be further interpreted. When subtracted from 1.0, Wilks's *lambda* can also be used to judge the overall goodness-of-fit of the discriminant model.

Respondents who gave nonsubstantive responses (no interest, no opinion, or don't know) to the question of Washington's power were coded as 0 and those with an opinion were scored 1. Each of the discriminating variables was either a dichotomy (coded 0 and 1) or coded as close as possible to an interval-level scale. The following were used as discriminating variables: age, gender, race (black or white), region (non-South or South), education (0 years of formal schooling to 17 or more years), family income (coded to the SRC-CPS's category midpoint), a five-category measure of strength of partisanship (from apolitical or other party to strong partisan), an opinion thermometer–based measure of the strength of ideological orientation,[1] and, for each year except 1970, a five-point political apathy index, which is a linear combination of general political interest and interest in the election campaign (S. E. Bennett, 1986). In 1970, only the item on campaign interest was available.

In SPSSX, the normal default is listwise deletion of cases with missing data, although an option exists that can substitute the predictors' means for purposes of classification only (Norusis, 1985). For purposes of discriminating between those with and without opinions, except in 1972 and 1984, the analyses are performed on the overwhelming majority of cases. Hence, missing data present no problem and can be ignored. In 1972 and 1984, there is a problem. In 1972, the federal government's power question was asked only of respondents to Form 2 of the CPS's questionnaire, which provides only 1,333 cases with which to work. In 1984, the question was asked of only the half-sample interviewed in person after the election, or 1,004 cases. In both years, the temptation is to substitute variable means for missing data to build up the number of cases. We have not "bitten the apple," for enough cases remain to make the analyses meaningful. When the concern is with distinguishing those with opinions who take different "sides," however, the problem of missing data must be considered anew.

Table A.1 presents the results of the multiple discriminant analyses of those with and without opinions on Washington's power between 1964 and 1988. Basically three things can be said. For the most part, the results confirm what earlier studies have found about the factors related to people's propensities for giving nonsubstantive responses on domestic public policy questions. Those who are most psychologically involved in public affairs—college graduates, men, strong ideologues, whites, the well-to-do, and the elderly—are most likely to have had an opinion on Washington's power over the past twenty-five years. Among the best discriminators are political interest, gender, education, and, to a slightly lesser degree, strength of ideology. Of lesser import but still consistently retained in the discriminant models are race, region, and age.

Thus far, the data in Table A.1 offer little surprise and make a good deal of sense. People who are more emotionally involved in public affairs use more mass media for political information and are much better informed (S. E. Bennett, 1986). We should expect, therefore, that those who are more politically interested would also be more likely to have opinions on the issue of government's power. Rapoport (1985) found girls and their mothers more likely to have no opinions on questions of public policy, and our data replicate his. Almond and Verba (1963: 379–382) noted the importance of education for political involvement and participation, and the evidence in Table A.1 is in keeping with their observations. Given the role of the federal government in forcing changes in race relations in the United States over the past three decades, it is not surprising that race as well as region would play a role in nonsubstantive responses about Washington's power. The evidence also strongly supports Glenn's (1969) contention that the elderly are not more likely to express no opinion on policy issues. Finally, given the importance attached by liberals and conservatives to the federal government's role, eyebrows should hardly rise when it is found, at least in the early going, that strong ideologues are consistently less likely than nonideologues to express nonsubstantive responses.

There is at least one surprise in the table. Given the partisan division on Washington's power, with Democrats emphasizing the central government and Republicans the states (Kessel, 1972), one would have expected strong partisans, who are more likely to be aware of and to endorse the party "line," to be more opinionated on this issue than independents and/or weak identifiers. But clearly this is not the case. The only time strength of partisanship emerges as even a minor predictor (1968) finds an inverse relation: Stronger supporters were more likely to have no opinion than independents and weak supporters.

There are some changes over the years. One is that the effect of age has grown considerably. In the 1960s and 1970s, age was either unimportant or only a minor discriminator. In the 1980s, however, it became one of the top three predictors of nonsubstantive responses. As we noted in Chapters 2 and 5, individuals who have come of age lately, after battles over the federal government's expansion have long since ended, may find the issue unimportant and thus are content either to avoid the question entirely or to be disinclined to upset the status quo.

Another change is the lessened importance in the 1980s of ideology. Although among the stronger predictors in 1964—when Goldwater tried to bring the issue of Washington's power to the center of the political agenda—by the 1980s, strength of ideological commitment was either of no importance or only a minor factor in nonsubstantive responses. Since Reagan sought to reinstill the question with both partisan and ideological vigor, the flaccidity of ideology as a discriminator of no opinion is interesting.

There is one other noteworthy change. In the 1960s, southerners were more likely to have opinions about Washington's power—not surprising, given that the "racial reorientation" of American politics (Carmines and Stimson, 1989) was occurring at the time. This pattern held true until 1976, when those living outside the South were less

Table A.1 Discriminating between Those with and without Opinions on the Federal Government's Power, for various years, 1964–1988

Variable[a]	Unstandardized Canonical Discriminant Function Coefficient	Standardized Canonical Discriminant Function Coefficient
1964		
Political apathy	0.498	0.552
Education	0.138	0.437
Gender	0.670	0.329
Ideology[b]	0.014	0.319
Region	0.310	0.148
Race	0.448	0.132
Age	0.007	0.111
Wilks's *lambda* = 0.858	Percentage of cases correctly classified = 66.71	(N = 1,391)
1966		
Political apathy	0.560	0.681
Education	0.065	0.210
Gender	0.524	0.258
Race	0.813	0.241
Ideology[b]	0.011	0.248
Family income	0.024	0.132
Region	0.200	0.091
Wilks's *lambda* = 0.859	Percentage of cases correctly classified = 66.98	(N = 1,183)
1968		
Political apathy	0.506	0.579
Gender	0.949	0.463
Race	1.143	0.329
Education	0.085	0.269
Ideology[b]	0.009	0.188
Partisanship[c]	− 0.144	− 0.137
Wilks's *lambda* = 0.869	Percentage of cases correctly classified = 66.45	(N = 1,223)
1970		
Campaign interest	0.482	0.682
Gender	0.893	0.442
Education	0.137	0.415
Region	0.687	0.324
Race	0.396	0.118
Wilks's *lambda* = 0.930	Percentage of cases correctly classified = 63.79	(N = 1,264)
1972		
Political apathy	0.522	0.579
Family income	0.049	0.402
Gender	0.673	0.333

Table A.1, *continued*

Variable[a]	Unstandardized Canonical Discriminant Function Coefficient	Standardized Canonical Discriminant Function Coefficient
Ideology[b]	0.008	0.181
Region	0.477	0.224
Education	0.082	0.237
Age	0.014	0.230
Partisanship[c]	−0.140	−0.136
Wilks's *lambda* = 0.903	Percentage of cases correctly classified = 63.78	(N = 831)

1976		
Political apathy	0.505	0.568
Gender	0.788	0.386
Education	0.107	0.301
Ideology[b]	0.013	0.278
Family income	0.017	0.198
Race	0.661	0.183
Region	−0.214	−0.098
Wilks's *lambda* = 0.869	Percentage of cases correctly classified = 67.34	(N = 1,919)

1978		
Political apathy	0.334	0.373
Ideology[d]	0.331	0.369
Gender	0.844	0.436
Education	0.128	0.348
Race	1.007	0.259
Age	0.013	0.194
Family income	0.009	0.111
Region	0.200	0.097
Wilks's *lambda* = 0.831	Percentage of cases correctly classified = 68.79	(N = 1,457)

1980		
Political apathy	0.454	0.492
Gender	0.903	0.443
Age	0.027	0.461
Education	0.143	0.356
Race	1.014	0.274
Wilks's *lambda* = 0.882	Percentage of cases correctly classified = 64.36	(N = 1,329)

1984		
Political apathy	0.564	0.609
Gender	0.631	0.312
Age	0.023	0.381
Education	0.126	0.307
Region	−0.303	−0.139

Table A.1, *continued*

Variable[a]	Unstandardized Canonical Discriminant Function Coefficient	Standardized Canonical Discriminant Function Coefficient
Ideology[b]	0.009	0.167
Race	0.445	0.132
Wilks's *lambda* = 0.864	Percentage of cases correctly classified = 65.07	(N = 752)

1988		
Political apathy	0.495	0.525
Gender	0.865	0.424
Education	0.158	0.438
Age	0.016	0.271
Race	0.427	0.133
Ideology[b]	0.083	0.104
Wilks's *lambda* = 0.890	Percentage of cases correctly classified = 62.66	(N = 1,516)

Source: Adapted from the University of Michigan's Survey Research Center–Center for Political Studies' National Election Studies.

[a]All variables are significant at less than .0001.

[b]Absolute difference between opinion-thermometer (OT) rating of liberals minus OT rating of conservatives.

[c]Ranges from apoliticals to strong party identifiers.

[d]Recoded self-placement on a measure of ideology; new variable ranges from "haven't thought much about this" to self-placement at scale positions 1 to 7.

likely to express nonsubstantive responses. It would have been reasonable to have expected the presence of the first southerner on a national ticket since the end of the Civil War to have stimulated greater involvement by southerners in the political fray. But, at least on the question of the national government's power, such was not the case. In 1978, with one of their own in the White House, southerners were again more likely to have opinions on the question. However, in the 1980s, either region was unimportant or nonsoutherners were more likely to hold opinions. Although these changes are significant, the central message of Table A.1 remains the constancy with which a few discriminating variables affect the likelihood of nonsubstantive responses being expressed about the central government's power.

The final point in the table is the modest discriminatory capacity of the discriminant functions. On average, just about two-thirds of the grouped cases are correctly classified. That figure might, at first blush, look good to students of surveys used to "explaining" only a fraction of the percentage of variance with a multivariate OLS regression equation, but the results of the discriminant analysis algorithm tend to exaggerate the model's goodness-of-fit (Klecka, 1980). There is disagreement on how best to deflate the classification results statistic (Grofman, 1978; Klecka, 1980; Daniels and Darcy, 1983; Sigelman, 1984). Resolution of the debate is beyond our scope. Suffice it to say that much of the same evidence can be obtained by subtracting the value of the U statistic in each segment of the table from 1.0. The resulting figure is an approximation to the total variance in the grouping variable accounted for by the combined effects of the discriminating variables and is analogous to the multiple coefficient of determination (R^2) produced by OLS regression. This done, as in 1984, the six predictors retained in the discriminant model together "explain" 13.6 percent of the variance in nonsubstantive responses on Washington's power. Similarly unimpressive results occur in each of the other nine years. For example, the final year, 1988, shows only 11 percent of explained variance.

Researchers confronted by such modest results, especially when a variety of discriminating factors known to shape the likelihood of expressing nonsubstantive responses on other domestic policy questions are included in the models, might justifiably throw up their hands in defeat. To do so, however, may be premature. Sometimes "nonfindings" have significance. As we stated, there are several reasons why the issue of the national government's role in American society and politics should be salient for a large portion of the population. However, we also pointed out (Figure 2.1) the large percentage of nonsubstantive responses on the question over the two decades. Now we know as well that factors thought to be important predictors of nonsubstantive responses in general are only modest discriminators of nonsubstantive responses on Washington's power. This could mean that the big government issue carries a much different connotation at the grass-roots level than at the elite level, as Philip Converse (1964) contends is the case for other public policy questions.

Perhaps the most important conclusion in Table A.1 is that expression of nonsubstantive responses on the question of Washington's power is not randomly distributed throughout the public. Rather, those with opinions tend to be among the most politically aware—the well-educated and well-heeled, whites, the middle-aged and elderly, and, to a lesser extent now than formerly, the ideologically committed. Moreover, as the percentage of the public giving nonsubstantive responses has increased in the late 1970s and 1980s, it has become more important to take into account the skewing of the expression of nonsubstantive responses on the issue. If Bishop and his associates (1983) are correct, the fact that those with opinions on the issue of the central government's power do not constitute an unbiased subset of the total public could significantly affect the distribution of views expressed on the issue, a point that has been ignored or overlooked by previous researchers.

Discovery of those most likely to have opinions about big government provides some clues about why some express nonsubstantive responses and others do not, but additional evidence is needed for a more complete explanation. What we need to know is whether nonsubstantive responses on the big government question is a special case or is correlated with nonsubstantive responses on other policy questions. To find out, we cross-indexed the governmental power item with a series of domestic and foreign policy questions in 1964, 1972, 1980, 1984, and 1988. For this set of analyses, all items were dichotomized: those with opinons and those without opinions.

In each year, nonsubstantive responses on the big government question reflect a similar tendency on other domestic and foreign policy issues. On domestic questions, there is a close relationship between nonsubstantive responses on the big government issue and those on New Deal–era questions involving government's role in the economy (governmental guarantee of jobs and living standards, 1964; governmental spending for social services, 1988), as well as responses on some of the issues that have arisen in the past two decades (government's role in dealing with industrial pollution, 1972; women's role in the economy and government, 1972, 1984, and 1988). Throughout, nonsubstantive responses on racial issues are also closely related to nonsubstantive responses on big government (governmental involvement in school integration, 1964; government helping blacks get equal access to jobs, 1964 and 1972; governmental aid to minorities, 1980, 1984, and 1988). The foreign policy issues run the gamut: foreign aid (1964), Vietnam (1972), and U.S. relations with the Soviet Union (1964, 1980, 1984, and 1988). In short, the same factors that account for nonsubstantive responses on other policy questions seem to underlie failure to express opinions about big government.

DIFFERENTIATING AMONG OPINIONS ON THE POWER OF THE CENTRAL GOVERNMENT

Since this section's goal is to determine the factors that distinguish those with opinions who feel Washington has become too powerful from those who believe it has not, discriminant analysis is again appropriate. The key question is determining which discriminating variables to include in the models. Given the federal government's role during the past twenty-five years in struggles relating to these variables, some are obvious: party identification, ideology, race, region, socioeconomic status (here tapped by education and family income), gender, and age.[2] Since Maddox and Lilie (1984: 42) believe that opinions on Washington's power tap "the public's response to taxes, regulation, government spending, and other economic issues," we also include an item asking the respondent to assess recent trends in his or her family's financial situation. Presumably, those who have been experiencing a downturn in financial fortunes would have different views about governmental intervention in the economy than those who think that lately they have been doing better.

Given the substance of the question, we also include two components of Americans' basic political orientations: trust in government and perceptions of governmental responsiveness.[3] Those who are cynical about government and think it does not respond to public opinion might be more likely to believe that the central government is too powerful. When data are available, we also include assessment of the incumbent president's performance in office.[4] Recent research indicates a connection between the public's assessment of presidential performance and trust in government (A. H. Miller, 1983; Lipset, 1985; Citrin and Green, 1986; Lipset and Schneider, 1987). It would also be reasonable to expect that the public's perception of how well a president is performing his job is related to its views on the amount of power the central government exercises. These variables are usually present on the SRC-CPS data sets over the years covered here.

Although the putative discriminatory variables plumb a wide range of social and psychological factors that allegedly affect opinions about the national government's role in society and politics, some important factors are left out. For example, Lipset (1979) posits a continuing tension in American political culture between egalitarianism, which inclines people toward support of governmental efforts to reduce inequality, and individualism, which leads to opposition to the expansion of governmental power. If it were possible to tap at least some element of an egalitarian ethic, such as sympathy for the poor or advocacy of greater social equality, would it be a significant predictor of opinions about Washington's power? Also, as we noted, the question on the federal government's power is unfocused. If a set of items dealing with various specific grants of power to the national government could be found, would opinions on them add substantially to comprehension of opinions on the more general item? Finally, if items dealing with feelings about the proper levels of federal spending for a variety of programs were tapped, how well would they relate to opinions about the federal establishment's power?

None of these is available on SRC-CPS's questionnaires prior to the 1980s. However, there are some variables available on a limited basis. In 1972, 1976, 1984, and 1988, the

CPS asked a series of questions about why some people are poor and others not and about equality of opportunity in the United States. Although the number and content of the questions varied from year to year, there was sufficient overlap for them to be profitably used as indicators of an egalitarian ethic. Also, in 1976, the CPS asked six items probing approval or disapproval of granting specific powers to the federal government. In 1984, the CPS asked ten items dealing with opinions about whether governmental spending for specific programs was "too little," "about right," or "too much." In 1988, a similar measure containing eight items about spending on domestic programs was entered.

The strategy for dealing with each set of items is the same. Each time a set was available, we performed a principal components factor analysis with orthogonal rotation that included the entire set. Variables loading on the first dimension at or above .35 were summed to create a scale; the contribution of each was weighted by its factor loading. This approach has its strengths and weaknesses. Chief among the latter is that with the egalitarianism measure in 1972, 1976, 1984, and 1988, different items composed it each time. This is more than offset by the scale's being unidimensional at each data point and sensitive to the contribution of its components to the underlying continuum.

Unlike the last section, missing data are a potentially serious problem here. Not only are 30 to 48 percent of the cases excluded by giving nonsubstantive responses on Washington's power, SPSSX's DISCRIMINANT program deletes cases with missing data on the discriminatory variables listwise, which often means the analysis is performed on a relatively small subset of cases.

There are several strategies for dealing with this situation. One is to replace the cases with missing data on each variable with the mean score. Given the very large percentage of nonsubstantive responses on the issue of Washington's power, one would have little confidence in any data produced this way. For issue items, Rapoport (1979) recommends random replacement of cases giving nonsubstantive responses. Again, given the proportions of the samples without opinions, interpretation would be dubious. More preferable would be to replace missing data with the mean only for the discriminating variables. Then the number of cases in each analysis would diminish only by those giving nonsubstantive responses on the grouping variable.

We prefer to report results of analyses in which missing data were not replaced, recognizing the implications of reduction in the number of cases upon which the data are computed. In 1964, 1972, 1984, and 1988, the analyses were redone in which missing data on the predictors were replaced by variable means. In each instance, no major substantive revisions in the initial findings (when missing data were not replaced) are required. Still, it is wise to temper conclusions somewhat when they stem from only a portion of the samples.

Table A.2 presents the results of the multiple discriminant analyses of opinions on the power of the federal government. Several important results can be derived from these data. Over the twenty-four years covered here, opinions about Washington's power reflect several factors and do not hinge upon either a single variable or even a small subset of variables. Hence, interpretations of opinions on this item as reflecting a single underlying dimension (Maddox and Lilie, 1984), or even a couple of dimensions (Nie, with Andersen, 1974; Nie, Verba, and Petrocik, 1979), are overly simplistic. As might be expected with an unfocused item that ties into elements of political culture, partisanship, and ideology, a wide variety of factors underlie opinions on the federal government's power.

Moreover, several of the factors discriminating among opinions on the issue are retained in the discriminant functions over all, or nearly all, of the twenty-four years: trust in government, race, ideology, and, to a lesser extent, partisanship and socioeconomic status. In addition, we suspect that had the item been available before 1968,

Table A.2 Discriminating among Those with Different Opinions on the Federal Government's Power, for various years, 1964–1988

Variable[a]	Unstandardized Canonical Discriminant Function Coefficient	Standardized Canonical Discriminant Function Coefficient
1964		
Party identification	0.272	0.557
Trust in government	0.464	0.495
Race	1.124	0.312
Region	0.758	0.362
Ideology[b]	− 0.007	− 0.208
Education	0.060	0.184
Family income	0.025	0.144
External political efficacy	− 0.116	− 0.085
Gender	0.153	0.077
Wilks's *lambda* = 0.714	Percentage of cases correctly classified = 74.94	(N = 858)
1966		
Party identification	0.260	0.511
Trust in government	0.322	0.361
Ideology[b]	0.013	0.383
Region	0.812	0.366
Race	1.009	0.263
Age	0.011	0.173
External political efficacy	− 0.147	− 0.117
Wilks's *lambda* = 0.751	Percentage of cases correctly classified = 72.54	(N = 766)
1968		
Presidential approval	0.354	0.359
Party identification	0.196	0.390
Trust in government	0.327	0.347
Race	1.282	0.321
Ideology[b]	− 0.009	− 0.266
Region	0.553	0.255
Gender	0.377	0.188
Education	0.045	0.141
Wilks's *lambda* = 0.811	Percentage of cases correctly classified = 69.32	(N = 811)
1970		
Trust in government	0.838	0.859
Race	1.377	0.492
Party identification	0.114	0.229
Age	0.013	0.210
Education	0.066	0.203
Wilks's *lambda* = 0.879	Percentage of cases correctly classified = 64.79	(N = 493)

Table A.2, *continued*

Variable[a]	Unstandardized Canonical Discriminant Function Coefficient	Standardized Canonical Discriminant Function Coefficient
1972		
Trust in government	0.677	0.745
Race	1.524	0.422
Region	0.767	0.361
Age	−0.012	−0.209
Party identification	0.139	0.281
Egalitarianism	0.210	0.285
Family income	0.025	0.223
External political efficacy	−0.256	−0.210
Wilks's *lambda* = 0.913 Percentage of cases correctly classified = 62.22 (N = 586)		
1976		
Trust in government	0.622	0.587
Ideology[b]	−0.014	−0.410
Race	1.161	0.301
Governmental powers scale	0.145	0.259
External political efficacy	−0.333	−0.277
Party identification	0.144	0.281
Region	0.617	0.277
Family income	0.016	0.196
Gender	0.357	0.196
Age	−0.006	−0.094
Wilks's *lambda* = 0.855 Percentage of cases correctly classified = 66.64 (N = 1,267)		
1978		
Trust in government	0.666	0.625
Party identification	0.122	0.229
Race	1.743	0.348
Presidential approval	0.358	0.308
Family economic situation	−0.165	−0.285
External political efficacy	−0.299	−0.299
Family income	0.009	0.111
Ideology[c]	0.102	0.197
Wilks's *lambda* = 0.851 Percentage of cases correctly classified = 68.42 (N = 750)		
1980		
Ideology[b]	−0.013	−0.391
Presidential approval	0.140	0.198
Trust in government	0.027	0.374
Race	0.143	0.251
Party identification	1.014	0.301
Age	0.017	0.270

Table A.2, *continued*

Variable[a]	Unstandardized Canonical Discriminant Function Coefficient	Standardized Canonical Discriminant Function Coefficient
Gender	0.366	0.183
Education	0.077	0.194
Family economic situation	0.098	0.171
Wilks's *lambda* = 0.879 Percentage of cases correctly classified = 68.45 (N = 626)		

1984		
Trust in government	0.709	0.699
Egalitarianism	− 0.307	− 0.402
Governmental spending scale	0.605	0.402
Age	0.015	0.235
Family income	− 0.013	− 0.269
Presidential approval	0.253	0.412
Ideology[b]	− 0.010	− 0.297
Race	0.889	0.235
Wilks's *lambda* = .796 Percentage of cases correctly classified = 68.62 (N = 367)		

1988		
Trust in government	0.883	0.871
Ideology	0.406	0.423
Gender	0.632	0.314
Race	0.984	0.282
Party identification	− 0.116	− 0.247
Education	0.057	0.155
Presidential approval	0.163	0.112
Wilks's *lambda* = 0.902 Percentage of cases correctly classified = 64.22 (N = 666)		

Source: Adapted from the University of Michigan's Survey Research Center–Center for Political Studies' National Election Studies.

[a]All variables are significant at less than 0.0001.
[b]Difference between opinion-thermometer (OT) rating of liberals minus OT rating of conservatives.
[c]Self-placement on a seven-point measure of ideology.

assessment of the incumbent president's performance would also have been a core predictor over the two decades. Opinions about Washington's power should be understood as reflecting a composite of different, and sometimes divergent, tendencies.

Most important among the discriminators over the long haul are trust in government and, if we may infer from the period before the item appeared on the questionnaire, assessment of the president's job performance, two dispositions already known to be related.[5] That opinions about Washington's power resonate with assessment of presidential job performance and political trust may explain why, under Reagan, both cynicism (A. H. Miller, 1983; Lipset, 1985; Citrin and Green, 1986; Lipset and Schneider, 1987) and wariness about Washington's power declined. It would also go a long way toward accounting for the rise between 1966 and 1980 in the percentage of the public believing that the central government had become too strong. A series of poor performances by presidents on a variety of issues (race relations, Vietnam, Watergate, the economy) gave rise to increasing cynicism, which in turn spurred progressively negative views of the federal government's power. Unfortunately, given that we have only cross-sectional survey data, it is not possible to sort out the causal ordering of the relationships.

There are also some important changes in the relative potency of the predictors over the years. In 1964, in addition to reflecting trust, opinions about Washington's power reflected partisan, ideological, racial (and, naturally, regional), and SES divisions in American politics. One sees in the data the major political battles of the day: Republicans, conservatives, whites, and southerners believed government was overgrown, while Democrats, liberals, blacks, and nonsoutherners demurred. At a considerably reduced level, one also sees the residue of the class struggles of the 1930s over expanded intervention by the central government in the nation's economic life. In the main, then, the 1964 data fit within the interpretation offered by Nie and his associates. Moreover, the pattern holds up fairly well through the rest of the 1960s, again in accord with Nie and his colleagues' view.

Still, "times were a-changing," although not in the way suggested by Nie and his associates. As early as 1970, with LBJ out of 1600 Pennsylvania Avenue and Nixon in, trust in government had become by far the strongest discriminator, followed by race and, at much weaker levels, partisanship and SES. The 1972 data show a similar pattern. What is significant is that in neither year is ideology, which Nie and his associates relied upon to interpret changes in opinions about Washington's power, a significant predictor. Perhaps what Nie et al. took to reflect increased ideological complexity of the issue of Washington's power was actually due to election of a Republican president and to growing discontent with government's performance at home and abroad. (Unfortunately, the question on assessment of presidential performance was not asked in 1970 and was only on Form 1 of the 1972 questionnaire.)

Whatever the reason, one of the more important discoveries in Table A.2 is the growing weakness after 1968 of party identification as a predictor of opinions about Washington's power. The only time thereafter that partisanship is entered early in the discriminant models, albeit at reduced potency, is 1978, when Carter was president. This supports our belief that replacement of a Democratic president by a Republican accounts for much of what Nie and his colleagues took to be growing ideological complexity. Given the uses put to big government under Republicans Nixon and Reagan, perhaps it is not surprising that the public has had increasing trouble deciding which party favors a stronger central government. In 1964, 36 percent of the public said the Democrats were more likely to favor a stronger central government, 8 percent picked the Republicans, 19 percent thought it would not make any difference, 7 percent did not know, and the rest gave nonsubstantive responses. By 1972, only 16 percent picked the Democrats, 18 percent chose the Republicans, 32 percent said it would not make any difference, 5 percent did not know, and 29 percent gave nonsubstantive responses. Finally, in 1988, 15 percent still thought the Democratic party would be more for a stronger national establishment, 14 percent said the Republicans would be, 24 percent thought it would make no difference, 1 percent did not know, and 46 percent gave no opinion. Because many people tend to support what they think is their party's position on policy questions, it is not surprising that as it became less and less obvious where the parties stood on Washington's power, partisanship was a less potent predictor of opinions. Of course, weakened attachments to the parties could have a similar result.

Another significant change over the years is the growing potency of age, especially in the 1980s. Two factors may account for this. One is the arrival on the national agenda of age-related issues: Social Security, Medicare, Medicaid, and so on. Much has been made lately in the mass media about a potential generational polarization, as young people are expected to shoulder increased financial burdens to pay for benefits for the elderly. How ironic, then, to discover in the 1980s that the elderly were more likely than the young to believe that the federal government had become too strong. Perhaps, as time passed, the old battles over expanded government lost their relevance to a generation that did not experience them, which explains the much higher rates of nonsubstantive responses among the young in the 1980s, and why among the young with opinions, strong central government has become more acceptable. The elderly, who can recall another era, still tend to harken to older symbolic cues.

Another interesting finding is that evaluations of personal and family financial fortunes are rarely important predictors of opinions on the issue of big government. The exceptions—1978 and 1980—happen to have been at the worst moments for the American economy between 1964 and 1984. Evidently, only when the economy is suffering both high unemployment and double-digit inflation do personal assessments of family financial trends affect opinions about the power of the national government.

There is one striking reversal in the sign of the discriminant function coefficients. In the 1960s, reflecting the battles of the 1930s and those still going on over governmental intervention in the economy, the well-to-do were more likely to view Washington as too powerful. This pattern held as recently as 1978. However, in 1984 and 1988, the wealthy were less likely to say that government was too strong. Critics of the Reagan administration charge that it has been most sensitive to the interests of the wealthy. Whether this is true is, for our purposes, moot. It is interesting, however, that under Reagan, the well-off became less fearful of the central government.

It is also important to note that when the measures are available, opinions about grants of specific powers to the federal government (1976), views about the proper levels of federal spending for various programs (1984), and egalitarian orientations (1972 and 1984) are modest discriminators of views about Washington's power. However, in 1976 and 1988, the egalitarianism scale was not retained in the discriminant model. Also, none of these dispositions approaches the predictive potency of trust in government.

Finally, a word is in order concerning the goodness-of-fit of the discriminant models. Taken together, the predictors can correctly classify somewhere from 75 percent (1964) to 62 percent (1972) of the grouped cases. As we pointed out, the actual successes of the discriminant models are a good deal less. Judged by the result of subtracting Wilks's *lambda* from 1.0, the models explain from just under 29 percent to slightly under 9 percent of the variance in opinions about the federal government. Equally important, classificatory power, once weakened, never returned to its 1964 level. The factors which divided opinions in the mid-1960s did not have the same capacity in the 1980s. What may have been, as late as the end of the 1960s, primarily a "position" issue became essentially a "valence" issue in the 1980s (Stokes, 1966).

This finding supports our contention that opinions about the central government's power in the abstract mean less and less, and that to understand how Americans feel about big government, it is necessary also to look at views on the myriad of specific programs that today make up the modern service state. Americans may from time to time tell pollsters they think the central establishment is too big, too intrusive, and even a potential threat at some unspecified future date. But many of these same people also expect their government to provide the services that are the heart of a large national establishment. Americans have come to terms with big government.

Notes

CHAPTER 1. A HISTORY OF AMBIVALENCE

1. On the average, Americans sixty-five to seventy-five can claim assets of $65,000, more than twice the national average. In the same age group, 77 percent own their own homes and 80 percent of these homeowners have paid off mortgages (*National Journal,* July 13, 1985: 1648).

CHAPTER 2. CHANGING VIEWS
ABOUT BIG GOVERNMENT, 1935–1989

1. How much confidence should be placed in public opinion data from the 1930s and 1940s, when the science of polling was in its infancy? Certainly, techniques for drawing samples were much cruder than they are today. The typical 1930s-1940s poll, for example, relied heavily on quota sampling techniques. The best surveys today rely strictly on probability methods to identify potential respondents. Some excellent nontechnical treatments of survey methods include Asher (1988), Bradburn and Sudman (1988), Crespi (1989), and Gallup (1972). For a good nontechnical description of polls in the early years, see Gallup and Rae (1940). In addition, pollsters knew less about how to construct unbiased questionnaires, although the best survey researchers knew a good deal more about the intricacies of questionnaire design than is sometimes appreciated today (see, for example, Cantril, 1944: Part 1). All things considered, it is best to use early polls with some caution. Still, scholars such as Erikson (1976) and Page and Shapiro (1982, 1983, and 1987) have shown that data from the early period of polling can shed valuable light on trends in public opinion.

2. The SRC-CPS data were released by the Inter-University Consortium for Political and Social Research to the University of Cincinnati's Behavioral Sciences Laboratory (BSL). Several Gallup polls were released to the BSL by the Roper Center for Public Opinion Research at the University of Connecticut, Storrs. Gallup's 1987 poll for the *Times Mirror* company was released directly to us by the Gallup organization. We are solely responsible for all analyses and interpretations.

3. Although there seems to be consensus that opinions about civil rights for blacks have changed substantially (see, for example, Carmines and Stimson, 1989; Schuman, Steeh,

and Bobo, 1985), the evidence of a rightward drift in public opinion and of increasing civil libertarianism is disputed (on the former, see Ferguson and Rogers, 1986; on the latter, see Sullivan, Piereson, and Marcus, 1982: Chap. 3).

4. Another potential result of an unfiltered Gallup question versus a filtered SRC-CPS one was uncovered by Bishop and his associates (1983: 539). After looking at the effects of adding filters to the substantive distributions on domestic policy issues, these researchers concluded that "the effect of using a filter question is to increase the percentage in favor of the more 'conservative' alternative." A comparison of the distributions in Figures 2.1 and 2.2 indicates that it is not a major problem here. On two of the three occasions when the SRC-CPS and Gallup asked their versions of the governmental power question in the same year (1964 and 1978), the former turned up a slightly larger percentage that thought government had become too strong. In 1984, the Gallup version identified a few more people worried about Washington having too much power. On each occasion, moreover, the differences were small (± 3–5 percent). In short, the unfiltered Gallup question does not seriously underestimate the percentage of the public subscribing to the belief that the central government has gotten too big.

5. Some confirmation of this comes from the Gallup item on big government, business, and labor as a threat to the nation. In August 1968, Republicans were slightly more likely than Democrats to pick big government as the most likely future threat (48 percent versus 41 percent; Gallup, 1973: 2154); in May 1979, they were even more likely to feel threatened by it (50 percent versus 36 percent; Gallup, 1980: 189). But by May 1981, big government was seen as the most likely threat by the same percentage of Democrats and Republicans (46 percent; Gallup, 1982: 218).

CHAPTER 3. THE TANGLED WEB OF IDEOLOGY

1. A recent study goes even further, claiming that "while Americans may respond to the *terms* 'liberal' and 'conservative,' these expressions have not only lost much of their traditional meaning, they do not even remotely come close to defining the nature of American public opinion" (*Times Mirror*, 1987: 1). Based on a 1987 Gallup poll, this study claims there are eleven distinct groups in the American public.

2. The obvious question is whether subtracting opinion thermometer ratings of conservatives from those of liberals constitutes a reliable and valid measure of ideology. For one thing, opinion thermometer ratings tend to be inflated—the positivity bias noted in evaluating political figures also extends to many political groups (Sears and Whitney, 1973). This means that ratings of liberals and conservatives are not as negatively correlated as one might imagine. In 1964 and 1966, for example, the Pearsonian correlation coefficient for the OT ratings of liberals and conservatives was only $r = -.10$. (Pearson's r measures the strength of the relationship between two interval-level variables. If its value is .0, there is no relationship; if it is 1.0, the relationship is perfect. It can be positive if high scores on variable 1 go with high scores on variable 2, or negative if high scores on variable 1 go with low scores on variable 2.) In 1968 and 1970, the correlations sagged to $-.04$ and $-.05$. Between 1972 and 1980, the correlations ranged from $-.22$ to $-.29$. However, in 1984 and 1986, they decreased to $-.06$ and $-.12$. In 1988, the correlation increased slightly to $-.19$. Although correlations as low as these suggest a reliability problem, there is a robust association between the OT-derived measure and the self-identification measure introduced by the CPS in 1972. Between 1972 and 1988, the correlations ranged from $r = .53$ to $.63$, and they averaged .59 over the seven observations. Hence, the OT-based measure of ideology can be used as a surrogate for the self-placement scale.

3. Extreme liberals are those who placed liberals 50 to 100 degrees warmer on the opinion thermometer than conservatives. Liberals rated liberals 10 to 49 degrees warmer than they rated conservatives. Moderates are those whose ranking of liberals and conservatives differed by 9 degrees or less. Conservatives rated conservatives 10 to 49 degrees warmer than they rated liberals. Extreme conservatives rated conservatives 50 to 100 degrees warmer than they rated liberals.

4. Missing data in key years complicate any attempt to uncover the meaning behind shifts in the relation between ideology and opinions about big government. The CPS did not ask the standard big government question in 1974, 1982, or 1986, and it did not include the OT ratings of liberals and conservatives in 1978. Absence of the big government item from CPS questionnaires in 1974, 1982, and 1986 prevents clear-cut testing of Nie et al.'s thesis about shifts in the meaning assigned by the public to the SRC-CPS's big government question. Still, some items are available in 1974 and 1982, and NORC asked a version of an old Gallup question on its 1985 GSS. At the appropriate point, each will be described.

5. Kendall's tau-c measures association for two ordinal level variables in a table having an unequal number of rows and columns. Tau-c ranges from -1.0 (indicating a perfect negative relationship), .0 (indicating complete independence), and 1.0 (indicating a perfect positive relationship).

6. Those who placed themselves at points 1–3 were classified as liberals, those at point 4 were considered moderates, and those choosing points 5–7 were labeled conservatives.

7. Liberals are those who rate liberals at least 10 degrees warmer than they rate conservatives on the opinion thermometer, conservatives rate conservatives at least 10 degrees warmer than they rate liberals, and moderates rate conservatives and liberals within 9 degrees of each other. Democrats include strong and weak identifiers and those who say they are independent but lean toward the Democratic party. Republicans include strong and weak partisans and independents who lean toward the GOP. Independents are those with no partisan leanings.

8. Liberals placed themselves at points 1–3 on the ideological scale, conservatives picked categories 5–7, and moderates selected category 4.

CHAPTER 4. DO WE REALLY WANT GOVERNMENT OFF OUR BACKS?

1. Factor analysis is a technique that allows researchers to identify dimensions underlying an array of variables, such as the ten we use here and the twenty-seven described in note 2. Although there are many different types of factor analysis, they all can be used to reduce the complexity of a large number of variables to one or more underlying but unmeasured components. See Kim and Mueller (1978a and 1978b) for good discussions of the different types of factor analysis. Maximum likelihood factor analysis enables a researcher to test hypotheses about the number and nature of dimensions undergirding an array of correlation coefficients. That is why it is called confirmatory factor analysis. When a factor analysis is rotated to a varimax solution, the dimensions that are uncovered in a correlation matrix are orthogonal, that is, completely unrelated to one another.

2. The twenty-seven items tapped opinions across the board, including civil libertarianism, the welfare state, feelings about big government, and trust in government and external political efficacy. The following is a sampling: The federal government should be able to overrule individual states on important matters; the federal government controls too much of our daily lives; governmental regulation of business usually does more harm

than good; when something is run by the government, it is usually inefficient and wasteful; dealing with a federal government agency is often not worth the trouble; people like me do not have any say about what the government does; elected officials in Washington lose touch with the people pretty quickly; the government is really run for the benefit of all the people; our society should do what is necessary to make sure that everyone has an equal opportunity to succeed; it is the responsibility of the government to take care of people who cannot take care of themselves; the government should help more needy people even if it means going deeper into debt; the government should guarantee every citizen enough to eat and a place to sleep; we should make every possible effort to improve the position of blacks and other minorities even if it means giving them preferential treatment; school boards ought to have the right to fire teachers who are known homosexuals; books that contain dangerous ideas should be banned from public school libraries; freedom of speech should not extend to groups like the Communist party or the Ku Klux Klan (KKK); the government ought to be able to censor news stories that it thinks threaten national security; the government should cut back federal spending for defense and military purposes; the government should change the laws to make it more difficult for a woman to get an abortion; a constitutional amendment should be passed to permit prayer in public schools; mandatory drug tests should be instated for government employees; environmental controls should be relaxed to allow more economic growth and development; and the federal income tax should be increased to reduce the federal deficit.

3. As we discuss in Chapter 6, a better measure of trust in government will show that this dimension does have a fairly straightforward relation to big government opinions.

CHAPTER 5. YOUNG PEOPLE, OLD QUESTIONS

1. Four items were drawn from the 1985, 1986, and 1987 NORC GSS to construct an index to tap the extent to which respondents believed that governmental help is appropriate for some problems. There was no change in question wording, and the four items "loaded" on a single dimension in a maximum likelihood factor analysis. People were asked to place themselves on five-point scales from approval of strong governmental action (1) to a belief that government should stay out (5): (1) "Some people think that the government in Washington should do everything possible to improve the standard of living of all poor Americans. . . . Where would you place yourself on this scale, or haven't you made up your mind on this?" (2) "Some people think the government in Washington is trying to do too many things that should be left to individuals and private businesses. Others disagree and think that the government should do even more to solve our country's problems. Still others have opinions somewhere in between." (3) "Some people think that it is the responsibility of the government in Washington to see to it that people have help in paying for doctors and hospital bills. Others think that these matters are not the responsibility of the federal government and that people should take care of these things themselves." (4) "Some people think that blacks have been discriminated against for so long that the government has a special obligation to help improve their living standards. Others believe that the government should not be giving special treatment to blacks."

2. The domestic spending index combined five items from the 1985, 1986, and 1987 NORC GSS. The introductory question was: "We are faced with many problems in this country, none of which can be solved easily or inexpensively. I'm going to name some of these problems, and for each one I'd like you to tell me whether you think we're spending too much money on it, too little money, or about the right amount." The issues used were

"improving and protecting the nation's health," "improving the nation's education system," "improving the conditions of blacks," welfare, and Social Security.

3. The welfare index from the 1986 NORC GSS was an additive index combining five items that shared this introduction: "Here are some opinions other people have expressed about welfare. For each of the following statements, please tell me whether you strongly agree, agree, disagree or strongly disagree with it." The statements were: (1) "Welfare makes people work less than they would if there wasn't a welfare system." (2) "Welfare helps people get on their feet when facing difficult situations such as unemployment, a divorce, or a death in their family." (3) "Welfare encourages young women to have babies before marriage." (4) "Welfare helps keep people's marriages together in times of financial problems." (5) "Welfare discourages young women who get pregnant from marrying the father of the child." All five items were coded in the same direction for our analysis.

4. The egalitarianism index was an additive index combining the following items in the 1984, 1986, and 1988 NES: (1) "Our society should do whatever is necessary to make sure that everyone has an equal opportunity to succeed." (2) "We have gone too far in pushing equal rights in this country." (3) "One of the big problems in this country is that we don't give everyone an equal chance." (4) "This country would be better off if we worried less about how equal people are." (5) "If people were treated more equally in this country we would have many fewer problems." (6) "It is not really that big a problem if some people have more of a chance in life than others." These items "loaded" on a single dimension in a maximum likelihood factor analysis. All items were coded in the same direction for analysis.

CHAPTER 6. COMING TO TERMS

1. The trust in government index is an additive combination of these items: (1) "Do you think that people in the government waste a lot of the money we pay in taxes, waste some of it, or don't waste very much of it?" (2) "Do you think that quite a few of the people running the government are a little crooked, not very many are, or do you think hardly any of them are crooked at all?" (3) "How much of the time do you think you can trust the government in Washington to do what is right—just about always, most of the time, or only some of the time?" (4) "Would you say the government is pretty much run by a few big interests looking out for themselves or that it is run for the benefit of all the people?"

APPENDIX. MULTIVARIATE ANALYSES
OF OPINIONS ABOUT BIG GOVERNMENT

1. To capture at least some facet of ideological orientation, the respondent's opinion thermometer rating of conservatives was subtracted from his or her OT rating of liberals. For purposes of discriminating between those with opinions and those without, the absolute value was used to test the presumption that strong ideologues, right or left, would be more concerned about Washington's power than the lukewarm. In 1978, OT ratings of liberals and conservatives were not asked, so we substituted the seven-point self-placement item introduced in 1972. The item was recoded so that those who "had not thought much about" ideology were coded 0, those who did not know where to place themselves were coded 1, and those who chose the most extreme categories were given

the highest code; those who selected more moderate categories were placed at some point in between. We do not use the self-placement variables in 1972, 1976, 1980, 1984, or 1988, because too many cases would have been lost.

2. Party identification is now indexed by the SRC-CPS's standard seven-point variable, which ranges from strong Democrat to strong Republican. Except in 1978, ideology is measured by the difference between the OT rating of conservatives subtracted from the OT rating of liberals. In 1978, self-placement on a seven-point variable is used. Race, region, education, and family income are coded as described in the previous section.

3. Trust in government is measured by a five-category index made up of four items: "Does government waste tax monies?" "How much of the time can government be trusted?" "Is government run for all the people or a few big interests?" "Are government people crooked?" The fifth item—"Are government people capable?"—ceased to load with the remainder after 1968 and is best not included in the index. The external political efficacy scale contains two items: "People like me have no say in what government does," and "Government officials don't care what people like me think." This follows the strategy recommended by Abramson (1983).

4. The wording of the item asking for assessment of presidential performance changes from time to time. The variable numbers used in each year are V47 in 1968, V3135 in 1976, V80 in 1978, V63 in 1980, V259 in 1984, and V140 in 1988.

5. Trust in government and assessment of presidential performance are not, however, so closely related as to be a multicollinear relationship. The average relationship between them is $r = .20$.

References

Abelson, Robert P., et al. (eds.). 1968. *Theories of Cognitive Consistency: A Sourcebook.* Chicago: Rand McNally & Co.

Abraham, Henry J. 1985. *Justices and Presidents: A Political History of Appointments to the Supreme Court.* New York: Oxford University Press.

Abramson, Paul R. 1983. *Political Attitudes in America: Formation and Change.* San Francisco: W. H. Freeman Co.

Abramson, Paul R., John H. Aldrich, and David W. Rohde. 1983. *Change and Continuity in the 1980 Elections.* Rev. ed. Washington, D.C.: Congressional Quarterly Press.

———. 1987. *Change and Continuity in the 1984 Elections.* Rev. ed. Washington, D.C.: Congressional Quarterly Press.

Abramson, Paul R., and Ada W. Finifter. 1981. "On the Meaning of Political Trust: New Evidence from Items Introduced in 1978." *American Journal of Political Science* 25 (May): 297–307.

Advisory Commission on Intergovernmental Relations (ACIR). 1983. *Changing Public Attitudes on Governments and Taxes, 1983.* Washington, D.C.: Advisory Commission on Intergovernmental Relations.

———. 1986. *Changing Public Attitudes on Governments and Taxes, 1986.* Washington, D.C.: Advisory Commission on Intergovernmental Relations.

———. 1987. *Changing Public Attitudes on Governments and Taxes, 1987.* Washington, D.C.: Advisory Commission on Intergovernmental Relations.

———. 1988. *Changing Public Attitudes on Governments and Taxes, 1988.* Washington, D.C.: Advisory Commission on Intergovernmental Relations.

Aldrich, John, and Charles Cnudde. 1975. "Probing the Bounds of Conventional Wisdom." *American Journal of Political Science* 19 (August): 571–608.

Alexander, Charles. 1975. *Holding the Line: The Eisenhower Era, 1952-1961.* Bloomington: Indiana University Press.

Almond, Gabriel A. 1988. "The Return to the State." *American Political Science Review* 82 (September): 853–874.

Almond, Gabriel A., and Sidney Verba. 1963. *The Civic Culture: Political Attitudes and Democracy in Five Nations.* Princeton, N.J.: Princeton University Press.

Asher, Herbert. 1988. *Polling and the Public: What Every Citizen Should Know.* Washington, D.C.: Congressional Quarterly Press.

Axelrod, Robert. 1973. "Schema Theory: An Information Processing Model of Perception and Cognition." *American Political Science Review* 67 (December): 1248–1266.

Barrett, Laurence I. 1989. "Giving the Public What It Wants." *Time,* October 23, p. 34.

Baskir, Lawrence M., and William A. Strauss. 1978. *Chance and Circumstance: The Draft, the War, and the Vietnam Generation.* New York: Alfred A. Knopf.

Beck, Paul Allen, Hal G. Rainey, Keith Nicholls, and Carol Traut. 1987. "Citizen Views of Taxes and Services: A Tale of Three Cities." *Social Science Quarterly* 68 (June): 223–243.

Beer, Samuel H. 1965. "Liberalism and the National Idea." In Robert A. Goldwin (ed.), *Left, Right, and Center: Essays on Liberalism and Conservatism in the United States* (pp. 142–169). Chicago: Rand McNally & Co.

———. 1978. "In Search of a New Public Philosophy." In Anthony King (ed.), *The New American Political System* (pp. 5–44). Washington, D.C.: American Enterprise Institute.

Bennett, Linda L. M., and Stephen Earl Bennett. 1986. "Opinions about the Power of the Central Government, 1964–1984." A paper prepared for the annual meeting of the American Political Science Association, Washington, D.C., August 27–31.

Bennett, Stephen E. 1973. "Consistency among the Public's Social Welfare Policy Attitudes in the 1960s." *American Journal of Political Science* 17 (August): 544–570.

———. 1986. *Apathy in America, 1960–1984: Causes and Consequences of Citizen Political Indifference.* Dobbs Ferry, N.Y.: Transnational Publishers.

Bennett, Stephen E., and Alfred J. Tuchfarber. 1975. "The Social-Structural Sources of Cleavage on Law and Order Policies." *American Journal of Political Science* 19 (August): 419–438.

Bennett, W. Lance. 1977. "The Growth of Knowledge in Mass Belief Studies: An Epistemological Critique." *American Journal of Political Science* 21 (August): 465–500.

———. 1980. *Public Opinion in American Politics.* New York: Harcourt, Brace Jovanovich.

Bentley, Arthur F. 1949. *The Process of Government.* Evanston: Principia Press of Illinois. (Original ed., 1908.)

Berelson, Bernard R., Paul F. Lazarsfeld, and William McPhee. 1954. *Voting.* Chicago: University of Chicago Press.

Berger, Raoul. 1977. *Government by Judiciary.* Cambridge, Mass.: Harvard University Press.

Berry, William D., and David Lowery. 1987. "Explaining the Size of the Public Sector: Responsive and Excessive Government Interpretations." *Journal of Politics* 49 (May): 401–440.

"Big Chill (Revisited), The, Or Whatever Happened to the Baby Boom?" 1985. *American Demographics* 7 (September): 23–29.

Birnbaum, Jeffrey H., and Alan S. Murray. 1987. *Showdown at Gucci Gulch: Lawmakers, Lobbyists, and the Unlikely Triumph of Tax Reform.* New York: Random House.

Bishop, George F. 1987. "Experiments with the Middle Response Alternative in Survey Questions." *Public Opinion Quarterly* 51 (Summer): 220–232.

Bishop, George F., Robert W. Oldendick, and Alfred J. Tuchfarber. 1980. "Experiments in Filtering Political Opinions." *Political Behavior* 2 (4): 339–369.

———. 1982. "Effects of Presenting One versus Two Sides of an Issue in Survey Questions." *Public Opinion Quarterly* 46 (Spring): 69–85.

————. 1983. "Effects of Filter Questions in Public Opinion Surveys." *Public Opinion Quarterly* 47 (Winter): 528–546.

Bishop, George F., Robert W. Oldendick, Alfred J. Tuchfarber, and Stephen E. Bennett. 1980. "Pseudo-Opinions on Public Affairs." *Public Opinion Quarterly* 44 (Summer): 198–209.

Bishop, George F., Alfred J. Tuchfarber, and Robert Oldendick. 1978a. "Effects of Question Wording and Format on Political Attitude Consistency." *Public Opinion Quarterly* 42 (Spring):81–92.

————. 1978b. "Change in the Structure of American Political Attitudes: The Nagging Question of Question Wording." *American Journal of Political Science* 22 (May): 250–269.

————. 1986. "Opinions on Fictitious Issues: The Pressure to Answer Survey Questions." *Public Opinion Quarterly* 50 (Summer): 240–250.

Bishop, George F., Alfred J. Tuchfarber, Robert Oldendick, and Stephen E. Bennett. 1979. "Questions about Question Wording: A Reply to Revisiting Mass Belief Systems Revisited." *American Journal of Political Science* 23 (February): 187–192.

Block, Fred, Richard A. Cloward, Barbara Ehrenreich, and Frances Fox Piven. 1987. *The Mean Season: The Attack on the Welfare State*. New York: Pantheon Books.

Bloom, Allan. 1987. *The Closing of the American Mind*. New York: Simon & Schuster.

Blum, John Morton. 1976. *V Was for Victory: Politics and American Culture during World War II*. New York: Harcourt, Brace & Jovanovich.

Bourgin, Frank. 1989. *The Great Challenge: The Myth of Laissez-Faire in the Early Republic*. New York: George Braziller.

Boyer, Ernest L. 1983. *High School: A Report on Secondary Education in America*. New York: Harper & Row.

Bradburn, Norman M., and Seymour Sudman. 1988. *Polls and Surveys: Understanding What They Tell Us*. San Francisco: Jossey-Bass.

Broder, David. 1984. "The Election That Didn't Happen." *Washington Post,* November 11, p. D7.

Brunk, Gregory G. 1978. "The 1964 Attitude Consistency Leap Reconsidered." *Political Methodology* 5 (3): 347–359.

Burns, James MacGregor. 1963. *The Deadlock of Democracy*. Englewood Cliffs, N.J.: Prentice-Hall.

————. 1966. *Presidential Government: The Crucible of Leadership*. Boston: Houghton Mifflin.

————. 1982. *The Vineyard of Liberty*. New York: Alfred A. Knopf.

————. 1989. *The Crosswinds of Freedom*. New York: Alfred A. Knopf.

Burns, James MacGregor, Jack Peltason, and Thomas Cronin. 1987. *Government by the People*. 13th ed. Englewood Cliffs, N.J.: Prentice-Hall.

Bush, George Herbert Walker. 1989. "Inaugural Address." In Gerald M. Pomper (ed.). *The Election of 1988: Reports and Interpretations* (pp. 207–211). Chatham, N.J.: Chatham House.

Caddell, Patrick H. 1979. "Crisis of Confidence, I: Trapped in a Downward Spiral." *Public Opinion* 2 (October/November): 2–8, 52–55, 58–60.

Campbell, Angus, Philip E. Converse, Warren E. Miller, and Donald E. Stokes. 1960. *The American Voter*. New York: John W. Wiley & Sons.

Campbell, Angus, Gerald Gurin, and Warren E. Miller. 1954. *The Voter Decides*. Evanston, Ill.: Row, Peterson & Co.

Cannon, Lou. 1982. *Reagan*. New York: Perigee.

Cantril, Hadley. 1944. *Gauging Public Opinion*. Princeton, N.J.: Princeton University Press.

Cantril, Hadley, with Mildred Strunk (eds.). 1978. *Public Opinion, 1935-1946*. Westport, Conn.: Greenwood Press. (Original ed., 1951.)

Carmines, Edward G., and James A. Stimson. 1989. *Issue Evolution: Race and the Transformation of American Politics*. Princeton, N.J.: Princeton University Press.

Carter, Jimmy. 1982. *Keeping Faith: Memoirs of a President*. New York: Bantam Books.

Citrin, Jack. 1974. "Comment: The Political Relevance of Trust in Government." *American Political Science Review* 68 (September): 973-988.

———. "Do People Want Something for Nothing: Public Opinion on Taxes and Government Spending." *National Tax Journal* 32, supplement (June): 113-129.

———. 1981. "The Changing American Electorate." In Arnold Meltsner (ed.), *Politics in the Oval Office* (pp. 31-61). San Francisco: Institute for Contemporary Studies.

Citrin, Jack, and Donald Philip Green. 1986. "Presidential Leadership and the Resurgence of Trust in Government." *British Journal of Political Science* 16 (October): 431-453.

Conover, Pamela Johnston, and Stanley Feldman. 1980. "Belief System Organization in the American Electorate: An Alternative Approach." In John C. Pierce and John L. Sullivan (eds.), *The Electorate Reconsidered* (pp. 49-67). Beverly Hills, Calif: Sage Publications.

———. 1981. "The Origins and Meaning of Liberal/Conservative Self-Identifications." *American Journal of Political Science* 25 (November): 617-645.

———. 1984. "How People Organize the Political World: A Schematic Model." *American Journal of Political Science* 28 (February): 95-126.

Converse, Jean M. 1976-77. "Predicting No Opinion in the Polls." *Public Opinion Quarterly* 40 (Winter): 515-530.

Converse, Philip E. 1964. "The Nature of Belief Systems in Mass Publics." In David E. Apter (ed.), *Ideology and Discontent* (pp. 206-261). New York: Free Press.

———. 1970. "Attitudes and Non-Attitudes: Continuation of a Dialogue." In Edward R. Tufte (ed.), *The Quantitative Analysis of Social Problems* (pp. 168-189). Reading, Mass.: Addison-Wesley.

———. 1975. "Public Opinion and Voting Behavior." In Fred I. Greenstein and Nelson W. Polsby (eds.), *Handbook of Political Science* (vol. 4, pp. 75-169). Reading, Mass.: Addison-Wesley.

———. 1980. "Comment: Rejoinder to Judd and Milburn." *American Sociological Review* 45 (August): 644-646.

Converse, Philip E., Aage R. Clausen, and Warren E. Miller. 1965. "Electoral Myth and Reality: The 1964 Election." *American Political Science Review* 59 (June): 321-336.

Converse, Philip E., and Gregory B. Markus. 1979. "Plus Ça Change . . . : The New CPS Election Study Panel." *American Political Science Review* 73 (March): 32-49.

Cooper, John Milton. 1983. *The Warrior and the Priest: Woodrow Wilson and Theodore Roosevelt*. Cambridge, Mass.: Harvard University Press.

Corwin, Edward S. 1957. *The President: Office and Powers*. New York: New York University Press.

Crespi, Irving. 1989. *Public Opinion, Polls, and Democracy*. Boulder, Colo.: Westview Press.

Croly, Herbert. 1964. *The Promise of American Life*. New York: Capricorn Books. (Original ed., 1909.)

Daniels, Mark R., and Robert Darcy. 1983. "Notes on the Use and Interpretation of Discriminant Analysis." *American Journal of Political Science* 27 (May): 359-381.

Davis, James A. 1975. "Communism, Conformity, Cohorts, and Categories: American

Tolerance in 1954 and 1972-73." *American Journal of Sociology* 81 (November): 491-513.

————. 1980. "Conservative Weather in a Liberalizing Climate: Change in Selected NORC General Social Survey Items, 1972-1978." *Social Forces* 58 (June): 1129-1156.

Delli Carpini, Michael X. 1986. *Stability and Change in American Politics: The Coming of Age of the Generation of the 1960s.* New York: New York University Press.

Delli Carpini, Michael, and Lee Sigelman. 1986. "Do Yuppies Matter? Competing Explanations of Their Political Distinctiveness." *Public Opinion Quarterly* 50 (Winter): 502-518.

Derthick, Martha, and Paul J. Quirk. 1985. *The Politics of Deregulation.* Washington, D.C.: Brookings Institution.

Devine, Donald J. 1972. *The Political Culture of the United States.* Boston: Little, Brown & Co.

"DeWitt, John." 1986. "Essays I and II." In Ralph Ketcham (ed.), *The Anti-Federalist Papers and the Constitutional Convention Debates* (pp. 189-198). New York: Mentor.

Easton, David. 1965. *A Systems Analysis of Political Life.* New York: John W. Wiley & Sons.

Edelman, Murray. 1985. *The Symbolic Uses of Politics.* Urbana: University of Illinois Press.

Ekirch, Arthur A., Jr. 1969. *Ideologies and Utopias: The Impact of the New Deal on American Thought.* Chicago: Quadrangle Books.

Erikson, Robert S. 1976. "The Relationship between Public Opinion and State Policy: A New Look Based on Some Forgotten Data." *American Journal of Political Science* 20 (February): 25-36.

Erikson, Robert S., Norman R. Luttbeg, and Kent Tedin. 1988. *American Public Opinion: Its Origins, Content, and Impact.* 3d ed. New York: Macmillan.

Exter, Thomas, and Frederick Barber. 1986. "The Age of Conservatism." *American Demographics* 8 (November): 30-38.

Fee, Joan Flynn. 1981. "Symbols in Survey Questions: Solving the Problem of Multiple Word Meanings." *Political Methodology* 7 (2): 71-95.

Ferguson, Thomas, and Joel Rogers. 1986. *Right Turn: The Decline of the Democrats and the Future of American Politics.* New York: Hill & Wang.

Field, John O., and Ronald E. Anderson. 1969. "Ideology in the Public's Conceptualization of the 1964 Election." *Public Opinion Quarterly* 33 (Fall): 380-398.

Flanigan, William H., and Nancy H. Zingale. 1987. *Political Behavior of the American Electorate.* 6th ed. Boston: Allyn & Bacon.

Francis, Joe D., and Lawrence Busch. 1975. "What We Know about 'I Don't Knows.'" *Public Opinion Quarterly* 39 (Summer): 207-218.

Free, Lloyd A., and Hadley Cantril. 1968. *The Political Beliefs of Americans: A Study of Public Opinion.* New York: Simon & Schuster.

Gallup, George. 1972. *The Sophisticated Poll Watcher's Guide.* Princeton, N.J.: Princeton University Press.

————. 1973. *The Gallup Poll: Public Opinion, 1935-1971.* 3 vols. New York: Random House.

————. 1978. *The Gallup Poll: Public Opinion, 1972-1977.* 2 vols. Wilmington, Del.: Scholarly Resources.

————. 1980. *The Gallup Poll: Public Opinion, 1979.* Wilmington, Del.: Scholarly Resources.

————. 1982. *The Gallup Poll: Public Opinion, 1981.* Wilmington, Del.: Scholarly Resources.

―――. 1984. *The Gallup Poll: Public Opinion, 1983.* Wilmington, Del.: Scholarly Resources.

Gallup, George, and Saul Forbes Rae. 1940. *The Pulse of Democracy.* New York: Simon & Schuster.

Gallup Report, The. 1984. Reports 220–221. January/February.

―――. 1985a. Report 234. March.

―――. 1985b. Report 235. April.

―――. 1985c. Report 237. June.

―――. 1986. Report 253. October.

―――. 1987. Report 263. August.

―――. 1988. Report 274. July.

―――. 1989. Reports 282–283. March/April.

Gerth, H. H., and C. Wright Mills (eds.). 1958. *From Max Weber: Essays in Sociology.* New York: Galaxy Books.

Ginsberg, Benjamin. 1986. *The Captive Public: How Mass Opinion Promotes State Power.* New York: Basic Books.

Glenn, Norval D. 1969. "Aging, Disengagement, and Opinionation." *Public Opinion Quarterly* 33 (Spring): 17–33.

―――. 1974. "Aging and Conservatism." *The Annals* 415 (September): 176–186.

―――. 1977. *Cohort Analysis.* Sage University Paper Series on Quantitative Applications in the Social Sciences, no. 07-005. Beverly Hills, Calif.: Sage Publications.

Gluck, Sherna Berger. 1987. *Rosie the Riveter Revisited: Women, the War, and Social Change.* New York: New American Library.

Goldwater, Barry. 1960. *The Conscience of a Conservative.* Shepherdsville, Ky.: Victor Publishing Co.

Goodwyn, Lawrence. 1978. *The Populist Moment.* New York: Oxford University Press.

Greenstein, Fred I. 1982. *The Hidden Hand Presidency: Eisenhower as Leader.* New York: Basic Books.

Grofman, Bernard. 1978. "A Comment on Dye and McManus' Use of Discriminant Function Analysis." *Political Methodology* 5 (2): 241–248.

Haas, Lawrence J. 1989. "The Terrifying T-Word." *National Journal* 21 (June): 1354–1357.

Hagner, Paul R., and John C. Pierce. 1982. "Correlative Characteristics of Levels of Conceptualization in the American Public, 1956–1976." *Journal of Politics* 44 (August): 779–807.

Hamby, Alonzo L. 1985. *Liberalism and Its Challengers: F.D.R. to Reagan.* New York: Oxford University Press.

Hamill, Ruth, Milton Lodge, and Frederick Blake. 1985. "The Breadth, Depth, and Utility of Class, Partisan, and Ideological Schemata." *American Journal of Political Science* 29 (November):850–870.

Hammond, John L. 1986. "Yuppies." *Public Opinion Quarterly* 50 (Winter): 487–501.

Hansen, Susan B. 1983. *The Politics of Taxation.* New York: Praeger.

Hastie, Reid. 1981. "Schematic Principles in Human Memory." In E. Tory Higgins, C. Peter Herman, and Mark P. Zanna (eds.), *Social Cognition: The Ontario Symposium* (vol. 1, pp. 39–88). Hillsdale, N.J.: Lawrence Erlbaum Associates.

Hayek, Friedrich A. 1944. *The Road to Serfdom.* Chicago: University of Chicago Press.

Hennessy, Bernard. 1970. "A Headnote on the Existence and Study of Political Attitudes." *Social Science Quarterly* 51 (December): 463–476.

Hero, Alfred O., Jr. 1969. "Liberalism-Conservatism Revisited: Foreign vs. Domestic Federal Policies, 1937–1967." *Public Opinion Quarterly* 33 (Fall): 399–408.

Higgs, Robert. 1987. *Crisis and Leviathan: Critical Episodes in the Growth of American Government.* New York: Oxford University Press.

Hill, David B., and Norman R. Luttbeg. 1983. *Trends in American Electoral Behavior.* 2d ed. Itasca, Ill.: F. E. Peacock.

Hoffman, David. 1988. "At Last, a President Who Ran as an Insider, Not an Outsider." *Washington Post National Weekly Edition*, December 26, p. 32.

Hofstadter, Richard. 1954. *The American Political Tradition.* New York: Vintage.

Holm, John D., and John P. Robinson. 1978. "Ideological Identification and the American Voter." *Public Opinion Quarterly* 42 (Summer): 235–246.

Howe, Irving. 1986. "The Spirit of the Times: Greed, Nostalgia, Ideology, and War Whoops." *Dissent* 33 (Fall): 413–425.

Huntington, Samuel P. 1981. *American Politics: The Promise of Disharmony.* Cambridge, Mass.: Harvard University Press.

Inglehart, Ronald. 1977. *The Silent Revolution: Changing Values and Political Styles among Western Publics.* Princeton, N.J.: Princeton University Press.

———. 1985. "Aggregate Stability and Individual-Level Flux in Mass Belief Systems: The Level of Analysis Paradox." *American Political Science Review* 79 (March): 97–116.

Ippolito, Dennis S. 1981. *Congressional Spending.* Ithaca, N.Y.: Cornell University Press.

Jackman, Mary R. 1978. "General and Applied Tolerance: Does Education Increase Commitment to Racial Integration?" *American Journal of Political Science* 22 (May): 302–324.

———. 1981a. "Education and Policy Commitment to Racial Integration." *American Journal of Political Science* 25 (May): 254–269.

———. 1981b. "Issues in the Measurement of Commitment to Racial Integration." *Political Methodology* 7 (3, 4): 160–171.

Jackson, John E. 1983. "The Systematic Beliefs of the Mass Public: Estimating Policy Preferences with Survey Data." *Journal of Politics* 45 (November): 840–865.

Jackson, Thomas H., and George E. Marcus. 1975. "Political Competence and Ideological Constraint." *Social Science Research* 4 (June): 93–111.

Janowitz, Morris. 1983. *The Reconstruction of Patriotism: Education for Civic Consciousness.* Chicago: University of Chicago Press.

Jennings, M. Kent, and Richard J. Niemi. 1981. *Generations and Politics: A Panel Study of Young Adults and Their Parents.* Princeton, N.J.: Princeton University Press.

Jones, Landon Y. 1980. *Great Expectations: America and the Baby Boom Generation.* New York: Ballantine Books.

Judd, Charles M., and Michael A. Milburn. 1980. "Structure of Attitude Systems in the General Public." *American Sociological Review* 45 (August): 627–643.

———. 1981. "Interpreting New Methods in Attitude Structure Research." *American Sociological Review* 46 (October): 675–677.

Kerlinger, Fred N. 1984. *Liberalism and Conservatism: The Nature and Structure of Social Attitudes.* Hillsdale, N.J.: Lawrence Erlbaum Associates.

Kessel, John H. 1972. "Comment: The Issues in Issue Voting." *American Political Science Review* 66 (June): 459–465.

Key, V. O., Jr. 1961. *Public Opinion and American Democracy.* New York: Alfred A. Knopf.

Key, V. O., Jr., with Milton C. Cummings, Jr. 1966. *The Responsible Electorate: Rationality in Presidential Voting, 1936–1960.* Cambridge, Mass.: Harvard University Press.

Kim, Jae-On, and Charles W. Mueller. 1978a. *Introduction to Factor Analysis: What It Is and How to Do It.* Sage University Paper Series on Quantitative Applications in the Social Sciences, no. 07-013. Beverly Hills, Calif.: Sage Publications.

———. 1978b. *Factor Analysis: Statistical Methods and Practical Issues.* Sage University Paper Series on Quantitative Applications in the Social Sciences, no. 07-014. Beverly Hills, Calif.: Sage Publications.

Kinder, Donald R. 1983. "Diversity and Complexity in American Public Opinion." In Ada W. Finifter (ed.), *Political Science: The State of the Discipline* (pp. 389–427). Washington, D.C.: American Political Science Association.

Kinder, Donald R., and David O. Sears. 1985. "Public Opinion and Political Action." In Gardner Lindzey and Elliot Aronson (eds.), *The Handbook of Social Psychology* (vol. 2, pp. 659–741). 3d ed. New York: Random House.

Klecka, William R. 1980. *Discriminant Analysis.* Sage University Paper Series on Quantitative Applications in the Social Sciences, no. 07-019. Beverly Hills, Calif.: Sage Publications.

Klingemann, Hans D. 1979. "Measuring Ideological Conceptualizations." In Samuel Barnes, Max Kasse et al. *Political Action: Mass Participation in Five Western Democracies* (pp. 215–254). Beverly Hills, Calif.: Sage Publications.

Kuklinski, James H., and Wayne Parent. 1981. "Race and Big Government: Contamination in Measuring Racial Attitudes." *Political Methodology* 7 (3, 4): 130–159.

Kuttner, Robert. 1980. *The Revolt of the Haves: Tax Rebellions and Hard Times.* New York: Simon & Schuster.

Ladd, Everett Carll, Jr. 1970. *American Political Parties: Social Change and Political Response.* New York: W. W. Norton & Co.

———. 1972. *Ideology in America: Change and Response in a City, a Suburb, and a Small Town.* New York: W. W. Norton & Co.

———. 1976–77. "Liberalism Upside Down: The Inversion of the New Deal Order." *Political Science Quarterly* 91 (Winter): 577–600.

———. 1978a. "The New Lines Are Drawn: Class and Ideology in America." *Public Opinion* 1 (July/August): 48–53.

———. 1978b. "The New Lines Are Drawn: Class and Ideology, Part II." *Public Opinion* 1 (September/October): 14–20.

———. 1979a. "Pursuing the New Class: Social Theory and Survey Data." In B. Bruce-Briggs (ed.), *The New Class?* (pp. 103–122). New York: McGraw-Hill Book Co.

———. 1979b. "The New Divisions in U.S. Politics." *Fortune*, March 26, pp. 88-96.

———. 1982. *Where Have All the Voters Gone?* 2d ed. New York: W. W. Norton & Co.

———. 1983. "Politics in the 80's: An Electorate at Odds with Itself." *Public Opinion* 5 (December/January): 2–5.

———. 1985. "Tax Attitudes." *Public Opinion* 8 (February/March): 8–10.

Ladd, Everett Carll, Jr., with Charles D. Hadley. 1978. *Transformations of the American Party System.* 2d ed. New York: W. W. Norton & Co.

Ladd, Everett Carll, Jr., et al. 1979. "The Polls: Taxing and Spending." *Public Opinion Quarterly* 43 (Spring): 126–135.

Lane, Robert E. 1962. *Political Ideology: Why the American Common Man Thinks What He Does.* New York: Free Press.

———. 1973. "Patterns of Political Belief." In Jeanne N. Knutson (ed.), *Handbook of Political Psychology* (pp.83–116). San Francisco: Jossey-Bass.

Lang, Gladys, and Kurt Lang. 1983. *The Battle for Public Opinion: The President, the Press, and the Polls during Watergate.* New York: Columbia University Press.

Lau, Richard R., and David O. Sears (eds.). 1986. *Political Cognition*. Hillsdale, N.J.: Lawrence Erlbaum Associates.

Lazarsfeld, Paul F., Bernard R. Berelson, and Hazel Gaudet. 1968. *The People's Choice*. 3d ed. New York: Columbia University Press.

Leff, Mark H. 1984. *The Limits of Symbolic Reform: The New Deal and Taxation, 1933–1939*. London: Cambridge University Press.

Lekachman, Robert. 1985–86. "Review of *Beyond Liberal and Conservative*, by William S. Maddox and Stuart A. Lilie." *Political Science Quarterly* 100 (Winter): 716.

Leuchtenburg, William E. 1983. *In the Shadow of FDR*. Ithaca, N.Y.: Cornell University Press.

Levitin, Teresa E., and Warren E. Miller. 1979. "Ideological Interpretations of Presidential Elections." *American Political Science Review* 73 (September): 751–771.

Light, Paul C. 1988. *Baby Boomers*. New York: W. W. Norton & Co.

Link, Arthur S. 1954. *Woodrow Wilson and the Progressive Era, 1910–1917*. New York: Harper & Row.

Lipset, Seymour Martin. 1977. "Why No Socialism in the United States?" In Seweryn Bialer and Sophia Sluzar (eds.), *Sources of Contemporary Radicalism* (pp. 31–149, 356–363). Boulder, Colo.: Westview Press.

———. 1979. *The First New Nation: The United States in Historical and Comparative Perspective*. Rev. ed. New York: W. W. Norton & Co.

———. 1981. *Political Man: The Social Bases of Politics*. Rev. ed. Baltimore: Johns Hopkins University Press.

———. 1983. "Socialism in America." In Paul Kurtz (ed.), *Sidney Hook: Philosopher of Democracy and Humanism* (pp. 47–63). Buffalo, N.Y.: Prometheus Books.

———. 1985. "Feeling Better: Measuring the Nation's Confidence." *Public Opinion* 8 (April/May): 6–9, 56–58.

Lipset, Seymour Martin, and William J. Schneider. 1983. "Confidence in Confidence Measures." *Public Opinion* 6 (August/September): 42–44.

———. 1987. *The Confidence Gap: Business, Labor, and Government in the Public Mind*. Rev. ed. Baltimore: Johns Hopkins University Press.

Littwin, Susan. 1986. *The Postponed Generation: Why American Youth Are Growing Up Later*. New York: William Morrow & Co.

"Long Queue for Government Assistance, A." 1989. *National Journal* 21 (May): 1209.

Lowi, Theodore J. 1979. *The End of Liberalism: The Second Republic of the United States*. 2d ed. New York: W. W. Norton & Co.

———. 1985. *The Personal President*. Ithaca, N.Y.: Cornell University Press.

Lubell, Samuel. 1956. *Revolt of the Moderates*. New York: Harper & Brothers.

Luskin, Robert C. 1987. "Measuring Political Sophistication." *American Journal of Political Science* 31 (November): 856–899.

Luttbeg, Norman R., and Michael M. Gant. 1985. "The Failure of Liberal/Conservative Ideology as a Cognitive Structure." *Public Opinion Quarterly* 49 (Spring): 80–93.

McClosky, Herbert. 1964. "Consensus and Ideology in American Politics." *American Political Science Review* 58 (June): 361–382.

McClosky, Herbert, and Alida Brill. 1983. *Dimensions of Tolerance: What Americans Believe about Civil Liberties*. New York: Russell Sage Foundation.

McClosky, Herbert, Paul J. Hoffman, and Rosemary O'Hara. 1960. "Issue Conflict and Consensus among Party Leaders and Followers." *American Political Science Review* 54 (June): 406–427.

McClosky, Herbert, and John Zaller. 1984. *The American Ethos: Public Attitudes toward Capitalism and Democracy.* Cambridge, Mass.: Harvard University Press.

McCoy, Drew. 1989. *The Last of the Fathers.* Cambridge, Mass.: Cambridge University Press.

McDonald, Forrest. 1979. *E Pluribus Unum: The Formation of the American Republic, 1776–1790.* Indianapolis: Liberty Press.

McElvaine, Robert S. 1987. *The End of the Conservative Era: Liberalism after Reagan.* New York: Arbor House.

Maddox, William S., and Stuart A. Lilie. 1984. *Beyond Liberal and Conservative: Reassessing the Political Spectrum.* Washington, D.C.: Cato Institute.

Mannheim, Karl. 1972. "The Problem of Generations." In Philip G. Altbach and Robert S. Laufer (eds.), *The New Pilgrims: Youth Protest in Transition* (pp. 101–138). New York: David McKay.

Marcus, George E., William Tabb, and John L. Sullivan. 1974. "The Application of Individual Differences Scaling to the Measurement of Political Ideologies." *American Journal of Political Science* 18 (May): 405–420.

Margolis, Michael. 1977. "From Confusion to Confusion: Issues and the American Voter (1956–1972)." *American Political Science Review* 66 (March): 31–43.

Margolis, Michael, and Khondaker E. Haque. 1981. "Applied Tolerance or Fear of Government? An Alternative Interpretation of Jackman's Findings." *American Journal of Political Science* 25 (May): 241–255.

Markus, Hazel, and R. B. Zajonc. 1985. "The Cognitive Perspective in Social Psychology." In Gardner Lindzey and Elliot Aronson (eds.), *Handbook of Social Psychology* (vol. 1, pp. 137–230). 3d ed. New York: Random House.

Martin, Steven S. 1981. "New Methods Lead to Familiar Results." *American Sociological Review* 46 (October): 670–675.

Matusow, Allen J. 1984. *The Unraveling of America: A History of Liberalism in the 1960s.* New York: Harper & Row.

Mauss, Armand L. 1971. "The Lost Promise of Reconciliation: New Left vs. Old Left." *Journal of Social Issues* 27 (1): 1–20.

Mead, Lawrence. 1986. *Beyond Entitlement: The Social Obligations of Citizenship.* New York: Free Press.

Merriam, Charles, and Harold Foote Gosnell. 1924. *Non-Voting.* Chicago: University of Chicago Press.

Merriman, W. Richard, and T. Wayne Parent. 1983. "Sources of Citizen Attitudes toward Government Race Policy." *Polity* 16 (Fall): 30–47.

Miller, Arthur H. 1974a. "Political Issues and Trust in Government." *American Political Science Review* 64 (September): 951–972.

———. 1974b. "Rejoinder to 'Comment' by Jack Citrin." *American Political Science Review* 64 (September): 989–1001.

———. 1983. "Is Confidence Rebounding?" *Public Opinion* 6 (June/July): 16–20.

Miller, Arthur H., and Warren E. Miller. 1976. "Ideology in the 1972 Election: Myth or Reality—A Rejoinder." *American Political Science Review* 70 (September): 832–849.

Miller, Arthur H., Warren E. Miller, Alden S. Raine, and Thad Brown. 1976. "A Majority Party in Disarray: Policy Polarization in the 1972 Election." *American Political Science Review* 70 (September): 752–778.

Miller, Warren E. 1979. "Crisis of Confidence, II: Misreading the Public Pulse." *Public Opinion* 2 (October/November): 9–16, 60.

Miller, Warren E., and Teresa E. Levitin. 1977. *Leadership and Change: Presidential Elections from 1972 to 1976.* Cambridge, Mass.: Winthrop Publishers.

Miller, Warren E., Arthur H. Miller, and Edward J. Schneider. 1980. *American National*

Election Studies Data Sourcebook, 1952–1978. Cambridge, Mass.: Harvard University Press.

Miller, Warren E., and J. Merrill Shanks. 1982. "Policy Directions and Presidential Leadership: Alternative Interpretations of the 1980 Presidential Election." *British Journal of Political Science* 12 (April): 299–356.

Mills, C. Wright. 1956. *The Power Elite.* New York: Oxford University Press.

Morris, Charles R. 1984. *A Time of Passion: America, 1960–1980.* New York: Harper & Row.

Moynihan, Daniel P. 1970. *Maximum Feasible Misunderstanding.* New York: Free Press.

Mueller, John E. 1973. *War, Presidents, and Public Opinion.* New York: John W. Wiley & Sons.

Murray, Alan, and Jeffrey H. Birnbaum. 1987. "Tax Reform: The Bill Nobody Wanted." *Public Opinion* 9 (March/April): 41–43, 60.

Neuman, W. Russell. 1986. *The Paradox of Mass Politics: Knowledge and Opinion in the American Electorate.* Cambridge, Mass.: Harvard University Press.

Newsweek. 1984. "The Challenger's Outlook." November 5, p. 29.

New York Times. 1986. "Workers for All Governments Found Up by 254,000 in 1985." October 14, p. Y13.

———. 1990. "A Dubious Reagan Achievement." January 4, p. Y22.

Nie, Norman H., with Kristi Andersen. 1974. "Mass Belief Systems Revisited: Political Change and Attitude Structure." *Journal of Politics* 36 (August): 540–591.

Nie, Norman H., and James N. Rabjohn. 1979a. "Revisiting Mass Belief Systems Revisited: Or, Doing Research Is Like Watching a Tennis Match." *American Journal of Political Science* 23 (February): 139–175.

———. 1979b. "Response." *American Journal of Political Science* 23 (February): 193.

Nie, Norman H., Sidney Verba, and John R. Petrocik. 1976. *The Changing American Voter.* Cambridge, Mass.: Harvard University Press.

———. 1979. *The Changing American Voter.* Rev. ed. Cambridge, Mass.: Harvard University Press.

National Opinion Research Center (NORC). 1987. *General Social Surveys, 1972–1987: Cumulative Codebook.* Storrs, Conn.: Roper Center for Public Opinion Research.

———. 1988. *General Social Surveys, 1972–1988: Cumulative Codebook.* Storrs, Conn.: Roper Center for Public Opinion Research.

———. 1989. *General Social Surveys, 1972–1989: Cumulative Codebook.* Storrs, Conn.: Roper Center for Public Opinion Research.

Nordlinger, Eric A., Theodore J. Lowi, and Sergio Fabbrini. 1988. "The Return to the State: Critiques." *American Political Science Review* 82 (September): 875–901.

Norusis, Marija J. 1985. *SPSSX: Advanced Statistics Guide.* New York: McGraw-Hill Book Co.

Nunn, Clyde Z., Harry J. Crockett, Jr., and J. Allen Williams, Jr. 1978. *Tolerance for Nonconformity.* San Francisco: Jossey-Bass.

O'Neill, William L. 1986. *American High: The Years of Confidence, 1945–1960.* New York: Free Press.

Page, Benjamin I., and Robert Y. Shapiro. 1982. "Changes in Americans' Policy Preferences, 1935–1979." *Public Opinion Quarterly* 46 (Spring): 24–42.

———. 1983. "Effects of Public Opinion on Policy." *American Political Science Review* 77 (March): 175–190.

———. 1987. "What Moves Public Opinion?" *American Political Science Review* 81 (March): 23–43.

Paine, Thomas. N.d. Common Sense *and* The Crisis. Garden City, N.Y.: Dolphin Books.

Parsons, Talcott. 1969. *Politics and Social Structure*. New York: Free Press.

Peffley, Mark A., and Jon Hurwitz. 1985. "A Hierarchical Model of Attitude Constraint." *American Journal of Political Science* 29 (November): 871–890.

Pennock, J. Roland. 1979. *Democratic Political Theory*. Princeton, N.J.: Princeton University Press.

People for the American Way. 1989. *Democracy's Next Generation: A Study of Youth and Teachers*. Washington, D.C.: People for the American Way.

Peters, B. Guy. 1986. *American Public Policy: Promise and Performance*. 2d ed. Chatham, N.J.: Chatham House.

Petrocik, John R. 1978. "Comment: Reconsidering the Reconsiderations of the 1964 Change in Attitude Consistency." *Political Methodology* 5 (3): 361–368.

———. 1980. "Contextual Sources of Voting Behavior: The Changeable American Voter." In John C. Pierce and John L. Sullivan (eds.), *The Electorate Reconsidered* (pp. 257–277). Beverly Hills, Calif.: Sage Publications.

Phillips, Kevin P. 1983. *Post-Conservative America: People, Politics, and Ideology in a Time of Crisis*. New York: Vintage Books.

Pierce, John C. 1970. "Party Identification and the Changing Role of Ideology in American Politics." *Midwest Journal of Political Science* 14 (February): 24–42.

Pious, Richard M. 1979. *The American Presidency*. New York: Basic Books.

Pollack, Norman. 1962. *The Populist Response to Industrial America*. New York: W. W. Norton & Co.

Pomper, Gerald M. 1972. "From Confusion to Clarity: Issues and American Voters, 1956–1968." *American Political Science Review* 66 (June): 415–428.

President's Committee on Administrative Management. 1937. *Administrative Management in the Government of the United States*. Washington, D.C.: Government Printing Office.

Price, Barbara A. 1984. "What the Baby Boom Believes." *American Demographics* 6: 31–33.

Public Opinion. 1982. "Opinion Roundup." 4 (December/January): 36.

———. 1983. "Opinion Roundup." 5 (April/May): 26.

———. 1985. "Opinion Roundup: Tax Americana." 8 (February/March): 19–29.

———. 1987. "Opinion Roundup: The Role of Government: An Issue for 1988?" 9 (March/April): 21–29.

Rapoport, Ronald B. 1979. "What They Don't Know Can Hurt You." *American Journal of Political Science* 23 (November): 805–815.

———. 1985. "Like Mother, like Daughter: Intergenerational Transmission of DK Response Rates." *Public Opinion Quarterly* 49 (Summer): 198–208.

Rasinski, Kenneth A. 1989. "The Effect of Question Wording on Public Support for Government Spending." *Public Opinion Quarterly* 53 (Fall): 388–394.

Ravitch, Diane. 1983. *The Troubled Crusade: American Education, 1945–1980*. New York: Basic Books.

———. 1985. *The Schools We Deserve*. New York: Basic Books.

Reagan, Michael D. 1987. *Regulation: The Politics of Policy*. Boston: Little, Brown & Co.

Reagan, Ronald W. 1981. "Inaugural Address of Ronald W. Reagan." In Marlene Michels Pomper (ed.), *The Election of 1980* (pp. 189–194). Chatham, N.J.: Chatham House.

———. 1985. "Second Inaugural Address." In Marlene Michels Pomper (ed.), *The Election of 1984* (pp. 185–190). Chatham, N.J.: Chatham House.

Reeves, Richard. 1985. *The Reagan Detour*. New York: Simon & Schuster.

Remini, Robert V. 1984. *Andrew Jackson and the Course of American Democracy, 1833–1845.* New York: Harper & Row.

Roberts, Steven V. 1989. "Reagan's Rating Is Best since 40's for a President." *New York Times,* January 18, p. Y1.

Robinson, John. 1984. "The Ups and Downs and Ins and Outs of Ideology." *Public Opinion* 7 (February/March): 12–15.

Robinson, John P., and John A. Fleishman. 1984. "Ideological Trends in American Public Opinion." *The Annals* 472 (March): 50–60.

Robinson, John P., and John Holm. 1980. "Ideological Voting Is Alive and Well." *Public Opinion* 3 (April/May): 52–58.

Ross, Irwin. 1969. *The Loneliest Campaign: The Truman Victory of 1948.* New York: New American Library.

Sanders, Arthur. 1986. "The Meaning of Liberalism and Conservatism." *Polity* 19 (Fall): 123–135.

Scammon, Richard E., and Ben J. Wattenberg. 1971. *The Real Majority.* New York: Coward, McCann & Geogehagen.

Schank, Robert, and Robert P. Abelson. 1977. *Scripts, Plans, Goals, and Understanding: An Inquiry into Human Knowledge Structures.* Hillsdale, N.J.: Lawrence Erlbaum Associates.

Schuman, Howard, and Stanley Presser. 1978. "The Assessment of 'No Opinion' in Attitude Surveys." In Karl F. Schuessler (ed.), *Sociological Methodology 1979* (pp. 241–275). San Francisco: Jossey-Bass.

———. 1981. *Questions and Answers in Attitude Surveys: Experiments on Question Form, Wording, and Context.* New York: Academic Press.

Schuman, Howard, Charlotte Steeh, and Lawrence Bobo. 1985. *Racial Attitudes in America: Trends and Interpretations.* Cambridge, Mass.: Harvard University Press.

Sears, David O., and Jack Citrin. 1985. *Tax Revolt: Something for Nothing in California.* Cambridge, Mass.: Harvard University Press.

Sears, David O., and Richard E. Whitney. 1973. *Political Persuasion.* Morristown, N.J.: General Learning Press.

Shapiro, Robert Y., and John M. Gillroy. 1984a. "The Polls: Regulation—Part I." *Public Opinion Quarterly* 48 (Summer): 531–542.

———. 1984b. "The Polls: Regulation–Part II." *Public Opinion Quarterly* 48 (Fall): 666–677.

Shapiro, Robert Y., Kelly D. Patterson, Judith Russell, and John T. Young. 1987. "The Polls: Public Assistance." *Public Opinion Quarterly* 51 (Spring): 120–130.

Sigelman, Lee. 1984. "Doing Discriminant Analysis: Some Problems and Solutions." *Political Methodology* 10 (1): 67–80.

Singer, Jerome E. 1968. "Consistency as a Stimulus Processing Mechanism." In Robert P. Abelson et al. (eds.), *Theories of Cognitive Consistency: A Sourcebook* (pp. 337–342). Chicago: Rand McNally & Co.

Smith, Eric R. A. N. 1989. *The Unchanging American Voter.* Berkeley: University of California Press.

Smith, Fred L. 1987. "Privatization at the Federal Level." In Steve H. Hanke (ed.), *Prospects for Privatization,* Proceedings of the Academy of Political Science (vol. 36, pp. 179–189). New York: Academy of Political Science.

Smith, Tom W. 1981. "General Liberalism and Social Change in Post–World War II America: A Summary of Trends." *Social Indicators Research* 10 (January): 1–28.

———. 1985a. "Atop a Liberal Plateau? A Summary of Trends since World War II." *Research in Urban Policy* 1 (1): 245–257.

————. 1985b. "The Polls: America's Most Important Problems, Part I: National and International." *Public Opinion Quarterly* 49 (Summer): 264–274.

————. 1987a. "That Which We Call Welfare by Any Other Name Would Smell Sweeter: An Analysis of the Impact of Question Wording on Response Patterns." *Public Opinion Quarterly* 51 (Spring): 75–83.

————. 1987b. "The Welfare State in Cross-National Perspective." *Public Opinion Quarterly* 51 (Fall): 404–421.

Smith, Tom W., and Paul B. Sheatsley. 1984. "American Attitudes toward Race Relations." *Public Opinion* 7 (October/November): 14–15, 50–53.

Sniderman, Paul M., and Richard A. Brody. 1977. "Coping: The Ethic of Self-Reliance." *American Journal of Political Science* 21 (August): 502–521.

Sniderman, Paul M., Michael G. Hagen, Philip E. Tetlock, and Henry E. Brady. 1986. "Reasoning Chains: Causal Models of Policy Reasoning in Mass Publics." *British Journal of Political Science* 16 (October): 405–430.

Sniderman, Paul M., and Philip E. Tetlock. 1986. "Interrelationship of Political Ideology and Public Opinion." In Margaret G. Hermann (ed.), *Political Psychology* (pp. 62–96). San Francisco: Jossey-Bass.

Stimson, James A. 1975. "Belief Systems: Constraint, Complexity and the 1972 Elections." *American Journal of Political Science* 19 (August): 393–417.

Stockman, David A. 1987. *The Triumph of Politics*. New York: Avon.

Stokes, Donald E. 1966. "Some Dynamic Elements of Contests for the Presidency." *American Political Science Review* 60 (March): 19–28.

Storing, Herbert J. 1981. *What the Anti-Federalists Were For*. Chicago: University of Chicago Press.

Sullivan, John L., James E. Piereson, and George E. Marcus. 1978. "Ideological Constraint in the Mass Public: A Methodological Critique and Some New Findings." *American Journal of Political Science* 22 (May): 233–249.

————. 1982. *Political Tolerance and American Democracy*. Chicago: University of Chicago Press.

Sullivan, John L., James E. Piereson, George E. Marcus, and Stanley Feldman. 1979. "The More Things Change, the More They Stay the Same: The Stability of Mass Belief Systems." *American Journal of Political Science* 23 (February): 176–186.

Sundquist, James L. 1983. *Dynamics of the Party System*. Rev. ed. Washington, D.C.: Brookings Institution.

Sussman, Barry. 1988. *What Americans Really Think: And Why Our Politicians Pay No Attention*. New York: Pantheon Books.

Taylor, Shelley, and Jennifer Crocker. 1981. "Schematic Bases of Social Information Processing." In E. Tory Higgins, C. Peter Herman, and Mark P. Zanna (eds.), *Social Cognition: The Ontario Symposium* (vol. 1, pp.89–134). Hillsdale, N.J.: Lawrence Erlbaum Associates.

Time. 1986. "The Making of a Miracle." August 25, pp. 12–18.

————. 1989. "The Can't-Do Government." October 23, pp. 28–32.

Times Mirror. 1987. *The People, Press, and Politics*. Los Angeles: Times Mirror Company.

————. 1988. "West Is Key to GOP Electoral College 'Lock' *Times Mirror*/Gallup Surveys Show." Press Release. Los Angeles: Times Mirror Company.

————. 1989. *The People, Press, and Economics*. Los Angeles: Times Mirror Company.

Tocqueville, Alexis de. 1969. *Democracy in America*. George Lawrence (trans.) and J. P. Mayer (ed.). Garden City, N.Y.: Doubleday Anchor Books.

Tolchin, Susan J., and Martin Tolchin. 1983. *Dismantling America: The Rush to Deregulate*. New York: Oxford University Press.

Truman, David B. 1971. *The Governmental Process*. 2d ed. New York: Alfred A. Knopf.

U.S. Department of Commerce. 1976. *Historical Statistics, Colonial Times to 1970*. Washington, D.C.: Bureau of Statistics.

———. 1986. *Statistical Abstract of the United States*. Washington, D.C.: Bureau of Statistics.

———. Bureau of the Census. 1988. *Statistical Abstract of the United States*. 108th ed. Washington, D.C.: Government Printing Office.

von Beyme, Klaus. 1985. ''The Role of the State and the Growth of Government.'' *International Political Science Review* 6 (January): 11–34.

Wattenberg, Martin P. 1986. *The Decline of American Political Parties, 1952–1984*. Rev. ed. Cambridge, Mass.: Harvard University Press.

Weinraub, Bernard. 1989. ''Bush and Governors Set Education Goals.'' *New York Times*, September 29, p. Y7.

Weisberg, Herbert F., and Bruce D. Bowen. 1977. *An Introduction to Survey Research and Data Analysis*. San Francisco: W. H. Freeman & Co.

Welch, Susan. 1985. ''The 'More for Less' Paradox: Public Attitudes on Taxing and Spending.'' *Public Opinion Quarterly* 49 (Fall): 310–316.

Wheaton, Blair, Bengt Muthén, Duane F. Alwin, and Gene F. Summers. 1977. ''Assessing Reliability and Stability in Panel Models.'' In David R. Heise (ed.), *Sociological Methodology, 1977* (pp. 84–136). San Francisco: Jossey-Bass.

White, John Kenneth. 1988. *The New Politics of Old Values*. Hanover, N.H.: University Press of New England.

White, Leonard D. 1956. *The Federalists*. New York: Macmillan.

———. 1958. *The Republican Era*. New York: Free Press.

Wildavsky, Aaron. 1982. ''The Three Cultures.'' *Public Interest* 69 (Fall): 45–58.

———. 1985. ''Equality, Spending Limits, and the Growth of Government.'' In C. Lowell Harriss (ed.), *Control of Federal Spending* (pp. 59–71). New York: Academy of Political Science.

Wilensky, Harold L. 1975. *The Welfare State and Equality*. Berkeley: University of California Press.

Wilson, L. A., II. 1983. ''Preference Revelation and Public Policy: Making Sense of Citizen Survey Data.'' *Public Administration Review* 43 (July/August): 335–342.

Wolfe, Tom. 1977. *Mauve Gloves and Madmen, Clutter and Vine*. New York: Bantam Books.

Wolfskill, George. 1962. *The Revolt of the Conservatives*. Boston: Houghton Mifflin.

Young, James Sterling. 1966. *The Washington Community, 1800–1828*. New York: Harcourt, Brace & World.

Index